When I get a little money I buy books.
And if any is left, I buy food and clothes.

Erasmus

Where is human nature so weak as in the bookstore?

Henry Ward Beecher

The Used Book Lover's Guide To New England

By
David S. and Susan Siegel

Book Hunter Press
P.O. Box 193
Yorktown Heights, NY 10598

Printed and bound in the United States of America

This guide is available at quantity discounts. For information, please contact Book Hunter Press, P.O. Box 193, Yorktown Heights, NY 10598, 914-245-6608.

Library of Congress Catalog Card Number: 92-097220

ISBN 0-9634112-0-9

Acknowledgments

We would like to thank the following state antiquarian bookseller associations for their assistance in researching this Guide.

Maine Antiquarian Booksellers Association
Massachusetts and Rhode Island Antiquarian Booksellers
New Hampshire Antiquarian Booksellers Association
Vermont Antiquarian Booksellers Association

We would also like to thank Helen Morrison of Old Number Six Book Depot and Frank Bequaert of Rainy Day Books for their help with the New Hampshire chapter, Barbara Falk for assistance with the Maine chapter and Roger Reid of Reid & Wright: An Antiquarian Book Center, Barbara DePalma of Deer Park Books and Bill Goring of Nutmeg Books for their assistance identifying Connecticut booksellers.

Last but not least, we would like to thank the more than six hundred book dealers listed in this Guide who patiently answered our questionnaire, responded to our phone calls, and chatted with us during our visits. Without their cooperation, this book would not have been possible.

Table of Contents

List of Maps

Genesis

Susan, my wife/partner, claims it's in my genes. She says I was born with a collector gene. My father was a collector and my children show signs of having inherited the gene.

My love of books goes back to a childhood of finding classic comics more interesting than Superman. I can still remember the thrill of discovering the world of Oz, Tarzan's jungle and London's Baker Street. In later years I discovered the joys of New York City's Fourth Avenue book shops: there was a time (many moons ago) when I thought I knew the location of every used book store in Manhattan. Though my professional life has been devoted to education, I have never missed an opportunity, whether on vacation or when attending a professional conference, to scour the yellow pages in the cities I was visiting to locate local used book stores.

But it was with my second marriage that my second life — my book hunting life — began in earnest. Although not quite the book person I am, Susan is a romantic and she enjoys searching out and exploring new places. Early in our courtship we discovered that spending weekends and vacation time visiting antiquarian book fairs and used books stores satisfied my hunger for books and our mutual desire to be together doing something that could be shared. We have even, if you can believe it, learned that reading aloud to one another is a sharing that brings us closer.

To guide us in our travels we have used a variety of sources, including the directories published by state antiquarian book seller associations and out-of-date guides we found in public libraries. We also learned that book dealers were most helpful in directing us to nearby shops that were not listed in any directory and which we would not otherwise have known about.

It was during our planning for a trip to England that we discovered *Drif's Guide To The Secondhand & Antiquarian Bookshops In Britain.* Like a light bulb appearing above our heads, it occurred to us that a labor of love and service to our fellow bibliomaniacs would be the publication of a comprehensive used book lover's guide to the United States. Why not, we thought, share the fruits of our book searches with other book lovers who, like ourselves, enjoy traveling in search of hidden treasures.

Too great a task for two mere mortals, we quickly decided that a regional approach would make more sense and that the New England region, a traditional cradle of literature, would be a good place to start.

If, we concluded, we could provide a truly comprehensive guide to the six New England states, and if such a guide proved useful to the world of book lovers, we could devote our silver years (we're saving the golden ones for our old age) to providing similar guides for other regions of the country: the mid Atlantic states, southeast, southwest, midwest and ultimately the farwest. We could become the Baedeker or Frommer of the used book world.

If this volume pleases you, we hope you will contact us with encouragement. If you find flaws but think the idea has merit, we hope you will contact us with constructive criticism. And if you think we should quit while we're behind, you can send us that message as well.

David S. Siegel
December, 1992

How To Get The Most From This Guide

This book is different from any other guide to the world of used and antiquarian book dealers.

In writing this book, our goal has been to provide book lovers with an easy-to-use, practical guide to the rich and often unknown world of used book dealers in New England. We also wanted to eliminate many of the uncertainties and anxieties associated with hunting for books in new places by providing the reader with helpful information not readily available anywhere else.

In the course of our travels through New England and elsewhere, we have discovered that used book sellers fall into three general categories:

Open shop dealers who maintain regular hours. These collections can vary in size from several hundred to 100,000+ books and can be either a general stock with a little of everything or a specialized collection limited to one or more specialty areas.

By appointment or chance dealers who generally, but not always, have smaller collections, frequently quite specialized. Most of these dealers maintain their collections in their own home. By phoning them in advance, avid book hunters can easily combine a trip to open shop dealers and by appointment dealers in the same region. In those instances where the dealers have indicated they are also available "by chance," the book hunter may wish to stop by even if he or she has not called ahead.

Mail order only dealers who issue catalogs and/or sell to people on their mailing list and frequently display their wares at used book fairs.

Since we believe that the majority of our readers will be people who enjoy taking book hunting trips, we have organized this guide by state and within each state by the category of book seller.

To help the reader locate specific stores, we have included at the beginning of each state chapter an alphabetical listing of all the dealers in the state as well as a listing by location.

In the *Open Shop* sections of each chapter, the number to the right of the shop name is the shop's map identification number. The number of the map on which the shop is located is included in the *Travel* directions.

We have also tried to include in each listing the kind of information about book sellers that we ourselves found useful in our own travels.

A description of the stock: are you likely to find the kind of book you are searching for in this shop?

The size of the collection: if the shop has a small collection, should you go out of your way to visit it?

Detailed travel directions: how can you find the shop?

Regional maps: what shops are located near each other?

Special services offered by the book seller: do they issue catalogs? Accept want lists? Do they have a search service?

Perhaps the most unique feature of this guide is the *Comments* section. Based on actual visits to almost every open shop in New England, as well as many of the "by appointment dealers" with large general stocks, our comments are designed not to endorse or criticize any of the establishments we saw but rather to place ourselves in the position of our readers and provide useful data or insights.

If you're interested in locating books in very specific categories, you'll want to take a close look at the *Specialty Index*. In addition to listing the open shops and by appointment dealers, the *Index* also includes mail order dealers you may want to contact.

A few caveats and suggestions before you begin your book hunting safari.

Even when an open shop lists hours and days open, we advise a phone call ahead to be certain that the hours have not changed and that the establishment will indeed be open when you arrive.

Is there a difference between an "antiquarian" book store, and a "used" book store? Yes and no. Many stores we visited call themselves antiquarian but their shelves contain a large stock of books published within the past ten or fifteen years. Likewise, we also found many older books in "used" book stores. For that reason, we have used the term "antiquarian" with great caution and only when it was clear to us that the book seller dealt primarily in truly older books, e.g., books published prior to the 20th century.

Some used book purists also make a distinction between "used" books and "out-of-print" books, a distinction which, for the most part, we have avoided. Where appropriate, however, and in order to assist the book hunter, we have tried to indicate the relative vintage of the stock and whether the collection consists of reading copies of popular works or rarer and more unusual titles.

The reader should also note that while we list shops that carry paperbacks, we do not include shops that sell exclusively paper.

After much consideration we decided to include a sampling of antique/collectible shops in the *Guide.* Although not on our original itineraries, we found them worth a visit when we came upon them. Although the size of the collections in these shops tends to be small, we have learned by experience that treasures can turn up in the most unlikely places. Many of these shops also rent space to used book dealers. In instances where the antique/collectible shop has a large collection, or more unusual books, we have listed the shop in the *Open Shop* section of the state listings. Other listings can be found at the end of the state chapter.

In almost all instances, the information regarding the size of the collection comes directly from the owner. While we did not stop to do an actual count of the collection during our visit, in the few instances where the owner's estimate seemed to be exaggerated, we made note of our observation in the *Comments* section.

And now to begin your search. Good luck and happy hunting.

Connecticut

Alphabetical Listing By Dealer

Alphabetical Listing By Location

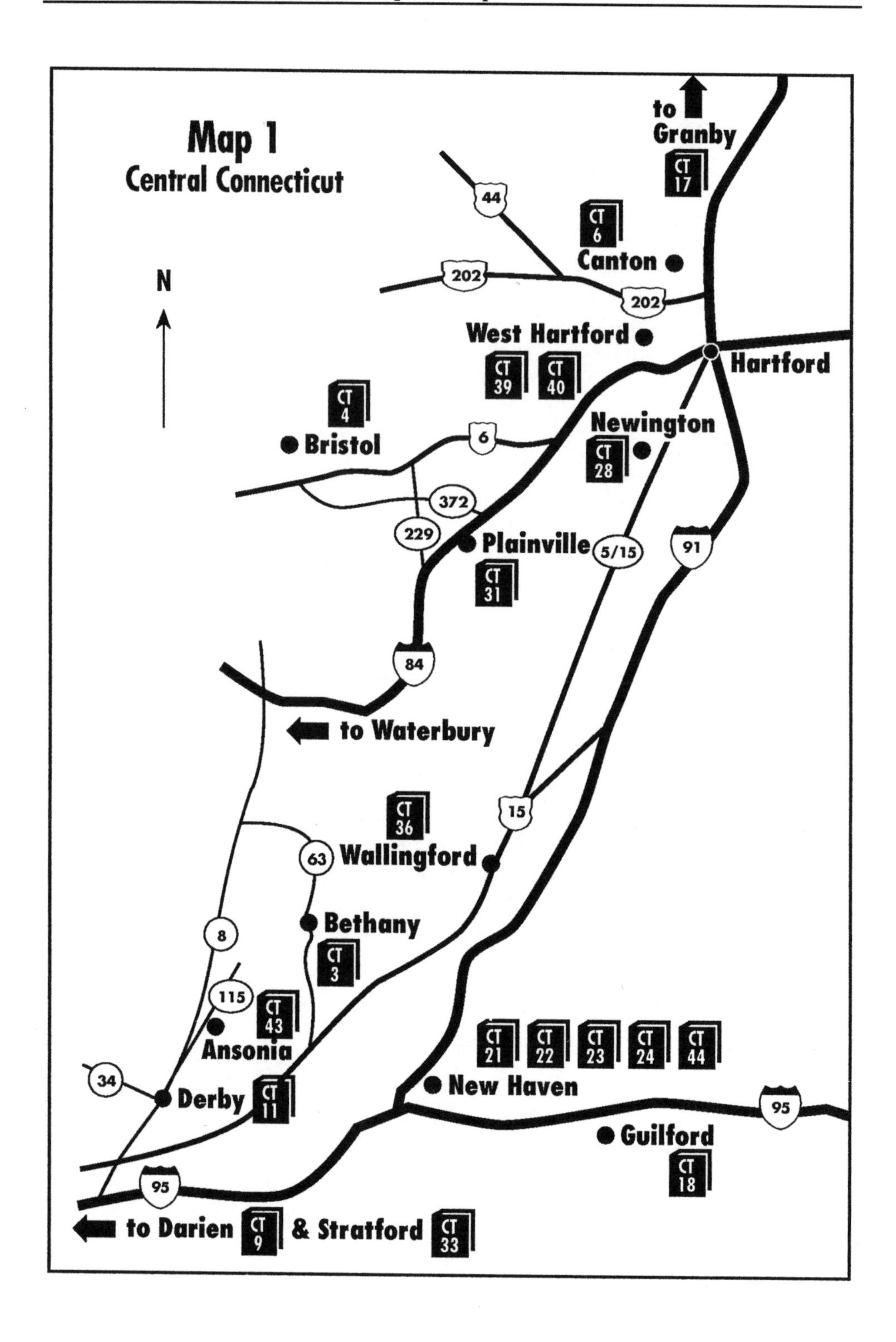

Map 1
Central Connecticut
N
to Granby
CT 17
44
CT 6
Canton
202
202
West Hartford
CT 39
CT 40
Hartford
CT 4
Bristol
6
Newington
CT 28
372
229
Plainville
5/15
91
CT 31
84
to Waterbury
CT 36
15
63
Wallingford
Bethany
8
CT 3
115
CT 43
Ansonia
CT 21
CT 22
CT 23
CT 24
CT 44
34
Derby
CT 11
New Haven
95
Guilford
CT 18
95
to Darien
CT 9
& Stratford
CT 33

Ansonia

Books by the Falls Annex (CT43) 203-734-1450
Ansonia Mall (Route 115) 06401

Collection: General stock and prints.
# of Volumes: 20,000
Hours: Monday-Friday 11-8. Saturday & Sunday 11-5.
Travel: Route 8 to Derby exit. Make right at exit onto Route 34. Proceed for 1/4 mile and make left onto Route 115 north. Shop is located on the right in an indoor mall. Map 1.
Owner: Ron Knox & Loretta Polka
Year Estab: 1991
Comments: This one year old shop, located in an indoor shopping mall, contains a good selection of inexpensively priced books and some comfortable chairs for the weary book browser. With the exception of the stock in the back room, the books are displayed in bins rather than on traditional book shelves. Despite this non traditional arrangement, the titles are easy to read. During our visit, the collection appeared smaller than the owner's estimate.

Bantam

Book Nook (CT1) 203-567-3188
895 Bantam Road (Route 202) 06750

Collection: General stock.
# of Volumes: 2,000+
Hours: Daily, 12-6. Some mornings from 10 AM and some evenings till 7 PM.
Travel: Located on Route 202, one block west of junction of Routes 202 and 209. Map 3.
Owner: Eugenia Dell
Comments: Located in a separate room off an antiques/collectibles shop, the books in this establishment are mainly library discards and/or other older books without either charm or value. The true book lover will find few bargains here and fewer still books of value. If you're visiting some of the other shops in the area, though, you may wish to stop here for a few minutes.

Victor Denette Books & Ephemera (CT2) 203-567-4074
Americana Mart, Route 202
Mailing address: P.O. Box 715 06750

Collection:	General stock and ephemera.
# of Volumes:	10,000
Hours:	Daily 9-5.
Services:	Appraisals, accepts want lists.
Travel:	On Route 202. Map 3.
Credit Cards:	No
Owner:	Victor Denette
Year Estab:	1990 (see comments)
Comments:	While some ephemera and a few signed and limited edition books are located in the front of this large antique and collectibles mart, most of the collection is displayed in a rear room. The books are of varied condition and type and with a few exceptions, they appear to be shelved with little rhyme or reason. There are, however, quite a few older items which might be of interest to the intrepid book hunter of scarce and out-of-print titles. If you have the patience to scan the numerous shelves, there is a better than even chance you might find an item or two of interest. Prices vary with a logic that alludes us. Although relatively new at this location, the owner has been in the book business for over 20 years.

Bethany

Whitlock Farm Booksellers (CT3) 203-393-1240
20 Sperry Road 06525

Collection:	General stock, ephemera, prints and maps.
# of Volumes:	50,000
Specialties:	Natural history; country life; early and curious; maps, prints.
Hours:	Tuesday-Sunday 9-5.
Services:	Appraisals, catalog.
Travel:	Exit 59 off Wilbur Cross Parkway. Left onto Route 69 for 4 1/2 miles. Left onto Morris Road. Take Morris to end. Bear right. Shop is first driveway on right. Map 1.
Credit Cards:	Yes
Owner:	Gilbert & Everett Whitlock

Year Estab: 1962

Comments: This quality collection is divided between two buildings, the larger of which contains sections representing almost all major areas of interest. The books are exceedingly well organized with the aisles clearly labeled and subcategories noted. Chairs and stools abound. The entrance is up a few steps. The shop's better books and some unusual items are located in an adjacent building. We have visited this shop on more than one occasion and each time we find it a most worthwhile stop. The Print Shop, located on the second floor of the larger building, is open Tuesday-Saturday.

Bristol

Omni Books & Comics (CT4) 203-589-3003
864 Farmington Avenue 06010

Collection: Specialty used and new, hardcover and paperback.
# of Volumes: 50,000 (see Comments)
Specialties: Science fiction; horror; mystery.
Hours: Monday-Friday 10-8. Saturday 10-5. Sunday 11-5.
Travel: Exit 31 off Route 84. Take Route 229 north to Route 6 east. Shop is 1/4 ahead on right in Bonnies Plaza. Map 1.
Credit Cards: Yes
Owner: Carol Theriault George Fietkiewwicz
Year Estab: 1987
Comments: This storefront shop offers mostly paperbacks with a scattering of hardcover titles in the specialty areas listed above, plus some literature and non fiction. This is not a store that any true hardcover used book lover would go out of his or her way to visit.

Canterbury

Stone of Scone Antiques, Books & Firearms (CT5) 203-546-9917
19 Water Street 06331

Collection: Specialty
# of Volumes: 3,500
Specialties: Connecticut; New England; natural history; firearms reference; Abraham Lincoln; western Americana.

Hours:	Tuesday-Friday 12-6. Saturday 10-6. Sunday-Tuesday 12-5.
Services:	Appraisals, search service, catalog, accepts want lists.
Travel:	I-395, exist 83A. Make left on Route 169 and proceed about 10 miles to Route 14. Turn left on Route 14 west and proceed 3 miles. Turn left onto Water Street. Shop is 500 feet ahead on left. Map 2.
Credit Cards:	Yes
Owner:	Tom & Jan Stratton
Year Estab:	1976
Comments:	A small, charming shop located in a garage like structure adjacent to the owner's home. The modest sized collection reflects the owner's interests in hunting and local history. The shop also stocks vintage guns and antiques.

Canton

Book Store (CT6) 203-693-6029
Route 44, Box 64 06019

Collection:	General stock.
# of Volumes:	10,000
Specialties:	Academic books.
Hours:	Wednesday-Friday 10-6. Saturday 10-5. Sunday 12-5.
Travel:	On Route 44/202 across from Davidson Chevrolet. Look for a cream colored, two story wood frame building. Map 1.
Credit Cards:	No
Owner:	Stephen Powell
Year Estab:	1970's
Comments:	A modest sized shop along a major thoroughfare with a collection of older and more recent used books that would be of interest to those with academic tastes. We noted a particularly nice collection on theology.

Coventry

Coventry Book Shop (CT7) 203-742-9875
1159 Main Street (Route 31)
Mailing address: P.O. Box 36 06238

Collection:	General stock.
# of Volumes:	15,000

Specialties: Americana; nautical.
Hours: Tuesday-Sunday 12-5.
Services: Appraisals, accepts want lists.
Travel: Located on Route 31. Look for a row of stores in a red one story building next to a white church. The book shop is the corner store closest to the church. Map 2.
Credit Cards: No
Owner: John R. Gambino
Year Estab: 1972
Comments: Books, books and more books are crammed into this roadside shop located in the heart of the village. The books, mostly reading copies (with many newer editions and a few oldies thrown in), are generally of the fairly common variety. The books are shelved from floor to almost ceiling with most shelves doubled layered and the overflow frequently stacked in the aisles blocking access to the lower shelves. The shop offers a little of everything with few subjects handled with any degree of depth. What you can be sure of finding are numbers, most likely more than the 15,000 estimate given by the owner. The shop offers what is probably one of the largest collections in this part of Connecticut. The books are quite reasonably priced.

The Golden Acorn (CT8) 203-742-0116
30 Mason Street
Mailing address: P.O. Box 67 06238

Collection: General stock of hardcover and paperback, records and ephemera.
# of Volumes: 25,000
Specialties: Biography; fiction; cookbooks; history; children's; poetry; science fiction; 19th century; religion.
Hours: Tuesday, Wednesday, Saturday, Sunday 12-5. Thursday & Friday 12-7 and by appointment.
Services: Appraisals, search service, accepts wants lists, mail order.
Travel: I-384 to junction of Routes 6 & 44. Take Route 44 north. After Route 44 joins with Route 31, follow signs for Route 31 which becomes Main Street in Coventry. Proceed on Route 31 for 5 miles. Make right turn on Mason Street. (Look for a house with a picket fence on one corner and the Coventry Antiques Center across the street.) Map 2.
Credit Cards: No

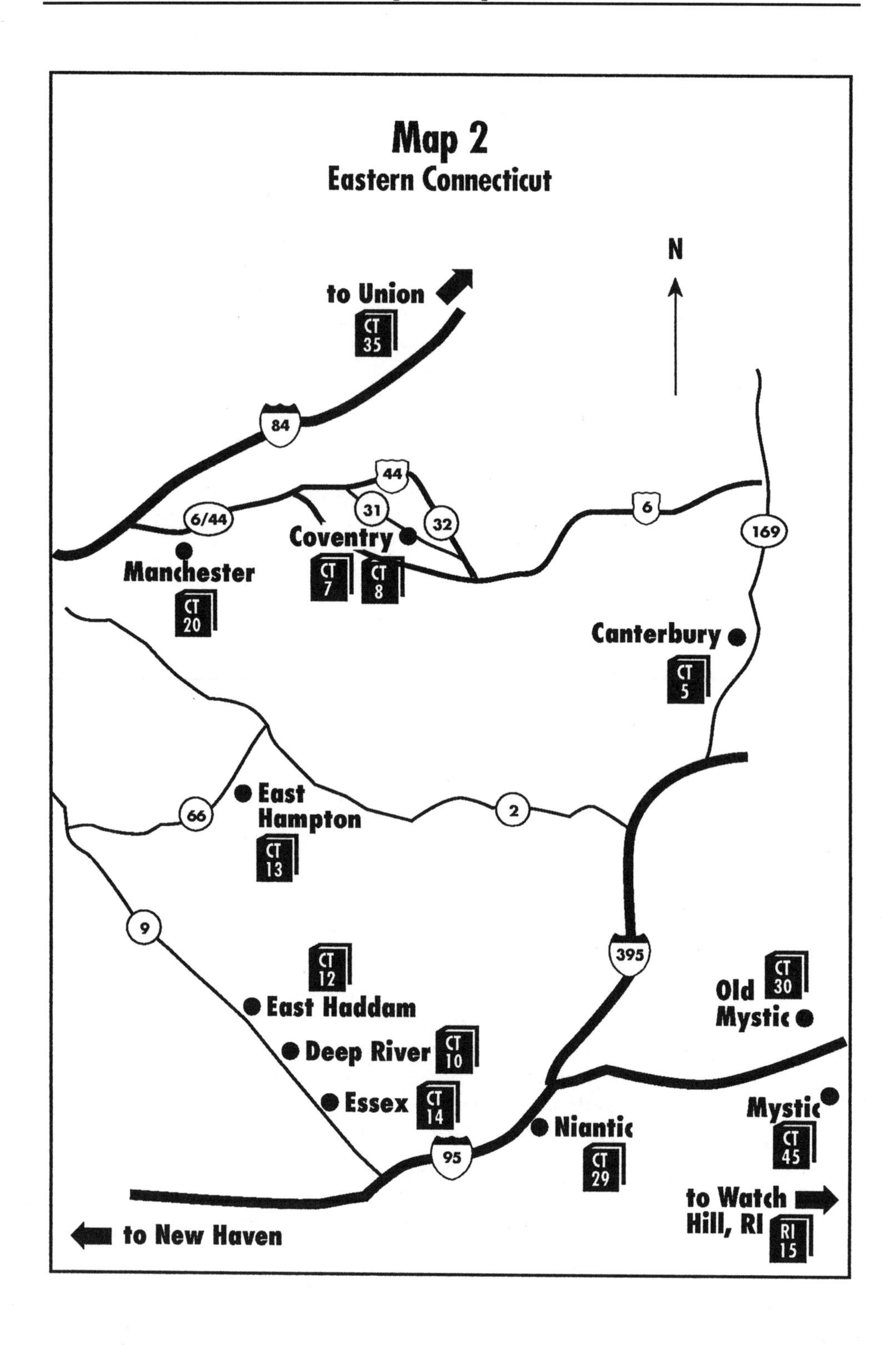

Map 2
Eastern Connecticut
N
to Union
CT 35
84
44
6/44
31
32
6
169
Coventry
CT 7
CT 8
Manchester
CT 20
Canterbury
CT 5
East Hampton
66
2
CT 13
9
395
CT 12
East Haddam
Deep River
CT 10
Essex
CT 14
Old Mystic
CT 30
Niantic
CT 29
95
Mystic
CT 45
to Watch Hill, RI
RI 15
to New Haven

Owner: Henry T. J. Becker
Year Estab: 1989
Comments: If a golden acorn will, as the owner claims, bring good luck, then visitors will not want to miss the tray of free golden acorns they will see as they enter the shop. Most of the shop's stock consists of reading copies generally found in a typical country used book shop atmosphere. Although we did spot a few antiquarian items, these were more the exception than the rule. While the shop does not offer a great deal in the way of rare literature, the buyer can make a large purchase and spend very little. On our visit, the stock appeared to be smaller then the 25,000 estimate given by the owner.

Darien

Gilann Books (CT9) 203-655-4532
895 Boston Post Road 06820

Collection: General stock and ephemera.
# of Volumes: 8,000
Specialties: Children's; leather bindings; illustrated; modern first editions; private press.
Hours: Tuesday-Sunday 11-5. (See Comments)
Services: Appraisals, accepts want lists.
Travel: On Post Road, 1/2 block from train station. Parking available in rear of shop. Map 1.
Credit Cards: Yes
Owner: Kathleen & Gil Rodriguez
Year Estab: 1975
Comments: This modest sized collection shares quarters with an antique shop. The stock contains some moderately priced interesting, rare and illustrated books. We also noted several interesting sets of antique bookends. The owner also operates a special summer book shop offering less expensive books around the corner at 4 West Street The summer shop is open Wednesday-Sunday 11-5.

Deep River (Winthrop)

W.B. Gottlieb - Books (CT10) 203-526-9462
385 Winthrop Road (Route 80) 06417

Collection: General stock.
# of Volumes: 3,000
Specialties: Literature; poetry.
Hours: Daily 12:30-5:30 or by appointment.
Travel: Exit 5 off Route 9 . Proceed on Route 80 to Winthrop Corners. Shop will be on left in an old barn.
Note: Although mailing address is Deep River, the shop is actually located in Winthrop. Map 2.
Credit Cards: No
Owner: William B. Gottlieb
Comments: While not large, this collection, housed in a bi-level barn adjacent to the owner's home, does offer some interesting and reasonably priced rarities. The titles in one bookcase containing reading copies are even more moderately priced. The majority of the collection is located on the first floor, with some mysteries and fiction shelved in a small balcony area.

Derby

Books by the Falls (CT11) 203-734-6112
253 Roosevelt Drive (Route 34) 06418

Collection: General stock and records.
# of Volumes: 40,000
Specialties: Poetry; classics; horror; science fiction.
Hours: Daily 9-5.
Services: Appraisals, search service.
Travel: Exit 15 off Route 8. Make left at exit and proceed west on Route 34 for about 7/10 of a mile. Shop is in an old red brick factory building on the right. Map 1.
Credit Cards: No
Owner: Ron Knox
Year Estab: 1980
Comments: This may not be the neatest shop we have visited but it is one with a good stock where the avid collector is likely to find some unusual titles at very reasonable prices. The

books are overflowing their shelves and in some aisles are piled on the floor blocking the lower shelves. Books are also shelved behind books. Don't miss the "overflow room" across the hall from the main shop area as the room contains enough books to stock a separate shop. Paperbacks and hardcover books are shelved together.

East Haddam

Connecticut River Bookshop (CT12) 203-873-8881
P.O. Box 461, Goodspeed Landing 06423

Collection: General stock and ephemera.
# of Volumes: 75,000
Specialties: Nautical; hunting; fishing; children's; New England; art; architecture.
Hours: Thursday-Saturday 11-5. Sunday 12:30-5.
Services: Catalog (nautical only), accepts want lists.
Travel: Exit 7 off Route 9. Left at blinking light, then right at traffic light. Continue over bridge into town. Shop is on right side, about 100 yards passed the Goodspeed Opera House. Entrance is in the rear of the building off the parking lot. Map 2.
Credit Cards: No
Owner: Frank Crohn
Year Estab: 1986
Comments: This well organized and well labeled collection is displayed in a series of small rooms, some involving a few steps. In addition to the specialties listed above, we noted an interesting bull fighting section. During our visit, some of the shelves looked rather threadbare, suggesting either that the shop has turned over a number of volumes or that the owner has not replenished his stock recently.

East Hampton

Bibliolatree (CT13) 203-267-8222
190 East High Street (Route 66)
Mailing address: P.O. Box 151 06424

Collection: General stock, with depth in many areas.
# of Volumes: 40,000+

Hours: Almost every afternoon 12-5:30. Best to call ahead.
Travel: Located on Route 66. Map 2.
Credit Cards: No
Owner: Paul O. Clark
Year Estab: 1977
Comments: Don't be fooled by the small room you'll encounter upon entering this unassuming but outstanding bi-level shop. While the first floor contains an excellent selection, the lower level is four times larger in size and consists of a maze of small rooms in which you're delighted to get lost in. You're likely to find a treasure around every corner. The cigar chomping owner knows his stock well and is always willing to help. Books overflow the shelves in some sections, and there are books on top of books, but the aisles are wide enough to avoid a cramped unorganized feeling.

Essex

Classic Books at Essex Antique Center (CT14) 203-388-4568
8 Main Street 06426

Collection: General stock.
# of Volumes: 1,000
Hours: Monday-Saturday 11-5. Sunday 1-4.
Travel: Exit 3 from Route 9. Follow signs to Essex. Bear left at fork. Shop is located on right in heart of village in a two story white frame building. Map 2.
Credit Cards: No
Owner: K.C. Whelen
Comments: This small collection of older books in reasonably good condition is displayed on the first floor of an antique shop. Some rare items are appropriately priced.

Falls Village

R & D Emerson (CT15) 203-824-0442
The Old Church, 103 Main Street 06031

Collection: General stock.
# of Volumes: 30,000+
Hours: Thursday-Monday 12-5.
Travel: Route 126 into village. Map 3.

Credit Cards: Yes
Owner: Robert & Dorothy Emerson
Year Estab: 1945
Comments: It's always interesting to see how a building designed for one use has been recycled to fit another purpose. This former church, located in the center of a quiet New England village, has lots of room to display its books. Our impression, however, is that the maze of small cubicles open to the public uses only half the available space. Most of the books are in good to fine condition. The shop can certainly and honestly claim to offer an excellent selection of rare and unusual titles The shop also stocks some typical used book store items. Few bargains to be had.

Gaylordsville

Deer Park Books (CT16) 203-743-2246
609 Kent Road (Route 7) 06755

Collection: General stock and ephemera.
# of Volumes: 3,000
Specialties: Signed and limited first editions; history; art reference; children's; illustrated; scarce non fiction.
Hours: Sunday 12-5 and Monday-Saturday by chance or appointment.
Services: Appraisals, search service, catalog, accepts want lists.
Travel: Route 7 north halfway between New Milford Center and Kent. Proceeding south, shop is on right, one mile south of intersection of Routes 7 & 55. Proceeding north, shop is on left, 6 miles from the New Milford bridge and after Cedar Hill Road. Shop is attached to owner's residence, a red one story house set back about 75 feet from the road. Map 3.
Credit Cards: No
Owner: Richard & Barbara DePalma
Year Estab: 1985
Comments: Interesting items abound in this modest sized shop and even the seasoned book hunter is likely to find a surprise item or two. When we visited, the owner was still settling in to this new location. Her plans include setting one room aside for a children's collection. A refreshing cup of coffee or tea always awaits the tired book hunter.

Granby

William & Lois Pinkney, Antiquarian Books (CT17) 203-653-7710
240 North Granby Road 06035

Collection: General stock.
# of Volumes: 12,000
Specialties: Limited editions club; fine bindings and sets; western Americana; Americana; New England; New York; natural history; first editions; sheet music; art; decorative arts; antiques.
Hours: Monday-Friday 9-5. Usually closed in January and February.
Services: Appraisals, catalog, accepts want lists, mail order.
Travel: Exit 40 off I-91. Proceed west on Route 20 to Granby, then 2 miles north on Route 189. Look for a private home with a small sign with the owner's name. Map 1.
Credit Cards: Yes
Owner: William & Lois Pinkney
Year Estab: 1964
Comments: This modest sized shop is located adjacent to the garage behind the owner's home. The books, in excellent condition, are neatly and tightly shelved in a dozen or so alcoves off a narrow aisle. The titles we observed were hardly run of the mill. This is not a shop that specializes in recent best sellers. Instead, what you'll find here are both the classics and some unusually rare non fiction titles. We strongly recommend a visit.

Guilford

Twenty Three Boston (CT18) 203-458-1155
23 Boston Street 06437

Collection: General stock.
# of Volumes: 3,000
Hours: Sunday, Monday, Wednesday, Thursday 8-8. Friday & Saturday 8-10 PM.
Services: Appraisals, search service, accepts want lists.
Travel: Exit 58 off I-95. Follow signs to Guilford. Shop is on the Green. Map 1.
Credit Cards: No

Owner: Joseph & Janis Abramo
Year Estab: 1992
Comments: A combination used book shop and expresso bar/tearoom. The modest collection, primarily fiction and biographies, consists mostly of newer used books, plus a glass display cabinet containing some rarer items. A small collection of paperbacks is located in a tiny alcove. If you're in the area and would like to relax with a cup of expresso or a sandwich, this would make for a most pleasant stop.

Litchfield

John Steele Book Shop (CT19) 203-567-0748
15 South Street near the Green Fax: 203-567-3394
Mailing address: P.O. Box 1091 06759

Collection: General stock and ephemera.
# of Volumes: 20,000
Specialties: New England history; New York history; fiction; technical.
Hours: Tuesday-Saturday 11-5. Sunday 1-5.
Services: Appraisals, search service, accepts want lists, mail order.
Travel: Exit 42 from Route 8. Shop is on Route 63 (South Street) near village green in a two story white frame house with a porch. Map 3.
Credit Cards: Yes
Owner: William W. Keifer
Year Estab: 1982
Comments: Located in the heart of historic Litchfield Village, this neat and well kept shop offers a moderate sized collection of books in generally good condition. The entrance is up a few steps.

Manchester

Books & Birds (CT20) 203-649-3449
519 East Middle Turnpike (Rts 6 & 44) 06040

Collection: General stock.
# of Volumes: 45,000+
Specialties: Birds.
Hours: Monday 10-3. Tuesday & Wednesday 10-4:30. Thursday 10-8. Friday & Saturday 10-5. Sunday by chance or appointment.

Services: Appraisals, search service, accepts want lists.
Travel: Located on Route 6/44. Map 2.
Credit Cards: Yes (over $30)
Owner: Gilbert J. Salk
Comments: A large warehouse like setting with the entrance several steps up. The shop offers an excellent selection of used and occasionally rare volumes with particular emphasis on nature, e.g, birds, dogs, horses, etc. The general stock contains a healthy representation of most subjects. We found ourselves spending much more time browsing here than in other shops with equally large collections because the wide aisles permitted us to move around easily and without feeling cramped or otherwise restricted. We also found the prices a bit higher than those we have seen in other shops with similar quality books.

Mystic

Trade Winds Gallery (CT45) 203-536-0119
20 West Main Street 06355

Collection: Specialty
Specialties: Antique maps and prints.
Hours: Monday-Saturday 10-2 & 3-6. Sunday 11-5.
Travel: Exit 89 off I-95. Make right at exit and a left onto U.S. 1 which becomes West Main Street at foot of the hill. The gallery is on left, before bridge. Map 1.
Credit Cards: Yes
Owner: Thomas K. Aalund
Year Estab: 1974
Comments: The gallery also sells marine art and art of New England.

New Haven

Arethusa Book Shop (CT21) 203-624-1848
87 Audubon Street 06511

Collection: General stock.
# of Volumes: 9,000
Specialties: Art; architecture; ancient history; cooking; philosophy; travel.
Hours: Monday-Saturday 10:30-6.

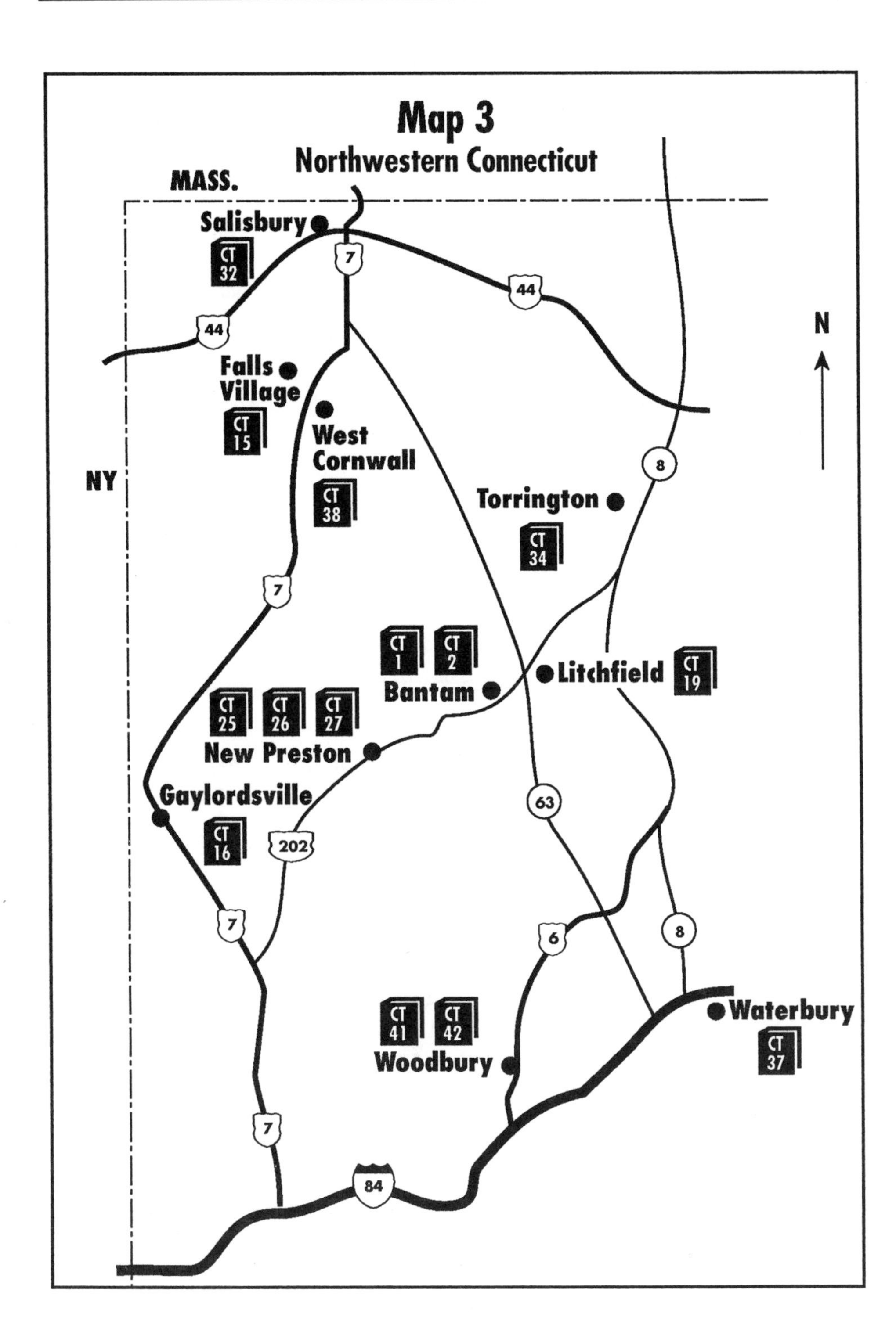
Map 3
Northwestern Connecticut
MASS.
NY
N
Salisbury
CT 32
Falls Village
CT 15
West Cornwall
CT 38
Torrington
CT 34
CT 1
CT 2
Bantam
Litchfield
CT 19
CT 25
CT 26
CT 27
New Preston
Gaylordsville
CT 16
CT 41
CT 42
Woodbury
Waterbury
CT 37
7
44
8
63
202
6
84

Travel: From I-95, exit 47 to second right (Church St.) After four lights, make right onto Audubon St. From I-91, exit 3 (Trumbull Street). Left at first light. Right at next light. Right at following light. Right onto Audubon Street. Map 1.
Credit Cards: Yes
Owner: John Gearty
Year Estab: 1988
Comments: Modest in size and moderately priced, this collection is displayed in a spacious and well lit shop located off a pedestrian mall. The titles are a mixture of older and more recent out-of-print books.

Bryn Mawr Book Shop (CT22) 203-562-4217
56 1/2 Whitney Avenue 06510

Collection: General stock.
# of Volumes: 20,000+
Hours: September-June: Wednesday-Friday 12-3. Saturday 10-1. July & August: Wednesday & Thursday 12-3. Closed last two weeks in August.
Travel: Exit 47 off I-95 or exit 3 off I-91. Shop is around the corner from the Arethusa Book Shop. Map 1.
Credit Cards: No
Year Estab: 1970
Comments: The shop is run by alumni. All proceeds go to the school's scholarship fund.

C.A. Stonehill, Inc. (CT44) 203-865-5141
282 York Street 06511

Collection: Speciality
# of Volumes: 5,000
Specialties: 17th & 18th century literature.
Hours: Monday-Friday 10-6. Saturday by appointment.
Services: Appraisals, catalog, accepts want lists.
Travel: Downtown exit off I-95. Map 1.
Credit Cards: No
Owner: Robert J. Barry
Year Estab: 1931
Comments: A true antiquarian shop with a collection of rare and one-of-a-kind English literature books. A place to locate works found nowhere else. Not a shop for casual browsing.

The shop is located on the second floor of a commercial building.

Coventry Books (CT23) 203-787-2581
75 Whitney Avenue 06511

Collection:	General stock.
# of Volumes:	30,000
Specialties:	Books with a scholarly focus.
Hours:	Tuesday-Saturday 10-6, except Thursday till 8.
Travel:	Exit 3 off I-91. Whitney is at the second light. Or, exit 47 off I-95. Shop is across the street from the Bryn Mawr shop.
Credit Cards:	Yes
Owner:	Kevin Epperson (Manager)
Comments:	A storefront shop with a neat and well organized collection. Although the owner does not list any specific specialties, we noted strong sections in history and books about other countries.

Whitlock's, Inc. (CT24) 203-562-9841
17 Broadway 06511

Collection:	General stock.
# of Volumes:	12,000+
Specialties:	Connecticut history; rare books.
Hours:	Monday-Saturday 9:30-5:30.
Services:	Search service, accepts want lists.
Travel:	Downtown exit off I-95. The shop is on the second floor of a two story commercial building. Look for the name on the door. Map 1.
Credit Cards:	Yes
Owner:	Reverdy Whitlock
Year Estab:	1900
Comments:	Located one flight up, this veteran New Haven book dealer carries a good general stock with some rather rare volumes. All the books are in good or better condition. The shop is definitely worth a visit.

New Preston

Britannia Bookshop (CT25) 203-868-0368
At The Waterfall
Mailing address: P.O. Box 295 06777

Collection:	General stock, prints and curios.
# of Volumes:	12,000
Specialties:	Britain; Ireland; travel; decorative arts.
Hours:	Friday-Sunday 11-5 and by appointment.
Services:	Mail order.
Travel:	Route 202 to Route 45 north. Make first turn on left onto Church Street. Shop is at the bridge and waterfall. Look for the Union Jack flag at the entrance. Map 3.
Credit Cards:	Yes
Owner:	Barbara Corey Tippin
Year Estab:	1984
Comments:	This bi-level shop with an abundance of ambience has found a home in an old cider mill overlooking a pond and waterfall. The combination of richly stained book shelves, Victorian Anglo prints, curios, a grand piano and other furniture gives the shop a charm and distinctiveness all its own. Other than the areas of specialization, the well cared for collection is limited in size. Even if you don't leave here with a book you've been searching for, you will have enjoyed your visit and you'll remember the sound of the waterfall as you drive away.

Timothy Mawson Books & Prints (CT27) 203-868-0732
Main Street 06777

Collection:	Speciality
# of Volumes:	5,000
Specialties:	Gardening; cooking; decorative prints.
Hours:	Thursday-Sunday 11-5 or by appointment.
Travel:	Route 202 to Route 45 north. Shop is located in heart of historic village at end of a row of stores. Map 3.
Owner:	Timothy Mawson
Comments:	A small, attractively decorated storefront shop that's worth a visit if you're interested in any of the shop's specialty areas.

Reid & Wright - An Antiquarian Book Center (CT26)
287 New Milford Turnpike (Route 202) 203-868-7706
Mailing address: P.O. Box 2370 06777 Fax: 203-868-1242

Collection: General stock.
# of Volumes: 15,000
Specialties: Architecture; antiques; British Isles; woodworking.
Hours: Weekdays except Tuesday 10-5. Saturday & Sunday 12-5:30.
Services: Appraisals, search service.
Travel: On Route 202, near Chuck Wagon Restaurant. Look for a stand alone "new" barn like building with a red telephone booth in front. Map 3.
Credit Cards: No
Owner: Roger & Marsha Reid
Year Estab: 1992
Comments: This group shop gives book hunters the opportunity to shop over 50 used book dealers in a single visit. Designed with the comfort of the book hunter in mind, browsers will appreciate the wide aisles and the ease with which they can reach titles on the top shelves. The collection consists of reasonably priced quality books in excellent condition. Book hunters interested in specific categories will also appreciate the carefully prepared subject and dealer index as well as the well marked bookcases. We agree with the owner when he says, "If you love to browse, you are probably about as close to heaven as you will get for a while." When you're planning your visit here, make sure you allow yourself ample time: as with other group shops, chances are you'll find many of the same subject categories duplicated in the individual dealer displays.

Newington

Science Fiction Book Shop (CT28) 203-666-0696
2453 Berlin Turnpike (Route 5/15) 06111

Collection: Speciality hardcover and paperback.
# of Volumes: 1,000
Specialties: Science fiction; horror; fantasy.
Hours: Monday-Friday 10-9. Saturday 10-6. Sunday 11-5.

Travel: Routes 5/15 south of Hartford. Shop is 1/3 mile passed McDonalds in Harvard Square Place Shopping Center on right. Entrance is through the Record Breaker shop. Map 1.
Credit Cards: No
Comments: Most of the stock in this roadside shop consists of harder to find paperbacks in the genre, plus some new hardcovers and paperbacks. The number of used hardcover titles is very limited. The shop's better quality used books are located behind the counter.

Niantic

Book Barn (CT29) 203-739-5715
41 West Main Street 06357

Collection: General stock.
# of Volumes: 14,000
Specialties: Military history; local history; nautical.
Hours: Daily 11-6.
Services: Catalog, accepts want lists.
Travel: Exit 72 off I-95. Left onto Route 156. Shop is about 2 miles ahead on left in an old barn. Map 2.
Credit Cards: No
Owner: Randi White
Year Estab: 1988
Comments: This is an expanding shop with a gregarious and enterprising young owner. Housed in a three story barn, the second and third floors of which have been remodeled with a modern sheet rock interior, the collection offers a potpourri of subjects. The books are in mixed condition and reasonably priced. Some interesting finds. The owner's future plans include creating a cafe in the third floor loft area.

Old Mystic

Paul Brown Books (CT30) 203-536-9689
Route 27, Box 163 06372

Collection: General stock (mostly non fiction).
# of Volumes: 8,000+
Specialties: Nautical; military; Americana.
Hours: Tuesday-Saturday 12-5. Sunday 8-5.

Services: Search service, accepts want lists.
Travel: Located at intersection of I-95 (southbound), exit 90 and Route 27 in Hedley Building Shopping Center. Look for a yellow two story frame building. The entrance is through the adjoining ice cream parlor. Map 2.
Credit Cards: No
Owner: Paul D. Brown
Year Estab: 1976
Comments: A small shop with narrow aisles and mostly newer used books. While the shop does not offer much in the way of rare items, the careful browser may find a few surprises.

Plainville

The Book Exchange (CT31) 203-747-0770
327 New Britain Avenue (Route 372) 06062

Collection: General stock of hardcover and paperback and records.
# of Volumes: 100,000+
Specialties: Literature; science fiction; mystery; occult; new age; history; biography; comics (collectible).
Hours: Saturday-Wednesday 10-6. Thursday & Friday 10-8.
Services: Accepts want lists.
Travel: Exit 34 off I-84. If heading west on I-84, turn right. If heading east, turn left. Proceed about 1/4 mile to end of road. Turn left. Shop is ahead on right in an old red farmhouse. Map 1.
Credit Cards: Yes
Owner: David & Paula Rose
Year Estab: 1970
Comments: One's initial impression upon entering this shop is that all of its stock is in the science fiction, horror and "far out" genre. Upon climbing the stairs to the second level, though, the persistent book hunter will discover a maze of rooms containing used hardcover books in other subject areas. The books are moderately priced and depending upon your area of interest, you might discover an item worth adding to your collection. We reiterate: don't be misled by your initial impression. The collection is large, but smaller than the owner's estimate as noted above.

Salisbury

Lion's Head Books (CT32) 203-435-9328
Academy Street 06068

Collection:	General stock of new and used books.
# of Volumes:	10,000 (combined)
Specialties:	20th century gardening; architecture.
Hours:	Monday-Saturday 10-5.
Services:	Appraisals, search service, accepts want lists.
Travel:	Route 44 or Route 41 to Salisbury. Academy Street is in heart of village. Map 3.
Credit Cards:	Yes
Owner:	Mike McCabe
Year Estab:	1972

Stratford

Ron's Reading Room (CT33) 203-378-7667
235 Wilbar Drive 06497

Collection:	General stock.
Specialties:	Americana; leather bindings; biography; travel; children's.
Hours:	See Comments section.
Services:	Appraisals, catalog, mail order.
Credit Cards:	Yes
Owner:	Ron Weston
Year Estab:	1987
Comments:	The owner's stock is displayed at the following Connecticut antique malls: Stratford Antique Center, 400 Honeyspot Road, Stratford; Chelsea Antiques, 293 Pequot Avenue, Southport; Mystic River Antiques Market, 14 Holmes Street; The Antiques Depot, 455 Boston Post Road, Old Saybrook.

Torrington

Nutmeg Books (CT34) 203-482-9696
354 New Litchfield Street 06790

Collection:	General stock and ephemera.

# of Volumes:	15,000
Specialties:	Non fiction.
Hours:	Saturday, Sunday & holiday Mondays 11-6. Other times by chance or appointment.
Services:	Appraisals, search service, catalog, accepts want lists.
Travel:	On Route 202 near intersection with Route 8. Look for a two story gray house. Map 3.
Credit Cards:	Yes
Owner:	Bill & Debby Goring
Year Estab:	1977
Comments:	The collection in this shop, located to the rear of the house, consists primarily of older and more recently used books in mixed condition. Reasonably priced. Limited fiction section. The owners like to "freshen up" their stock in selected categories by periodically selling off entire categories and beginning anew.

Union

Traveler Restaurant Book Cellar (CT35) 203-684-9042
I-84, Exit 74
Mailing address: 1257 Buckley Highway 06076

Collection:	General stock.
# of Volumes:	20,000
Hours:	Daily 10-8, except Saturday 8-8.
Services:	Accepts want lists.
Travel:	Exit 74 off I-84. Restaurant/bookstore is visible from exit on south side of highway. Map 2.
Credit Cards:	Yes
Owner:	Martin W. Doyle
Year Estab:	1985
Comments:	The unique setting for this book store is the basement of a family restaurant where every diner gets to select a free book to take home. The collection is well organized with most subjects available. Most of the books are inexpensive reading copies. The restaurant is decorated with photos and short biographies of contemporary writers.

Wallingford

Bell Ringer Books (CT36) 203-269-5044
134 East Main Street 06492

Collection: General stock, ephemera and prints.
# of Volumes: 1,500
Hours: Monday, Wednesday, Friday 1-5, but best to call ahead. Other times by appointment.
Services: Appraisals
Travel: Exit 14 off I-91 north runs directly into East Main Street. Collection housed in owner's home, a red house immediately after light. From I-91 south, use exit 15. Map 1.
Credit Cards: No
Owner: Joseph H. Riotte
Year Estab: 1962
Comments: The owner states that his book selling endeavors are operated more as a hobby than a money making enterprise and that "collectors interests are considered over dealers' bargain hunting exploits".

Waterbury

The John Bale Book Company (CT37) 203-757-6531
108 Grand Street 06702

Collection: General stock.
# of Volumes: 3,000-5,000
Hours: Monday-Friday 8:30-5:30. Saturday 10-3. Sunday 10-1.
Services: Accepts want lists, search service, mail order.
Travel: Exit 21 off I-84. Eastbound, turn right onto Meadow, then right onto Grand. Westbound, turn right onto Field, then right onto Grand. Map 3.
Credit Cards: No
Owner: Donato Gaeta
Year Estab: 1992
Comments: This storefront shop located directly across from the main post office in downtown Waterbury houses a fledgling used book store that, in our view, offers great promise. The collection is modest in size but makes every effort to cover

most subjects. The books range from more recent vintage to collectibles. Rarer books are kept in a glass cabinet. There's also a scattering of paperbacks. Prices are reasonable.

West Cornwall

Barbara Farnsworth, Bookseller (CT38) 203-672-6571
Route 128
Mailing address: P.O. Box 9 06796

Collection:	General stock, prints and drawings.
# of Volumes:	40,000
Specialties:	Horticulture; cooking; modern first editions; English history; European history; natural history.
Hours:	Saturday 9-5. Weekdays by chance or appointment.
Services:	Occasional catalog, accepts want lists.
Travel:	1/4 mile east of covered bridge on Route 128. Map 3.
Credit Cards:	Yes
Owner:	Barbara Farnsworth
Year Estab:	1978
Comments:	This absolutely delightful shop is a must for any true used book afficionado. The books are beautifully displayed on both floors of this former Masonic Temple. The books are easy to view and reach, there's ample room between shelves and comfortable chairs are always in sight. The books are in immaculate condition and most reasonably priced. Rarer books are kept in a separate private room. The only unfortunate feature of this store is that the only time a book lover can be certain it is open is on Saturdays. But, because the owner says she is frequently on the premises other days, we suggest a call if you're in the area. It would be a pity to miss this charming stop.

West Hartford

The Jumping Frog/Hartford Book Center (CT39) 203-523-1622
585 Prospect Avenue 06105

Collection:	General stock and ephemera.
# of Volumes:	60,000+

Specialties: Modern first editions; Americana; art; photography; exploration; transportation; nature; cookbooks; presidents.
Hours: Tuesday-Saturday 12-8. Sunday 12-6. Monday by chance or appointment.
Services: Appraisals, search service, mail order.
Travel: Exit 44 off I-84. Proceed north on Prospect Avenue. Shop is on left. Map 1.
Credit Cards: Yes
Owner: Bill McBride
Year Estab: 1983
Comments: The authors visited the owner's new group shop during its first month or so of business and returned two years later to find it had grown in both quality and quantity. The shop's interior is a book browser's delight: wide aisles, moderate height bookcases, comfortable seating, a chess table waiting for players, a large children's play area, and one of the very few shops we have visited that prominently displays signs for rest rooms for the comfort and convenience of its customers. The collection covers virtually all subject areas and for the most part, the books are in excellent condition and are reasonably priced.

West Hartford Book Shop (CT40) 203-232-2028
322 Park Road 06119

Collection: General stock.
# of Volumes: 15,000
Specialties: Literature; leather bindings; gardening; travel; sets.
Hours: Monday-Saturday 11-6. Thursday till 9. Most Sundays 11-5.
Services: Appraisals, search service, accepts want lists, book repairs.
Travel: Exit 43 off I-84. Right turn at end of exit. Proceed through 2 lights. Shop is fourth store on left. Map 1.
Credit Cards: Yes
Owner: Michael Polasko
Year Estab: 1976
Comments: While this small shop has a healthy sized collection, it is easy for a book hunter to develop a sense of claustrophobia while browsing. In order to make the maximum possible use of his limited space, the owner has created a series of compact alcoves off a narrow center aisle. The cramped

quarters should not dissaude the determined book lover from visiting, though. The stock consists of more recently used books with a limited selection of older and very rare materials. We also noted some first editions.

Woodbury

Books About Antiques (CT41) 203-263-0241
139 Main Street South 06798

Collection:	Specialty new and used books.
# of Volumes:	350 (used)
Specialty:	Antiques and collectibles
Hours:	Monday-Saturday 10-5:30. Sunday 12-4. Closed Tuesday during July & August.
Services:	Accepts want lists.
Travel:	Exit 15 off I-84. Proceed east on Route 6 for 5.8 miles. Map 3.
Credit Cards:	Yes
Owner:	Greg Johnson
Year Estab:	1988

Bygone Books (CT42) 203-266-0123
289 Main Street South
Mailing address: P.O. Box 854 06798

Collection:	General stock.
# of Volumes:	3,000-3,500
Hours:	Tuesday, Thursday, Sunday 10-4. Wednesday, Friday, Saturday 10-5.
Services:	Search service, accepts want lists.
Travel:	Exit 15 off I-84. Proceed north on Route 6 for about 5 miles into Woodbury. Shop is on right in a two story gray building. The entrance is one flight up. Map 3.
Credit Cards:	No
Owner:	Terri Hale
Year Estab:	1992

Bethany

The Antiquarium 203-393-2723
166 Humiston Drive 06524

Collection: Specialty books and ephemera.
# of Volumes: 8,000
Specialties: Scholarly and research material; Iceland; Haiti, bibliography; natural history; Mervyn Peake; Arthur Quiller-Couch.
Services: Appraisals, accepts want lists.
Credit Cards: No
Owner: Lee & Marian Ash
Year Estab: 1958

Bethel

Bethel Bibliophiles 203-790-8588
8 Highland Avenue 06801

Collection: Specialty and small general stock.
# of Volumes: 9,000
Specialties: Science fiction; fantasy; modern first editions.
Services: Search service, accepts want lists.
Credit Cards: No
Owner: Christopher Grahame-Smith
Year Estab: 1985

Branford

Richard Blacher 203-481-3321
209 Plymouth Colony, Alps Road 06405

Collection: Specialty
# of Volumes: 2,000-3,000
Specialties: Roycroft Shop and other American private presses.
Services: Search service, accepts want lists.
Credit Cards: No
Owner: Richard Blacher
Year Estab: 1978

Branford Rare Books 203-488-7477
Box 2088 06405

Collection: Specialty books and ephemera.
# of Volumes: 500
Specialties: Americana; maps; 19th century ephemera.
Services: Appraisals, search service, accepts want lists, mail order.
Credit Cards: Yes
Owner: John R. Elliott
Year Estab: 1978

Brookfield

Boyson Book Nook 203-775-0176
23 Cove Road 06804

Collection: General stock.
# of Volumes: 4,000
Specialties: Children's; illustrated; science; technology; travel; non fiction.
Services: Search service, accepts want lists.
Credit Cards: No
Owner: Bert Boyson
Year Estab: 1982
Comments: Additional books may be seen at Bittersweet Antiques, Route 7, Gaylordsville, CT. Open daily (except Wednesday) 10-5. Sunday 12-5.

Canterbury

Marjorie M. Hall 203-546-9933
124 Elmdale Road 06331

Collection: Specialty books and ephemera.
# of Volumes: 2,000
Specialties: Regional Americana; American art; maritime.
Services: Catalog, accepts want lists.
Credit Cards: No
Owner: Marjorie Hall
Year Estab: 1965

Colebrook

Colebrook Book Barn 203-379-3185
657 North Colebrook Road (Route 183) 06021

Collection:	General stock.
# of Volumes:	20,000
Specialties:	Americana; American literature; first editions.
Hours:	By chance 10-5 or by appointment.
Services:	Appraisals
Travel:	Approximately 8 miles from junction of Routes 8 & 44. Take Route 44 west to Route 183 north.
Credit Cards:	No
Owner:	Robert S. Seymour
Year Estab:	1955

Collinsville

Country Lane Books 203-489-8852
P.O. Box 47 06022

Collection:	Specialty
# of Volumes:	1,000
Specialties:	British & American first editions; western Americana; children's.
Services:	Catalog, appraisals, accepts want lists.
Credit Cards:	No
Owner:	Edward T. Myers
Year Estab:	1967

Lawrence Golder, Rare Books 203-693-8631
P.O. Box 144 06022 Fax: 203-693-8110

Collection:	Specialty
# of Volumes:	150
Specialties:	Rare general Americana; voyages; travel; exploration; arctic; rare books in most fields.
Services:	Appraisals, catalog.
Credit Cards:	No
Owner:	Lawrence Golder
Year Estab:	1970

Cos Cob

The Book Block 203-629-2990
8 Loughlin Avenue 06807 Fax: 203-629-1051

Collection:	Specialty
# of Volumes:	500
Specialties:	Private press; fine bindings; literature; illustrated; Sir Richard F. Burton; early printed books.
Services:	Appraisals, catalog, restoration, conservation and bookbinding.
Credit Cards:	Yes
Owner:	David Block
Year Estab:	1979

Danbury

Orpheus Books 203-792-4990
4 Abbott Avenue 06810

Collection:	Specialty
# of Volumes:	3,500
Specialties:	Classic music, including opera, history, theory, biography.
Services:	Catalog, search service.
Credit Cards:	No
Owner:	Irving & Rita Goldstein
Year Estab:	1986

Fairfield

Kemet Books 203-255-5015
1700 Post Road, P.O. Box 662 06430

Collection:	General stock.
# of Volumes:	5,000
Specialties:	Egypt
Hours:	By chance Tuesday-Saturday 12-5 or by appointment.
Services:	Catalog, accepts want lists, search service.
Travel:	Exit 21 (Mill Plain Road) off I-95. Make left onto Route 1 (Boston Post Road). At first light, turn left into shop's parking lot.
Credit Cards:	Yes

Owner: Steve P. Turi
Year Estab: 1991

A. Lucas, Books 203-259-2572
89 Round Hill Road 06430

Collection: General stock.
# of Volumes: 14,000
Specialties: First edition literature.
Services: Appraisals, search service, accepts want lists, mail order.
Credit Cards: No
Owner: Alexander Lucas
Year Estab: 1972

Museum Gallery Book Shop 203-259-7114
360 Mine Hill Road 06430

Collection: Specialty
# of Volumes: 5,000
Specialties: Art; illustrated.
Services: Catalog (occasional), accepts want lists.
Credit Cards: No
Owner: Henry B. Caldwell
Year Estab: 1977

Goshen

Angler's and Shooter's Bookshelf 203-491-2500
Box 173 06756

Collection: Specialty
# of Volumes: 12,000-15,000
Specialties: Hunting; angling.
Services: Catalog, appraisals.
Credit Cards: No
Owner: Col. Henry A. Siegel
Year Estab: 1967

Granby

Fin N' Feather Gallery 203-653-6557
36 Lakeside Drive 06035

Collection:	Specialty
# of Volumes:	6,000
Specialties:	Hunting; fishing.
Services:	Search service, catalog, accepts want lists.
Credit Cards:	Yes
Owner:	Barry Small

Greenwich

Melvin Milligan Rare Books 203-869-0852
8 Glen Court 06830 Fax: 203-869-5820

Collection:	Specialty
# of Volumes:	3,000
Specialties:	Middle East; Africa; Asia; Sir Richard F. Burton.
Services:	Accepts want lists.
Credit Cards:	No
Owner:	Melvin & Betty Milligan
Year Estab:	1988

Hamden

American Worlds Books 203-776-3558
Box 6305, Whitneyville Station 06517

Collection:	Speciality
# of Volumes:	9,000+
Specialties:	American literature; American cultural history.
Services:	Catalog, accepts want lists, search service.
Credit Cards:	Yes
Owner:	Nolan E. Smith
Year Estab:	1970

Antique Books 203-281-6606
3651 Whitney Avenue 06518

Collection:	General stock.

# of Volumes:	30,000
Specialties:	History; science; Civil War; religion; early school books, literature; agriculture. Most books are over 100 years old.
Hours:	By chance or appointment.
Credit Cards:	No
Owner:	Willis O. Underwood
Year Estab:	1975

McBlain Books 203-281-0400
2348 Whitney Avenue
Mailing address: P.O. Box 5062 06518

Collection:	Specialty with very small general stock.
# of Volumes:	6,000
Specialties:	Africa; Asia; black America; Latin America; Middle East, Eastern Europe; travel; travel guides.
Services:	Catalog
Credit Cards:	Yes
Owner:	Philip & Sharon McBlain
Year Estab:	1971

Hartford

Richard F. Murphy, Jr. 203-951-9266
P.O. Box 375 06141

Collection:	Specialty books and ephemera.
# of Volumes:	10,000
Specialties:	Estate libraries; Americana; magazines.
Services:	Appraisals, mail order, accepts want lists.
Credit Cards:	No
Owner:	Richard F. Murphy, Jr.

Mansfield Center

Sheila B. Amdur, Books 203-423-3176
130 Sawmill Brook Lane 06250

Collection:	Specialty and small general stock.
# of Volumes:	3,000
Specialties:	Connecticut; New England; history of medicine and psychiatry.

Services: Accepts want lists, mail order.
Credit Cards: No
Owner: Sheila B. Amdur
Year Estab: 1976

Marlborough

Considine Books 203-295-0526
41 South Main Street 06447

Collection: General stock.
# of Volumes: 3,000
Specialties: Philosophy; modern literature.
Services: Search service, accepts want lists, catalog.
Credit Cards: No
Owner: Nancy Considine
Year Estab: 1989

Meriden

Dunn & Powell Books 203-235-0480
251 Baldwin Avenue
Mailing address: P.O. Box 2544 06450

Collection: Specialty
# of Volumes: 12,000
Specialties: Detective; Ayn Rand first editions; anarchism; atheism.
Services: Catalog
Credit Cards: Yes
Owner: Steve Powell & William Dunn
Year Estab: 1991 (see Comments)
Comments: Formerly Dunn's Mysteries and Steve Powell Books. The business operates a second office in Bar Harbor, ME. See Maine listing.

New Haven

David M. Lesser, Fine Antiquarian Books 203-787-5910
400 Orange Street
Mailing address: P.O. Box 1729 06507-1729

Collection: Specialty

# of Volumes: 5,000
Specialties: 18th and 19th century Americana.
Services: Catalog
Credit Cards: No
Owner: David M. Lesser
Year Estab: 1989

William Reese Co. 203-789-8081
409 Temple Street 06511 Fax: 203-865-7653

Collection: Specialty
# of Volumes: 20,000
Specialties: Americana; travel; voyages; American and English literature.
Services: Appraisals, catalog.
Credit Cards: No
Owner: William Reese
Year Estab: 1979

R.W. Smith - Bookseller 203-776-5564
51 Trumbull Street 06510

Collection: Specialty books and ephemera.
# of Volumes: 15,000
Specialties: American art; architecture; photography; design; decorative arts; cartoons.
Services: Search service, catalog, accepts want lists.
Credit Cards: No
Owner: Raymond W. Smith
Year Estab: 1975

New London

J. T. Smart Books 203-443-2123
P.O. Box 544 06320

Collection: Specialty
# of Volumes: 5,000+
Specialties: 19th century books only. Books with wood engraved, steel engraved, etched, chrome lithograph and hand colored plates; travel; biography; English history; natural history; poetry.

Services: Appraisals, catalog, accepts want lists.
Credit Cards: Yes
Owner: Todd Weyman & Jennifer Gershon
Year Estab: 1990
Comments: The owners also display a small general stock of 19th century books at the Library Antiques Center in Williamstown, MA.

New Milford

Scarlett Letter Books 203-354-4181
155 Candlewood Mountain Road 06776 203-350-1766

Collection: General stock, prints and original art.
# of Volumes: 2,000
Specialties: Children's; medical; cooking; etiquette; illustrated.
Hours: October 1-May 1 only.
Services: Appraisals
Credit Cards: No
Owner: Kathleen & Michael Lazare
Year Estab: 1971
Comments: Owners operate an open shop, The Pansy Patch, in St. Andrews, New Brunswick, Canada, from May 15 to September 15.

New Preston

Trebizond Rare Books 203-868-2621
Main Street, P.O. Box 2430 06777

Collection: Specialty
# of Volumes: 2,500
Specialties: English, American and continental literature; voyages; travel; 18th century British books.
Hours: By chance or appointment.
Services: Appraisals, catalog, accepts want lists.
Credit Cards: No
Owner: Williston R. Benedict
Year Estab: 1975

Newtown

American Political Biography 203-270-9777
39 Boggs Hill Road 06470

Collection: Specialty
# of Volumes: 5,000
Specialties: Biographies of American statesman, especially United States presidents.
Services: Search service, catalog, accepts want lists.
Credit Cards: No
Owner: Jeffrey R. Speirs
Year Estab: 1970

Bancroft Book Mews 203-426-6338
86 Sugar Lane 06470

Collection: Specialty
# of Volumes: 3,000-5,000
Specialties: Performing arts.
Services: Catalog, search service, accepts want lists.
Credit Cards: No
Owner: Eleanor Bancroft
Year Estab: 1980

The Pages of Yesteryear 203-426-0864
9 Old Hawleyville Road 06470

Collection: Non fiction only.
# of Volumes: 1,000
Specialties: History
Services: Appraisals, mail order.
Credit Cards: No
Owner: John Renjilian
Year Estab: 1964

Pomfret Center

Pomfret Book and Print Shop 203-928-2862
Box 214 (Routes 44 & 169) 06259

Collection: General stock and ephemera.

# of Volumes:	4,000-5,000
Specialties:	New England; town maps; atlases; postcards; prints.
Services:	Accepts want lists, appraisals.
Credit Cards:	No
Owner:	Roger & Judith Black
Year Estab:	1967

Ridgefield

Timeless Books 203-431-0203
159 Sleepy Hollow Road 06877

Collection:	Specialty
# of Volumes:	6,000+
Specialties:	Children's; children's series.
Services:	Accepts want lists, mail order.
Credit Cards:	No
Owner:	Dorothy & Tony Saia
Year Estab:	1987

South Windsor

John Woods Books 203-289-3927
347 Main Street 06074

Collection:	Specialty
# of Volumes:	10,000
Specialties:	Medicine; dentistry.
Services:	Catalog, accepts want lists.
Credit Cards:	No
Owner:	John A. Woods
Year Estab:	1976

Southbury

Chiswick Book Shop, Inc. 203-264-7599
Professional Building, Village Street 06488

Collection:	Specialty
Specialties:	Printing; typography; private presses. All books are old or rare.
Services:	Catalog

Credit Cards: No
Owner: Herman & Aveve Cohen
Year Estab: 1931

Stevenson

Starr Book Works 203-268-3921
82 Pachaug Trail
Mailing address: P.O. Box 825 06491

Collection: General stock in fine bindings.
# of Volumes: 1,000+
Specialties: 17th, 18th 19th century fine bindings.
Services: Custom bookbinding and restoration work done on premises.
Travel: Route 34 to Route 111 to Cottage Street. Turn right onto Downs Road to Pachaug Trail.
Credit Cards: No
Owner: Chris & Donna Starr
Year Estab: 1991

Stonington

Battersea Books 203-535-1622
106 Water Street 06378

Collection: General stock.
# of Volumes: 10,000
Specialties: Nautical; literature.
Hours: By chance or appointment.
Services: Search service.
Travel: Exit 92 off I-95. Right at end of ramp then immediate left into village. Shop is in rear of building through a side gate.
Credit Cards: No
Owner: Grace Jones
Year Estab: 1981
Comments: A quaint shop with narrow aisles and overflowing shelves. The books are in fairly good condition and are moderately priced. The entrance is up a few steps.

Storrs

Rainbow Books 203-429-5343
146 Moulton Road 06268

Collection:	Specialty and some general stock.
# of Volumes:	4,000
Specialties:	Children's, including picture books, folk tales and classics. About one third of collection is adult general stock.
Services:	Search service, accepts want lists.
Credit Cards:	No
Owner:	Caroline C. Lucal
Year Estab:	1986

Washington

Crofter's Books 212-769-4213
P.O. Box 1236 06793

Collection:	Specialty
# of Volumes:	10,000
Specialties:	Film; aeronautic; Orwell; labor.
Services:	Search service, accepts want lists, mail order.
Credit Cards:	Yes
Owner:	B. Parkman
Year Estab:	1976

West Cornwall

Deborah Benson Bookseller 203-672-6614
62 River Road 06796 Fax: 203-672-6615

Collection:	Specialty
# of Volumes:	7,000
Specialties:	Early medical; diabetes; modern first editions; Alice in Wonderland.
Services:	Appraisals, accepts want lists.
Credit Cards:	No
Owner:	Deborah Covington
Year Estab:	1948

West Hartford

David E. Foley, Bookseller 203-561-0783
76 Bonnyview Road 06107

Collection:	Specialty
# of Volumes:	3,000
Specialties:	Hunting; fishing, firearms, archery, fox hunting; sporting dogs; natural history as it relates to sporting subjects.
Services:	Appraisals, search service, catalog, accepts want lists.
Credit Cards:	No
Owner:	David E. Foley

Windsor

Cedric L. Robinson - Booksellers 203-688-2582
597 Palisado Avenue 06095

Collection:	Specialty
# of Volumes:	15,000
Specialties:	Americana; American literature; manuscripts; maps; prints; photography.
Hours:	Between 9-5, Monday-Saturday.
Services:	Appraisals, catalog, accepts want lists.
Credit Cards:	No
Owner:	Cedric & William Robinson
Year Estab:	1946

Stephen Auslender 203-762-3455
P.O. Box 122 Wilton 06897

Collection:	Specialty
# of Volumes:	500
Specialties:	Military, including history and technology.
Services:	Catalog
Credit Cards:	No
Owner:	Stephen Auslender

Bankside Books 203-255-5379
372 Greens Farms Road Westport 06880

Collection:	Specialty
# of Volumes:	2,000
Specialties:	Mark Twain; American and British first editions; press books.
Services:	Search service.
Credit Cards:	No
Owner:	Richard A. Lowenstein
Year Estab:	1980

Warren Blake Books 203-459-0820
308 Hadley Drive Trumbull 06611

Collection:	General stock.
# of Volumes:	1,250
Specialties:	Astronomy
Services:	Catalog
Credit Cards:	No
Owner:	Warren Blake
Year Estab:	1972

Book Troves 203-754-7589
197 Draher Street Waterbury 06708

Collection:	Specialty
# of Volumes:	4,000
Specialties:	Nautical; Americana.
Services:	Search service, catalog, accepts want lists.
Credit Cards:	No
Owner:	Yvonne Cronauer
Year Estab:	1991

Philip Buchanan, Bookdealer 203-498-8333
P.O. Box 6458 Hamden 06517

Collection: General stock.
# of Volumes: 10,000
Specialties: Abraham Lincoln; Civil War; scholarly music.
Services: Catalog, search service, accepts want lists.
Credit Cards: No
Owner: Philip Buchanan
Year Estab: 1986

Marc Chabot 203-263-3783
72 Joshua Hill Road Woodbury 06798

Collection: Specialty
# of Volume: Under 500
Specialty: Art reference
Services: Accepts want lists.
Credit Cards: No
Owner: Marc Chabot
Year Estab: 1990

George H. Davis 203-438-8473
82 Soundview Road Ridgefield 06877

Collection: Specialty
# of Volumes: 1,000+
Specialties: Fiction, including, E. Phillips Oppenheim, Joseph C. Lincoln, James Oliver Curwood, C.S. Forester.
Services: Appraisals, accepts want lists.
Credit Cards: No
Owner: George H. Davis
Year Estab: 1986

Michael C. Dooling 203-758-8130
P.O. Box 1047 Middlebury 06762

Collection: Specialty
# of Volumes: 1,500
Specialties: Art; architecture; fine bindings; travel; exploration; science; medicine; rare books.

Services: Appraisals, catalog.
Credit Cards: No
Owner: Michael C. Dooling
Year Estab: 1978

Ed McDonald's Mostly Mystery 203-380-1699
111 Boston Avenue Stratford 06497

Collection: Specialty
Specialties: Mystery; science fiction; horror. Signed first editions and reading copies.
Services: Catalog, accepts want lists.
Owner: Ed McDonald
Year Estab: 1992

Elliot's Books 203-484-2184
799 Forest Road, P.O. Box 6 Northford 06472 Fax: 203-484-7644

Collection: General stock.
# of Volumes: 100,000
Specialties: Scholarly out-of-print; university presses; anthropology; linguistics; Asia, Africa; Latin America; social studies; economic development; science; humanities.
Services: Appraisals, search service, accepts want lists.
Credit Cards: No
Owner: E. M. Ephraim
Year Estab: 1957

Extensive Search Service 203-774-1203
51 Squaw Rock Road Danielson 06239 Fax: 203-774-2949

Collection: Specialty
Specialties: Disneyana; cartoon animation and original art; Walt Kelly; Wizard of Oz; Batman animation art; television and movie memorabilia; Civil War maps.
Services: Search service, catalog.
Credit Cards: Yes
Owner: David Haveles
Year Estab: 1970

Fourth Estate Plus 203-447-1361
P.O. Box 866 New London 06320

Collection:	General stock and ephemera.
# of Volumes:	5,000
Specialties:	Nautical; Connecticut; children's; newspapers; prints; postcards; magazines.
Services:	Subject lists, search service (children's and magazines only), accepts want lists.
Credit Cards:	No
Owner:	Jim & Jeanne Kontoleon
Year Estab:	1986

Shirley Gold Books 203-525-9639
56 Coolidge Street Hartford 06106

Collection:	General stock.
# of Volumes:	8,000-9,000
Specialties:	Americana; Middle East; Connecticut; Russia; Japan; China; Southeast Asia; American literature; art.
Services:	Appraisals, search service, accepts want lists.
Credit Cards:	No
Owner:	Shirley Gold
Year Estab:	1965

Charles E. Gould, Jr. 203-927-3017
P. O. Box 543 Kent 06757

Collection:	Specialty
# of Volumes:	300-500
Specialties:	P.G. Wodehouse only: first and rare editions, later issues, reprints, ephemera, autographs, sheet music.
Services:	Catalog, accepts want lists.
Credit Cards:	No
Owner:	Charles E. Gould, Jr.
Year Estab:	1980

Hop River Books
P.O. Box 261 Columbia 06237

Collection:	General stock (mostly non fiction).
# of Volumes:	12,000-13,000

Specialties: Natural history.
Services: Search service, catalog, accepts want lists.
Credit Cards: No
Owner: Ken & Marilyn Bowen

George Kassis 203-656-0849
P.O. Box 1131 Darien 06820

Collection: Speciality
Specialties: Pre 1900 Middle East books, maps and prints.
Services: Accepts want lists.
Credit Cards: No
Owner: George Kassis

David Ladner Books 203-288-6575
P.O. Box 6179 Whitneyville 06517

Collection: General stock.
# of Volumes: 5,000
Specialties: Books about books; art; architecture; illustrated; Russia; foreign language books.
Services: Appraisals, search service, catalog, accepts want lists.
Credit Cards: No
Owner: David Ladner
Year Estab: 1976

L. Lyon 203-673-5044
P.O. Box 1031 Avon 06001

Collection: Specialty
Specialties: Americana; American history; Connecticut; Hartford, CT.
Services: Accepts want lists.
Credit Cards: No
Owner: L. Lyon
Year Estab: 1979

Julian J. Nadolny 203-225-5353
121 Hickory Hill Road Kensington 06037

Collection: Specialty
# of Volumes: 5,000
Specialties: Natural history.

Services: Catalog, appraisals.
Credit Cards: No
Owner: Julian J. Nadolny

New England Books 203-393-0789
16 Brinton Road Bethany 06524

Collection: General stock.
# of Volumes: 5,000
Specialties: Early New England and American imprints; New England; New England authors; 19th & 20th century literature; leather bindings; 17th & 18th century American and English theology.
Services: Accepts want lists.
Credit Cards: No
Owner: Donald R. Menzies
Year Estab: 1981

William Peters, Bookseller 203-429-1970
P.O. Box 442 Willington 06279

Collection: Specialty
# of Volumes: 5,000-7,000
Specialties: Contemporary first editions; poetry; small press; 20th century theology.
Services: Catalog, accepts want lists.
Credit Cards: No
Owner: William Peters
Year Estab: 1981

E. Tatro, Bookseller 203-563-7884
60 Goff Road Wethersfield 06109

Collection: Specialty
# of Volumes: 1,000
Specialties: Sports (baseball, boxing, football, golf, olympic games, wrestling, strong men, strength, weight lifting, physical culture.)
Services: Catalog, accepts want lists.
Credit Cards: No
Owner: E. Tatro
Year Estab: 1965

Town's End Books 203-529-3896
132 Hemlock Drive Deep River 06417

Collection:	Specialty
# of Volumes:	1,500-2,000
Specialties:	Natural history writers (fiction and non fiction) including Eric Sloane, Peter Matthiessen, John McPhee, Kenneth Roberts and Ian Fleming.
Services:	Accepts want lists.
Credit Cards:	No
Owner:	John D. & Judy Townsend
Year Estab:	1992

Treasure Hunters 203-487-0240
P.O. Box 463 Mansfield Center 06250

Collection:	Specialty books and ephemera.
Specialties:	Radio
Services:	Accepts want lists.
Credit Cards:	No
Owner:	Barbara Davies
Year Estab:	1986

Turkey Hill Books 203-938-8833
4 Packer Brook Road Redding 06896 Fax: 203-259-8062

Collection:	General stock.
# of Volumes:	5,000
Specialties:	First, signed and limited editions; illustrated; children's; art.
Services:	Appraisals, search service, accepts want lists.
Credit Cards:	No
Owner:	Jack Grogins
Year Estab:	1972

Barbara Weindling 203-746-2514
60 Ball Pond Road Danbury 06811

Collection:	Specialty
# of Volumes:	5,000
Specialties:	Cookbooks
Services:	Search service, catalog, accepts want lists.

Credit Cards: No
Owner: Barbara Weindling
Year Estab: 1972

Robert Williams 203-393-1488
57 Lacey Road Bethany 06525

Collection: Specialty
# of Volumes: 5,000
Specialties: Dogs; hunting; fishing.
Services: Accepts want lists, search service.
Credit Cards: No
Owner: Robert Williams
Year Estab: 1977

The World War II Historian 203-423-8194
763 Brooklyn Turnpike
Mailing address: P.O. Box 327 Scotland 06264

Collection: Specialty
# of Volumes: 5,000
Specialties: World War II.
Services: Catalog, accepts want lists.
Credit Cards: No
Owner: Thomas W. Heinonen
Year Estab: 1986

Antique Dealers

Verde Antiques & Books 203-379-3135
64 Main Street (Route 44) Winstead

Maine

Alphabetical Listing By Dealer

Alphabetical Listing By Location

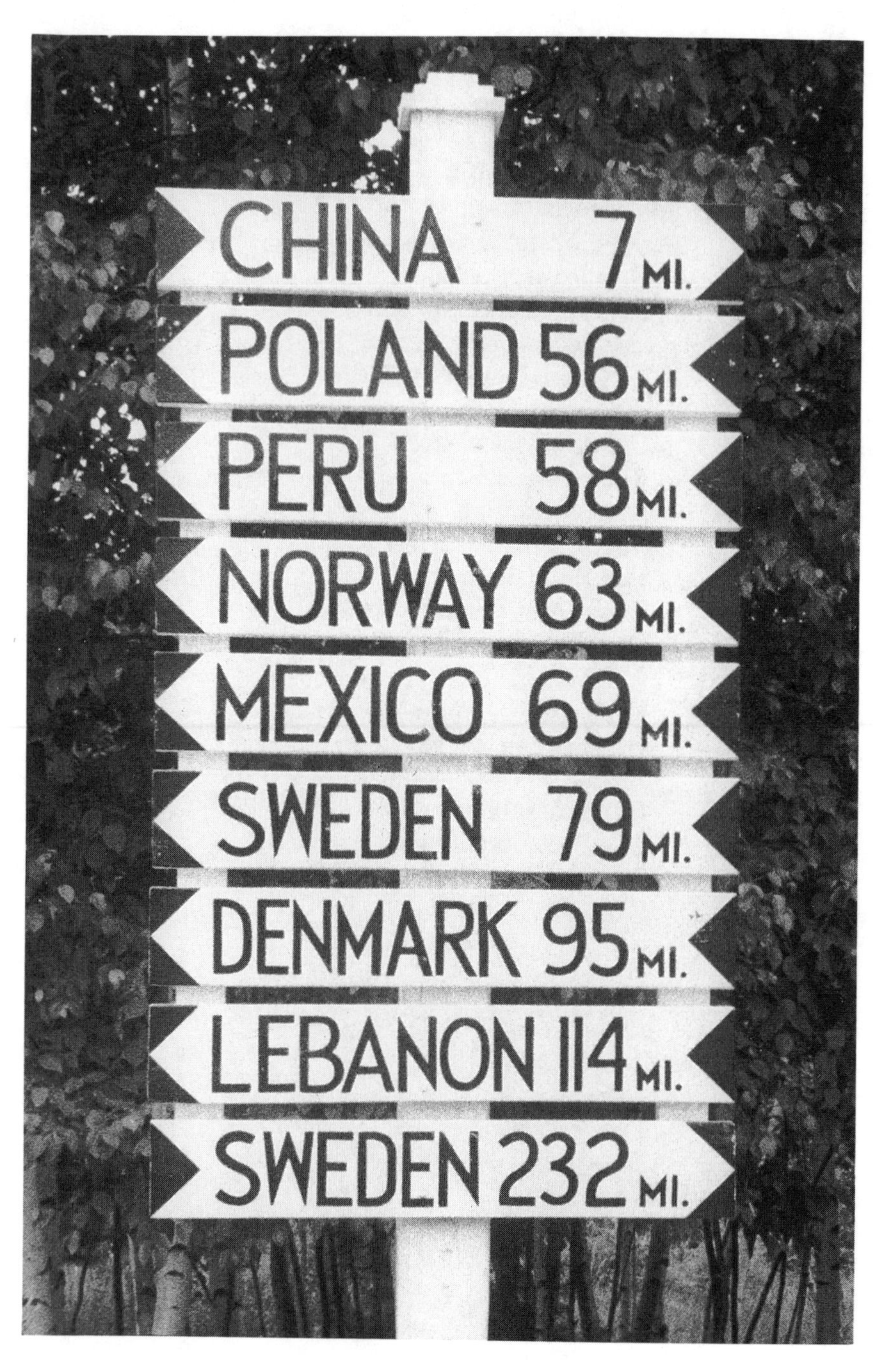

Book hunting in Maine

Augusta

Memory Lane (ME1) 207-622-1791
Outer Western Avenue 04330

Collection:	General stock and ephemera.
# of Volumes:	5,000+
Specialties:	Americana; children's; poetry; history; war.
Hours:	Monday-Thursday 9-5. Friday 9-3. Saturday & Sunday by chance or appointment.
Services:	Search service, accepts want lists, mail order.
Travel:	From Augusta, proceed west on Route 202 1 1/2 miles. Shop is on left at Drummond Motors. Map 4.
Credit Cards:	Yes
Owner:	Pamela S. Drummond
Year Estab:	1989
Comments:	A roadside used book/collectibles shop with a modest sized collection that appeared to be smaller than the owner's estimate when we visited. Worth a stop if you're in the area.

Bangor

Lippincott Books (ME2) 207-942-4398
624 Hammond Street 04401

Collection:	General stock, ephemera and pulps.
# of Volumes:	15,000
Specialties	Maine; Canada and North Woods; philosophy; metaphysics; poetry; literature; mystery; science fiction; Stephen King; some uncommon books.
Hours:	Monday-Friday 10-5:30. Saturday 10-5.
Services:	Appraisals
Travel:	Exit 46 off I-95. Shop is 1/2 mile from exit, across from a Subway fast food restaurant. Map 6.
Credit Cards:	Yes
Owner:	Bill Lippincott
Year Estab:	1975
Comments:	Don't be fooled by the sign on the outside of this one story shop that reads: "Old Books & Comic Books." The shop houses an excellent and reasonably priced general stock as well as an in depth collection of rare and older books in the fantasy/mystery/horror genre.

Pro Libris Bookshop (ME3) 207-942-3019
10 Third Street 04401

Collection:	General stock of paperback and some hardcover.
# of Volumes:	20,000+
Specialties:	Literature; science fiction; mystery; romance; westerns.
Hours:	Monday-Saturday 10-6. Sunday 12-4.
Travel:	1 block south of intersection of U.S. Route 2 and Maine Route 222, across the street from shopping center parking lot. Map 6.
Credit Cards:	No
Owner	Eric Furry
Year Estab:	1980
Comments:	A neat shop with a well organized collection.

Bar Harbor

Treasures, Bargains & Books (ME4) 207-359-2106
37 1/2 Cottage Street
Mailing address: P.O. Box 26 Sedgwick 04676

Collection:	General stock, ephemera, records and collectibles.
# of Volumes:	3,000
Hours:	Summer: Daily 9AM-10PM. Fall & Spring: Daily 11-5. Winter: Saturday only.
Travel:	Downtown Bar Harbor next to the Criterion Theatre. Map 6.
Credit Cards:	No
Owner:	Paul Volenik
Year Estab:	1991
Comments:	This small, tightly packed shop offers an interesting cornucopia of books, ephemera and collectibles. The book collection is modest in size and scope. If you have children, bring them along. They'll enjoy browsing through the shop's unusual display of memorabilia.

Belfast

The Booklover's Attic (ME5) 207-338-2450
RFD #2, Box 8 04915

Collection:	General stock (primarily non fiction) and records.
# of Volumes:	20,000
Specialties:	Aviation; maritime; military; music; science fiction; American first editions; photography; architecture; children's. Records range from classical to popular and jazz.
Hours:	April 15-October 15: Monday-Saturday 10-6. Sunday 11-5. Remainder of year by chance or appointment.
Services:	Appraisals, search service, accepts want lists.
Travel:	Just over the Belfast Bridge proceeding north on Route 1. Shop is on left. Map 6.
Credit Cards:	No
Owner:	Peter & Estelle Plumb
Year Estab:	1975
Comments:	Easy to find along a major road, this fine collection is housed in a two story addition to the owner's home. A large music section (books and records) occupies a separate upstairs room. An excellent science fiction collection, including many first editions, is located on the first floor.

Frederica deBeurs Books (ME6) 207-338-4122
42 Cedar Street 04915

Collection:	General stock.
# of Volumes:	12,000
Specialties:	Maine authors; fine and decorative arts; mathematics; science; technology.
Hours:	Wednesday-Sunday 10-5.
Services:	Catalog, accepts want lists, mail order.
Travel:	From Route 1 take exit Route 3. Proceed to downtown Belfast. Cedar Street is fifth street on right after Shop n' Save. Map 6.
Credit Cards:	No
Owner:	Frederica deBeurs
Year Estab:	1980
Comments:	Located in a two story frame house in a residential neighborhood, this immaculately kept shop offers an interesting collection of moderately priced books. The lower shelves in

the children's section contain some inexpensive books that should interest the younger browsers in the family.

Blue Hill

Bliss House Books (ME7) 207-374-2259
Pleasant Street 04614

Collection:	General stock.
# of Volumes:	4,000
Hours:	June-October: Thursday, Friday, Saturday 12-5 and by appointment any time.
Services:	Appraisals, accepts want lists.
Travel:	Route 1 to Route 15 (Pleasant Street) into Blue Hill. House is 1/3 of a mile from Main Street. Map 6.
Credit Cards:	No
Owner:	Anthony Baker
Year Estab:	1989

Brunswick

Gordon's Book Shop (ME8) 207-725-2500
14 Center Street 04011

Collection:	General stock.
# of Volumes:	10,000
Specialties:	World War II; art.
Hours:	Monday-Friday 10-3. Saturday 10-1, but best to call ahead.
Services:	Appraisals, accepts want lists.
Credit Cards:	No
Owner:	Marilyn A. Gordon
Year Estab:	1968

Old Books (ME9) 207-725-4524
136 Maine Street 04011

Collection:	General stock of hardcover and paperback.
# of Volumes:	25,000
Specialties:	Literature; fiction.
Hours:	Monday-Saturday except Thursday 10-5.
Travel:	I-95 to exit 22. Proceed via Pleasant Street toward down-

	town Brunswick. At second light make left turn onto Maine Street. Shop is at far end of first block on the left over the new book store "Its Academic." Map 8.
Credit Cards:	No
Owner:	Clare C. Howell
Year Estab:	1977
Comments:	One flight up in the heart of downtown Brunswick, this collection is neatly organized in a series of small rooms. A comfortable seating area encourages leisurely browsing. Children's books and paperbacks are located in a separate room. Because of its second story location, the shop is easy to miss if you're not looking for it.

Bryant Pond

Mollockett Books & Collectibles (ME10) 207-665-2397
Box 36 04219

Collection:	General stock, ephemera and records.
# of Volumes:	20,000
Specialties:	New England and its writers; 20th century fiction; sociology; nature.
Hours:	Mid May-mid October: Daily except Tuesday & Wednesday 10-5. Remainder of year by chance or appointment.
Services:	Appraisals
Travel:	Shop is located on Route 26 across from Citgo station, about 1/4 miles passed sign "Entering Bryant Pond" and junction of Route 232. Map 9.
Credit Cards:	No
Owner:	Basil Seguin
Year Estab:	1968
Comments:	This mid 19th century country store has been converted into a used book shop where book hunters can find many bargains in a collection of old, but not necessarily antiquarian, books that are somewhat dusty. The owner has a charming downeast accent and book collectors old enough to remember Old Time Radio might think they were speaking with Titus Moody. The shop also sells collectibles. The entrance is one fight up.

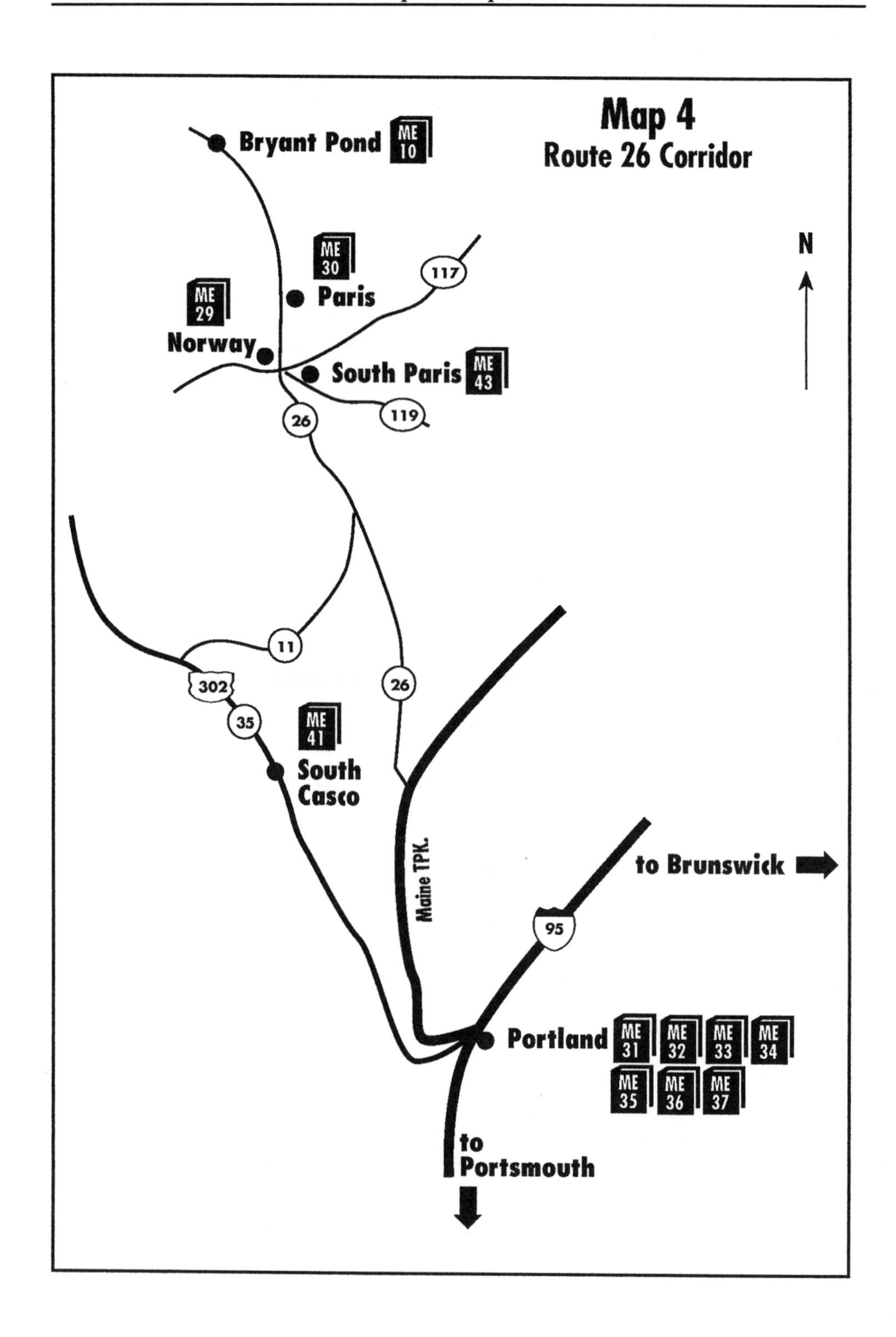

Map 4
Route 26 Corridor
N
Bryant Pond
ME 10
ME 30
Paris
ME 29
Norway
South Paris
ME 43
117
119
26
11
302
35
26
ME 41
South Casco
Maine TPK.
to Brunswick
95
Portland
ME 31
ME 32
ME 33
ME 34
ME 35
ME 36
ME 37
to Portsmouth

Camden

ABCDEF Bookstore (ME11) 207-236-3903
23 Bay View Street 04843

Collection: General stock and ephemera.
# of Volumes: 50,000+
Specialties: Americana; European history; literature; music; art; rare and contemporary first editions; *Harper's* magazine circa 1860's.
Hours: April 1-January 15: Daily 10:30-5.
Travel: Located in downtown Camden. Bay View is a sharp right turn off Route 1 (Main Street). Shop is half way down street on right. Map 6.
Credit Cards: Yes
Owner: Lillian Berliawsky
Year Estab: 1950's
Comments: This storefront shop houses an extensive quality collection that is particularly strong in non fiction but also offers a good fiction section. This long-time dealer loves her books, treating them almost like her own children. Her special books are kept in a separate room and upstairs in her private "inner sanctum".

Dolphin Books (ME12) 207-236-3283
78 Elm Street
Mailing address: P.O. Box 582 04843

Collection: General stock.
# of Volumes: 12,000+
Specialties: Art; architecture; Americana; history; biography.
Hours: April 15-December 15: Daily 10-5.
Services: Accepts want lists.
Travel: On Route 1 proceeding north, shop is on right just before heart of downtown Camden. Map 6.
Credit Cards: Yes
Owner: Leon H. & Elizabeth Ballou
Year Estab: 1977
Comments: A cat, soft music and a pot bellied stove welcome book hunters to this attractively decorated bi-level shop. The owners make the most of their limited space to display a good general collection of books in very good condition.

Stone Soup Books (ME13)
35 Main Street 04843

Collection: General collection of hardcover and paperback.
# of Volumes: 25,000
Specialties: Maritime; photography; Civil War; biography.
Hours: May-October: Daily 10:30-5. Winter: Monday-Saturday 10:30-5.
Services: Accepts want lists, mail order.
Travel: Downtown Camden above Marriner's Restaurant. Map 6.
Credit Cards: No
Owner: Paul Joy
Year Estab: 1982
Comments: One flight up, the collection in this shop is crowded into two small rooms. The majority of the stock is paperback with about 2,000-5,000 hardcover books. The owner is planning to expand.

Castine

Barbara Falk - Bookseller (ME14) 207-326-4036
Route 166A
Mailing address: Box 356 04421

Collection: General stock and ephemera.
# of Volumes: 12,000
Specialties: Women; poetry; children's.
Hours: Tuesday-Saturday 10-5.
Travel: From Route 1 at Bucksport, take Route 175 south to Route 166. At fork in road (look for "Entering Castine" sign), follow Route 166A. House is a short distance ahead on right just before a large red barn. The name Falk is on the mailbox. Map 6.
Credit Cards: No
Owner: Barbara Falk
Year Estab: 1957
Comments: This modest sized shop adjoining the owner's home offers some unusual and interesting finds, all of which are in excellent condition. Some first editions. The charm and friendliness of the owner, along with her insights into the Maine used book market, make this out of the way shop worth a visit.

Damariscotta Mills

Barn Stages Bookshop (ME15)
Route 215, Bay View Road
Mailing address: Pump Street Newcastle 04553

Collection:	Speciality
# of Volumes:	7,000
Specialties:	Children's
Hours:	Mid May-mid October: Sundays only 1-5.
Travel:	Route 215, two miles north of Business Route 1 in Newcastle. Shop is in former Damariscotta Mills Library building near Alewives Fabrics store. Map 8.
Credit Cards:	No
Owner:	Barbara W. Yedlin
Year Estab:	1990
Comments:	Sales are limited to the general public only. The owner will not knowingly sell to dealers. The owner divides her time between this shop and shops in Newcastle and Wiscasset.

Deer Isle

Skeans & Clifford (ME16) 207-348-2660
Main Street
Mailing address: P .O. Box 725 04627

Collection:	General stock and framed fine prints.
# of Volumes:	5,000
Specialties:	Fine and applied arts; Americana; literature; travel.
Hours:	Mid May-Mid October: Monday-Saturday 12-6. Remainder of year by chance or appointment.
Services:	Appraisals
Travel:	Route 15 at Bucksport to Deer Isle. Shop is on right as you enter village. Map 6.
Credit Cards:	No
Owner:	Stanley Clifford
Year Estab:	1992
Comments:	This small storefront shop carries a modest sized collection of used books that look like new. Because of its size, the shop may not be worth going out of your way for. However, if you enjoy exploring the back roads, then you'll want to add this establishment to your list.

Dresden

Mathom Bookshop (ME17) 207-737-8806
Blinn Hill Road, P.O.Box 161 04342

Collection:	General stock.
# of Volumes:	4,000
Specialties:	Contemporary poetry; signed books; Maine; New England; Women's studies; history; scholarly.
Hours:	July & August: Daily 9-5. September-June: By chance or appointment.
Services:	Book repair and rebinding, appraisals, accepts want lists.
Travel:	From Route 27, Blinn Hill Road is around the corner from Dresden Texaco. Second house on left. Map 4.
Credit Cards:	No
Owner:	Lewis Turco
Year Estab:	1979
Comments:	The shop is in a private house that dates back to 1754.

East Lebanon

Lebanon Book Barn (ME18) 207-457-1042
RFD 1, Box 116 04027

Collection:	General stock.
# of Volumes:	25,000
Specialties:	Medicine; discovery and exploration.
Hours:	Thursday-Sunday 9-6. Other times by chance or appointment. Closed month of May.
Credit Cards:	No
Owner:	Hugh S. Morris
Comments:	Only a portion of the owner's collection is on display in this shop, located in a one room barn plus the owner's adjoining house. Additional stock is packed away in boxes that are not readily accessible. If you're interested in the owner's specialties, the shop should be right up your alley. If, however, you're interested in a more general stock, while it is here, we do not recommend your going out of the way to find it. And, if you're looking for something special, a phone call would probably do as well. The owner is gregarious, an intellect, and one with whom you might enjoy spending the afternoon.

Edgecomb

Edgecomb Book Barn (ME19) 207-882-7278
Cross Point Road 04556

Collection:	General stock.
# of Volumes:	30,000
Specialties:	Maritime; Maine; children's; travel.
Hours:	May-November: Daily 11-6.
Services:	Appraisals, mail order.
Travel:	Traveling northeast from Wiscasset, right turn onto Eddy immediately after bridge. Left turn at dead end. Right turn at Cross Point Road. Barn is 3 miles ahead on left. If coming from opposite direction, follow signs. Map 8.
Credit Cards:	No
Owner:	Frank McQuaid
Year Estab:	1952
Comments:	A large barn with reasonably priced books that are somewhat worn. The patient browser may be able to come up with some rare finds. In addition to the specialties listed above, we noted a large mystery collection

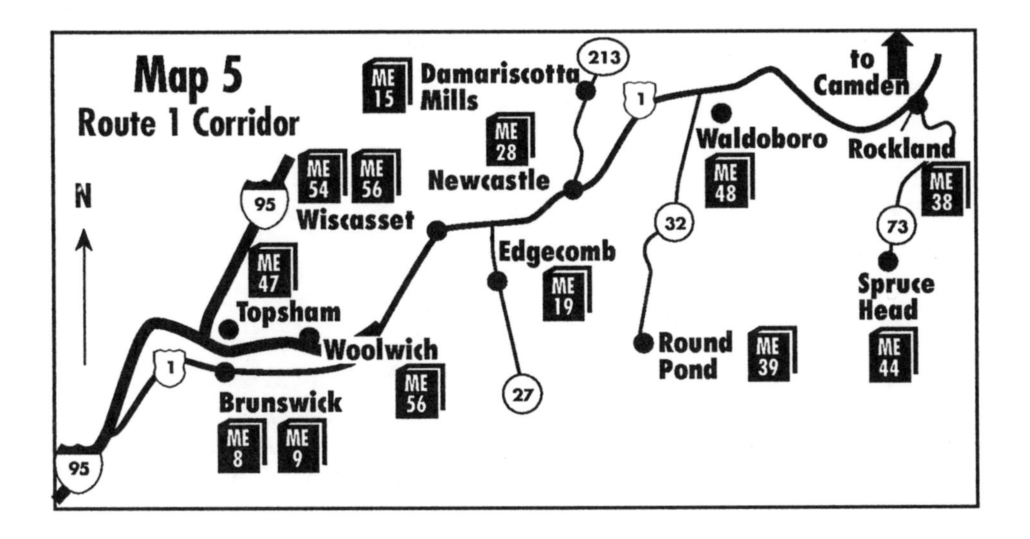

Ellsworth

Big Chicken Barn Books (ME20) 207-667-7308
Route 3, Box 150A 04605

Collection: General stock of hardcover, paperback and ephemera.
# of Volumes: 100,000+
Hours: Open daily throughout year. Spring & Fall: 9-5. Summer 9-7. Winter 10-4.
Travel: On Route 3, between Bucksport and Bangor. Heading east, approximately 8 miles before Ellsworth. You can't miss the barn on right. Map 6.
Credit Cards: Yes
Owner: Annagret Cukierski
Comments: If you're a serious book collector, don't get your hopes up even though this establishment has a vast collection. Located on the second floor of a huge barn, most of the titles here are quite common and few, if any, rare books are to be found. If you are a browser, you will certainly enjoy walking through aisles and aisles and aisles of books and magazines, all appropriately categorized. While you're browsing, the other members of your party might enjoy walking through the lower level where an equally large stock of antiques and collectibles are offered for sale.

Hallowell

Merrill's Bookshop (ME21) 207-623-2055
108 Water Street
Mailing address: 9 Coughlin Street Augusta 04330

Collection: General stock.
# of Volumes: 5,000+
Specialties: Literature; history; unusual items in a variety of categories.
Hours: Open daily but call ahead as hours may vary.
Services: Appraisals, search service, accepts want lists, mail order.
Travel: From Augusta, follow Routes 27/201 south. Water Street is Route 201. Map 4.
Credit Cards: Yes
Owner: John R. Merrill
Year Estab: 1988
Comments: For a relatively small store, the owner has assembled a rich general collection.

Riverbooks (ME22) 207-626-2726
113 1/2 Water Street 04347

Collection:	General stock.
# of Volumes:	3,000+
Specialties:	Foreign language books, including Estonian and German.
Hours:	June 1-Labor Day: Monday-Saturday 12-4. Remainder of year by chance or appointment.
Services:	Appraisals, accepts want lists, mail order.
Travel:	From Augusta, follow Routes 27/201 south. Water Street is Route 201. Map 4.
Credit Cards:	Yes
Owner:	Edda Briggs
Year Estab:	1991
Comments:	Although the collection in this tiny storefront shop is modest in size, the shop is worth a stop when visiting the other book shops on Water Street. The owner stores additional books at home.

Leon Tebbetts Book Store (ME23) 207-623-4670
164 Water Street 04347

Collection:	General stock of hardcover and some paperback.
# of Volumes:	30,000
Hours:	Monday-Saturday 10-5. Sunday 12-4.
Services:	Search service, accepts want lists, mail order.
Travel:	From Augusta, follow Routes 27/201 south. Water Street is Route 201. Map 4.
Credit Cards:	No
Owner:	Leon Tebbetts
Year Estab:	1959
Comments:	The owner of this long established street level shop makes the most of every square inch of space to house a good healthy general collection. The books are shelved in a maze of small cubicles off narrow aisles.

Houlton

Mountain & Meadow Books (ME24) 207-532-9285
59 Bangor Street 04730 Fax: 207-532-4038

Collection:	General stock.

# of Volumes: 3,000
Hours: Monday-Friday 9-5. Saturday 9-2.
Travel: At Houlton exit off I-95 proceed south for 1 mile. Turn right at bridge and traffic light. Shop is 1/2 mile ahead on right in rear of John's Audio & CB Repair Shop.
Credit Cards: Yes
Owner: John Folsom
Year Estab: 1990

Lincolnville Beach

Goose River Exchange (ME25) 207-789-5241
Route 1, Box 20 04849 Fax: 207-236-8670

Collection: General stock and ephemera.
# of Volumes: 3,000
Hours: Memorial Day-Columbus Day: Daily 10-6.
Services: Mail order.
Travel: On Route 1, 4 miles north of Camden across from Lobster Pound restaurant. Map 6.
Credit Cards: No
Owner: Ken Shure
Year Estab: 1977

Machias

Eastern Maine Books (ME26) 207-255-4908
65 Main Street
Mailing address: P.O. Box 527 04654

Collection: General stock of used and new books.
# of Volumes: 4,000
Specialties: Maine; genealogy; automobiles; maritime.
Hours: Monday-Saturday 9-5.
Travel: Route 1 is Main Street. Shop is located in Ferris Wheel Emporium. Map 6.
Credit Cards: Yes
Owner: Richard Lindsey
Year Estab: 1989

Madison

Books Bought and Sold, Records Too! (ME27) 207-696-3138
125 Main Street 04950

Collection:	General stock and records.
# of Volumes:	10,000+
Hours:	Monday-Saturday 9-5.
Travel:	At junction of Routes 8/201A & 43/148. Map 4.
Credit Cards:	No
Owner:	Colby J. Seams
Year Estab:	1985
Comments:	If you can find your way through the maze of crowded small rooms, you'll find a solid collection of hardcover books (and some paperbacks) in this shop. Our only caveat is that both the books and the shop are somewhat dusty.

Newcastle

Barn Stages Book Shop (ME28) 207-563-8335
Pump Street, R.R. 1, Box 749 04553

Collection:	General stock.
# of Volumes:	10,000
Hours:	Mid May-mid October: Monday-Friday 7-9 PM. Also by appointment.
Travel:	Pump Street is off Business Route 1. Look for ambulance station at foot of street. Map 8.
Credit Cards:	No
Owner:	Barbara W. Yedlin
Year Estab:	1985
Comments:	Sales are limited to the general public only. The owner will not knowingly sell to dealers. The owner divides her time between this shop and shops in Wiscasset and Damaroscotta Mills.

Norway

Books and Other Treasures (ME29) 207-743-7908
251 Main Street 04268

Collection:	General stock.

# of Volumes:	10,000
Hours:	Saturday & Sunday 9-6. Weekdays and evenings by chance or appointment.
Services:	Mail order, search service, accepts want lists.
Travel:	In heart of village, at corner of Main and Bridge Streets and across the street from Advertiser-Democrat building. Map 9.
Credit Cards:	No
Owner:	Joan Marr
Year Estab:	1989
Comments:	Shop also sells collectibles and antiques.

Paris

The Haunted Bookshop (ME30) 207-743-6216
73 Lincoln Street
Mailing address: P.O. Box 34 04271

Collection:	General stock.
# of Volumes:	3,000+
Hours:	Summer: Tuesday-Friday 10-4. Remainder of year by chance or appointment.
Services:	Mail order.
Travel:	3 miles from Route 26 north of South Paris heading toward West Paris. Shop is located in historic village of Paris Hill. (Village is listed on National Historic District Registry.) Map 9.
Credit Cards:	No
Owner:	Wini Mott
Year Estab:	1979

Portland

Carlson and Turner Books (ME31) 207-773-4200
241 Congress Street 04101

Collection:	General stock.
# of Volumes:	50,000
Specialties:	Americana; social thought; fine printing; technology; travel; the unusual and eclectic; scholarly.
Hours:	January-April: Saturday 10-5. Sunday 12-5. May to December: Monday-Saturday 10-5, Sunday 12-5, or by appointment.

Services: Appraisals, search service, occasional catalogs, accepts want lists.
Travel: Route 95 to Route 295. Take Franklin Street exit to Congress Street. Make left on Congress and go 3 blocks. Store is on left across from cemetery. Map 5.
Credit Cards: Yes
Owner: David John Turner & Norma C. Carlson
Year Estab: 1974
Comments: A street level shop with a solid collection of scholarly books. The basement level is devoted primarily to paperbacks.

Cunningham Books (ME32) 207-775-2246
762 Congress Street 04102

Collection: General stock.
# of Volumes: 10,000+
Hours: Monday-Saturday 10-5:30. Sundays by chance.
Travel: Downtown Portland. Map 5.
Credit Cards: Yes
Owner: Joan Pickard
Year Estab: 1979
Comments: A spacious storefront shop with comfortable seating. The collection consists mostly of newer used books in spotless condition.

J. Glatter Books (ME33) 207-773-4033
20-34 Danforth Street 04101

Collection: General stock.
# of Volumes: 15,000
Specialties: Art; photography; technical.
Hours: Tuesday-Friday 11-5. Saturday 12-4. Other times by chance or appointment.
Services: Accepts want lists, mail order.
Travel: Approximately four blocks from heart of Old Port Exchange district. Map 5.
Credit Cards: No
Owner: Jack Glatter
Year Estab: 1982

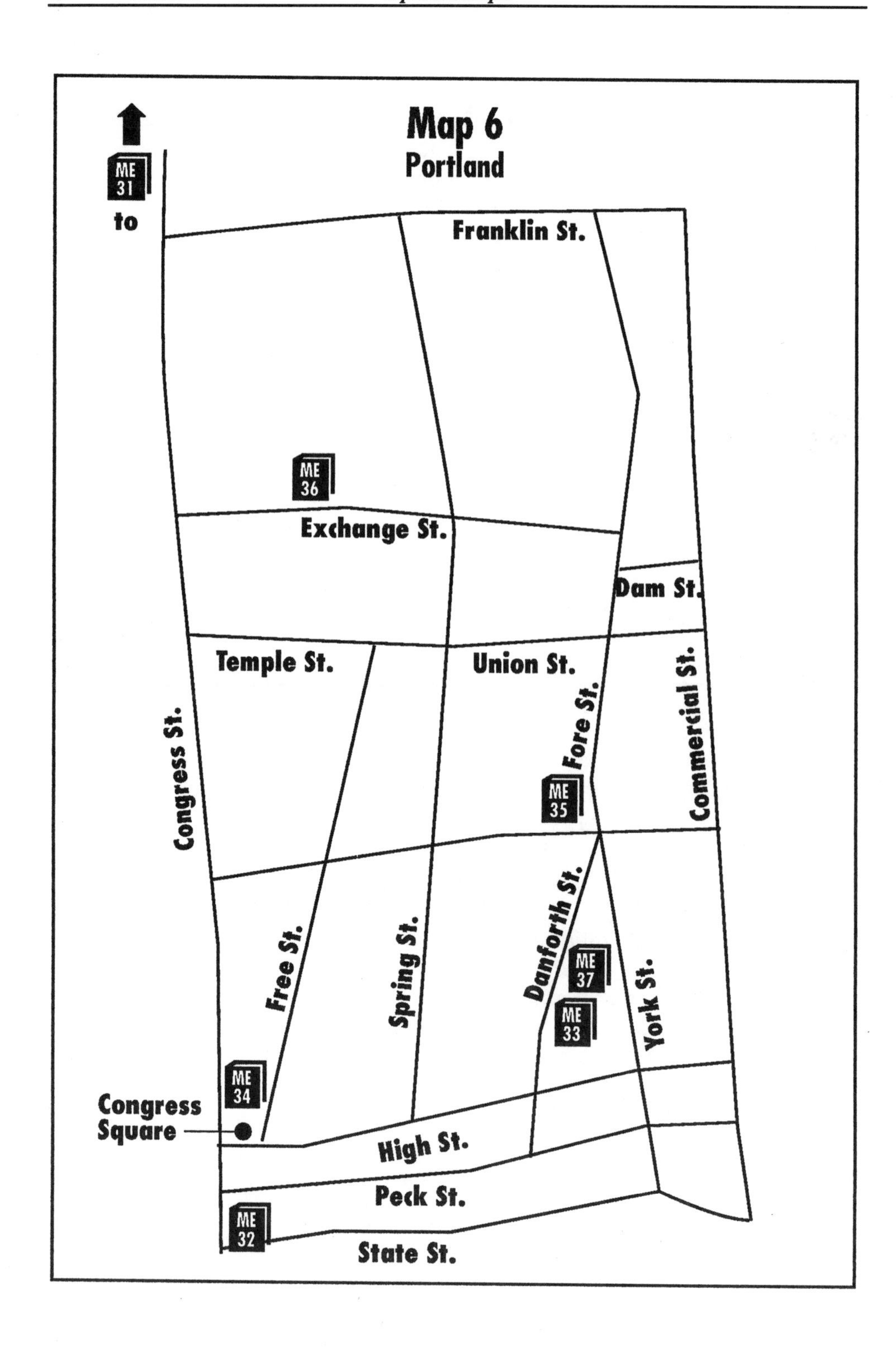
Map 6
Portland
ME 31
to
Franklin St.
ME 36
Exchange St.
Dam St.
Temple St.
Union St.
Fore St.
Commercial St.
Congress St.
ME 35
Danforth St.
Free St.
Spring St.
ME 37
ME 33
York St.
ME 34
Congress Square
High St.
Peck St.
ME 32
State St.

Harding's Book Shop (ME34) 207-761-2150
594 Congress Street 04102

Collection: General stock.
# of Volumes: 50,000+
Specialties: Art; maritime; local history; maps.
Hours: Monday-Saturday 9:30-5:30 and till 9 on Thursday. Sunday 12-5.
Services: Appraisals, search service, accepts want lists.
Travel: In downtown Portland across the street from Portland Museum of Art and Children's Museum of Maine. Map 5.
Credit Cards: Yes
Owner: Douglas N. Harding
Year Estab: 1950's
Comments: Located in a three story flat iron building dating back to 1823, this well organized collection is displayed in a series of rooms, all on street level, including a separate children's room. The books are in good condition and are reasonably priced. The owner operates a second store in Wells, ME.

Little Nemo's World of Books (ME35) 207-874-2665
420 Fore Street 04101 eve: 603-433-4406

Collection: Speciality books, prints and pre 1900 maps.
# of Volumes: 6,000
Specialties: Art; literature; travel; antique maps and images; 19th century poetry.
Hours: Daily 11-7.
Services: Appraisals, accepts want lists, search service.
Travel: Located in heart of Old Port Exchange district across from municipal parking lot. Map 5.
Credit Cards: Yes
Owner: Brian DiMambro
Year Estab: 1989
Comments: A shop that offers mostly used but also some new books. Some unusual finds. The books are reasonably priced and in excellent condition.

Allen Scott/Books (ME36) 207-774-2190
89 Exchange Street 04101

Collection: General stock.
# of Volumes: 17,000

Specialties: First editions; leather volumes; art; architecture; children's; Americana; maritime; literature; natural history.
Hours: Monday-Saturday 11-6 and by appointment.
Services: Appraisals, search service, accepts want lists.
Travel: Franklin Street exit off I-295. Stay on Franklin for 2 miles. Make right onto Congress. Proceed 3 blocks and make left onto Exchange. Map 5.
Credit Cards: Yes
Owner: Allen Scott
Year Estab: 1971
Comments: A narrow, but not cramped, street level store in the historic Old Port Exchange district, this shop offers a quality collection of books in pristine condition. A comfortable seating area encourages relaxed browsing.

Yes Books (ME37) 207-775-3233
20 Danforth Street 04101

Collection: General stock, ephemera and records.
# of Volumes: 20,000
Hours: Monday-Friday 11-5:30. Saturday 12-7:30. Sunday 12:30-5:30.
Services: Appraisals, mail order.
Travel: Approximately four blocks from heart of Old Port Exchange district. Map 5.
Credit Cards: No
Owner: Pat Murphy
Year Estab: 1983
Comments: Located in a renovated building that also houses a cafe and display of original art works, this shop offers mostly newer used books in good condition. Both the collection and general atmosphere of the shop and building are somewhat bohemian.

Rockland

Dooryard Books (ME38) 207-594-2500
436 Main Street 04841

Collection: General stock.
# of Volumes: 15,000
Specialties: Art; maritime; Maine; history; photography; do-it-yourself.

Hours: Monday-Saturday 12-5. Best to call if coming from a distance.
Services: Accepts want lists.
Travel: Map 8.
Credit Cards: No
Owner: Steve Stevens
Year Estab: 1988

Round Pond

Carriage House (ME39) 207-529-5555
Route 32, Box 71 04564

Collection: General stock (primarily non fiction), ephemera and antiques.
# of Volumes: 15,000
Specialties: Americana; maritime; illustrated.
Hours: June-October: Daily 10-5. Remainder of year by chance or appointment.
Services: Accepts want lists.
Travel: From Route 1 in Waldoboro, take Route 32 directly to Round Pond. From Route 1 in Damariscotta, take Routes 129/130 to Bristol. Make left turn immediately after Town Hall onto an unmarked road for about 3 miles. At end of road, make right turn onto Route 32. Shop is just ahead on right. Map 8.
Credit Cards: No
Owner: Roy & Jean Gillespie
Year Estab: 1961
Comments: This moderately priced collection is housed in a series of rooms in a barnlike extension on the owner's house. Unlike other shops that combine books with antiques and collectibles, this shop is primarily books. Don't overlook the special bargain section.

Sargentville

Wayward Books (ME40) 207-359-2397
Route 15, RFD 26B 04673

Collection: General stock.
# of Volumes: 14,000

Specialties:	Literature; modern first editions; women's studies; cookbooks; gardening; natural history; history; politics; civil liberties.
Hours::	Mid May-December: Monday-Friday 10-5. Saturday 12-5. Remainder of year by appointment.
Services:	Search service, accepts wants lists.
Travel:	On Route 15, 1/4 mile before the bridge to Deer Isle. Shop is on left. Map 6.
Credit Cards:	Yes
Owner:	Sybil Pike
Year Estab:	1976
Comments:	A spacious and well lit shop with comfortable chairs on either side of a pot bellied stove. New books are mixed in with used. There's also a table of remainders. According to the owner, "visiting the shop is always a crapshoot."

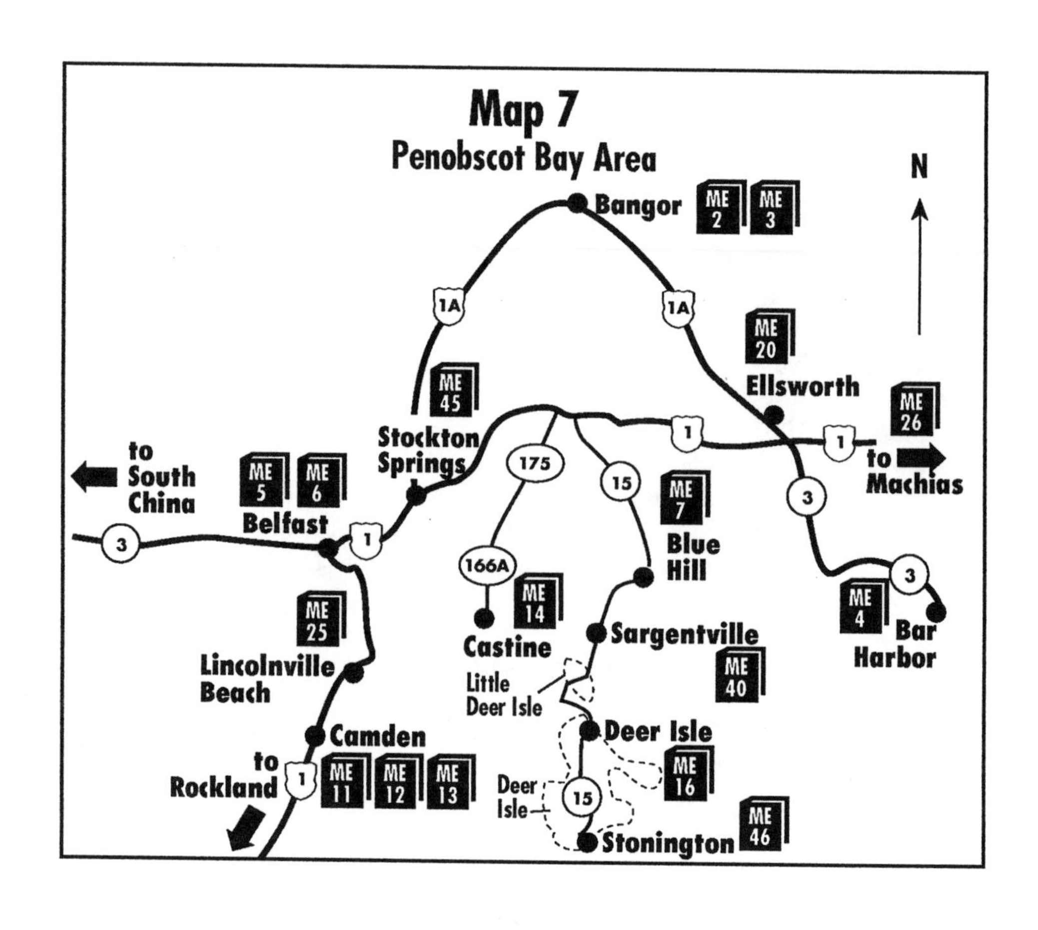

South Casco

Varney's Volumes (ME41) 207-655-4605
Quaker Ridge Road
Mailing address: P.O. Box 84 04077

Collection:	General stock.
# of Volumes:	10,000
Specialties:	Children's; Christmas; Maine.
Hours:	July & August: Daily except Wednesday and Sunday 10-5. By appointment remainder of year.
Services:	Catalog, accepts want lists, mail order.
Travel:	25 miles northwest of Portland on Route 302. Right turn at Cry-of-the Loon gift shop. Proceed 1/4 mile on Quaker Ridge road. Shop is third house on left. Map 9.
Credit Cards:	No
Owner:	A. Lois Varney
Year Estab:	1978

South China

Gray Matter Service (ME42) 207-445-2245
Box 381 04358

Collection:	General stock.
# of Volumes:	30,000+
Hours:	May-October: Monday-Thursday 10-4:30. Friday-Sunday 1-4:30. March-April: Saturday & Sunday only 1-4:30.
Travel:	On Route 3, approximately 11 miles east of Augusta next to Border Bank. Map 4.
Credit Cards:	No
Owner:	Mabel Charles
Comments:	The gracious owner of this shop, located in a one story stand alone building, takes pride in providing her public with a large stock of reading copies. The books are clean and reasonably priced. An interesting collection to browse.

South Paris

Downtown Bookshop (ME43) 207-743-7245
6 Western Avenue 04281

Collection: General stock of new and used books.
# of Volumes: 5,000 (combined)
Specialties: Primarily fiction (used books).
Hours: Monday-Friday 9:30-5. Saturday 9:30-3.
Services: Appraisals
Travel: Map 9.
Credit Cards: Yes
Owner: Theresa Geissler
Year Estab: 1985
Comments: The shop also sells gifts and greeting cards.

Spruce Head

Lobster Lane Book Shop (ME44) 207-594-7520
04859

Collection: General stock.
Hours: June 1-September 30: Thursday-Sunday 12:30-5. October-May: Sunday only. Best to call ahead.
Travel: Map 8.
Credit Cards: No
Owner: Vivian York
Comments: We're sorry we didn't get to visit this little known but well respected shop as it was not open when we were in the area. Both the shop's owner and collection were highly praised by other dealers in the area.

Stockton Springs

Victorian House/Book Barn (ME45) 207-567-3351
East Main Street
Mailing address: P.O. Box 397 04981

Collection: General stock.
# of Volumes: 10,000+
Specialties: Maine.

Hours: May-November: Daily 8-8. Remainder of year by chance or appointment.
Services: Search service, accepts want lists, mail order.
Travel: East Main Street runs parallel to Route 1 for about one mile with entrances at each end. Map 6.
Credit Cards: No
Owner: Andrew B. W. MacEwen
Year Estab: 1960
Comments: Book hunters will find a typical book barn atmosphere when visiting this shop — a good selection of well worn but somewhat dusty books. Few bargains.

Stonington

Stonington Book Store (ME46) 207-367-5821
6 West Main Street
Mailing address: P.O. Box 279 04681

Collection: General stock of used and new books and fine art prints.
# of Volumes: 3,000
Specialties: Maritime; American history; American literature; biography; poetry; cookbooks, Maine; politics; mysteries.
Hours: Memorial Day-Columbus Day: Daily 9-5.
Services: Mail order.
Travel: From Route 1 at Bucksport, take Route 15 south. Shop is across from Opera House. Map 6.
Credit Cards: Yes
Owner: Bob Freeman
Year Estab: 1988
Comments: A small shop that carries newer used and new books, primarily non fiction, with some older books displayed in a glass case. Worth a stop if you enjoy visiting out of the way shops along scenic back roads.

Topsham

Coastal Book Search (ME47) 207-729-3053
at Antiques at Topsham Mall
Mailing address: P.O. Box 118 04086

Collection: General stock.
# of Volumes: Under 500

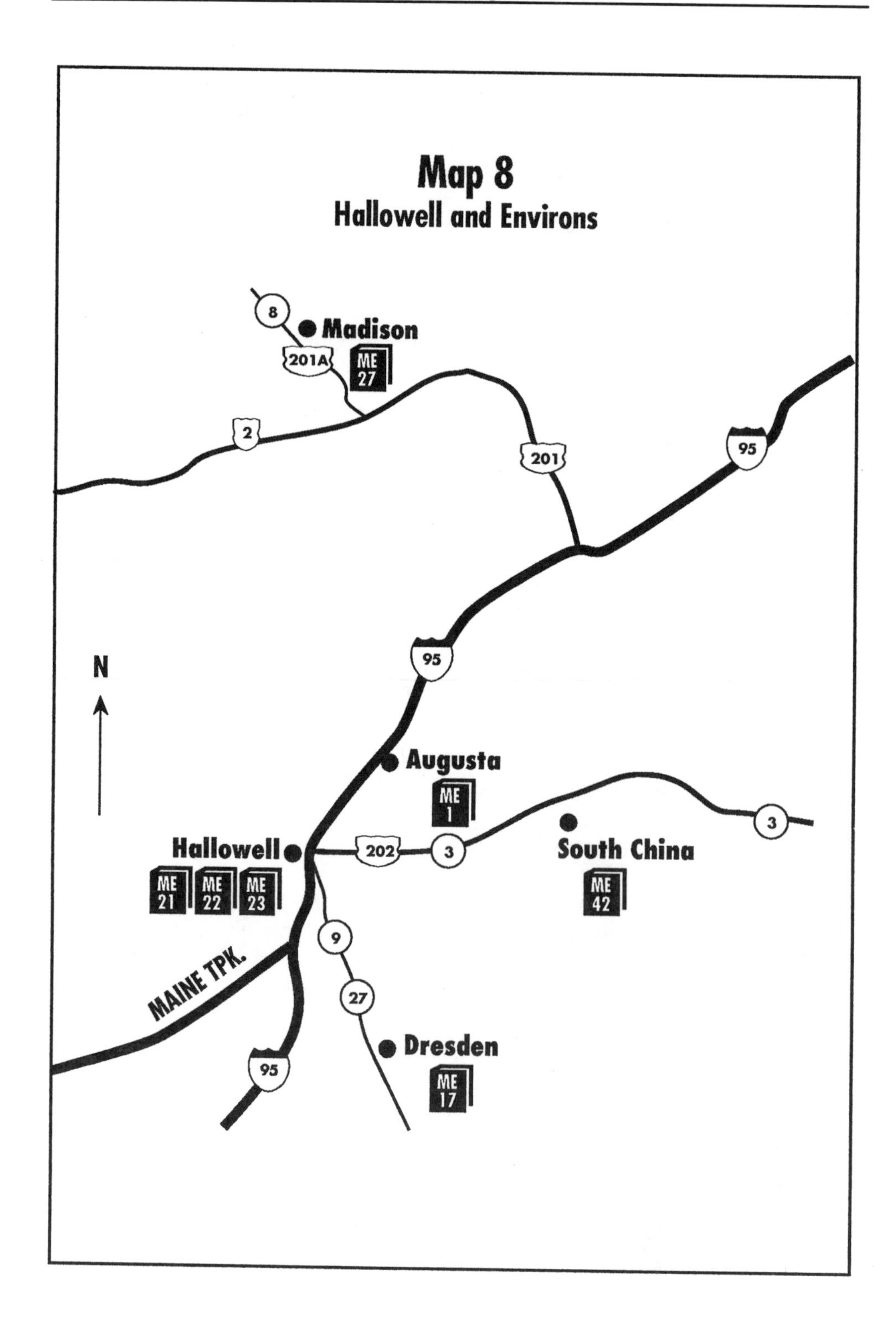
Map 8
Hallowell and Environs
8
Madison
201A
ME 27
2
201
95
N
95
Augusta
ME 1
3
Hallowell
202
3
South China
ME 21
ME 22
ME 23
ME 42
9
MAINE TPK.
27
Dresden
95
ME 17

Hours: Monday-Saturday 9:30-5:30. Sunday 12-5.
Travel: Exit 24 off I-95. Shop located in shopping center. Map 8.
Credit Cards: Yes
Owner: Charles & Susan Crosby
Comments: This modest collection of books is on display at an antique/ collectible shop. The owner also does book auctions and operates a search service for rare books, manuscripts, autographs and photographs.

Waldoboro

Bill's Cafe & Bookstore (ME48) 207-832-4613
235 Jefferson Street 04572

Collection: General stock of mostly used hardcover and paperback.
# of Volumes: 5,000
Specialties: Children's.
Hours: Daily 7 AM-8 PM.
Travel: Route 1 to Waldoboro. Make right at Irving gas station onto Jefferson Street. Cafe is about 1/4 mile ahead on right. Map 8.
Credit Cards: Yes
Owner: William & Barbara Howlett
Year Estab: 1991

Wells

The Arringtons (ME49) 207-646-4124
Route 1, P.O. Box 160 04090

Collection: General stock and ephemera.
# of Volumes: 30,000
Specialties: Military history (all periods and countries), including unit histories; U.S. & world history.
Hours: Daily 10-5, except closed Tuesday & Wednesday January-March.
Services: Appraisals, accepts want lists.
Travel: I-95 to exit 2. Left turn off exit ramp onto Route 109. At light, turn left onto Route 1. Shop is about one mile ahead on left. Map 10.
Credit Cards: Yes
Owner: George & Eleanor Arrington

Year Estab: 1988
Comments: A bi-level shop with quality books on the street level and reading copies and paperbacks upstairs. Well organized.

Austin's Antiquarian Books (ME50) 207-646-4883
Route 1 Fax: same
Mailing address: P.O. Box 3010 04090

Collection: General stock and ephemera.
# of Volumes: 20,000
Specialties: Americana; western Americana; George Armstrong Custer bindings.
Hours: June 1-September 15: Daily 10-6. Remainder of year by chance or appointment.
Services: Appraisals, search service, catalog, accepts want lists.
Travel: I-95 to exit 2. Left off exit and proceed 1 mile to Route 1. Right turn onto Route 1. Shop is 2/10 mile ahead on left across from public library. Map 10.
Credit Cards: Yes
Owner: Gary & Karen Austin
Year Estab: 1979
Comments: A spaciously laid out shop offering reasonably priced books of higher quality than typically found in "book barn" collections.

The Book Barn (ME51) 207-646-4926
Route 1
Mailing address: P.O. Box 557 04090

Collection: General stock of hardcover and some paperback, comics and supplies for books and comics.
# of Volumes: 20,000-30,000
Specialties: Comics; autographs.
Hours: April 15-October 15: Daily 10-5. Remainder of year: Saturday & Sunday 10-5 or by chance or appointment.
Services: Catalog
Travel: I-95 to exit 2. Left off exit ramp onto Route 109. At light, turn right onto Route 1. Shop is on left next to shopping center. Map 10.
Credit Cards: Yes
Owner: Harry & Ann Polizzi

Year Estab:	1984
Comments:	A two story "new" barn with the entrance one flight up. Hardcover and paperbacks are intershelved in some categories. A special bargain section offers hardcover books for $1.00-$3.00 with discounts for quantity purchases. When we visited, the size of the collection seemed more in the 10,000-15,000 range.

East Coast Books (ME52) 207-646-3584
Depot Street
Mailing address: P.O. Box 849 04090

Collection:	General stock, ephemera and framed and unframed fine art.
# of Volumes:	20,000
Specialties:	Mail auction bids of autographs and historical Americana; theater playbills; local history.
Hours:	May-November: Daily 10-6.
Services:	Accepts want lists, catalog.
Travel:	I-95 to exit 2. Make left off exit ramp onto Route 109. Depot Street is on left just before road ends at Route 1. Map 10.
Credit Cards:	Yes
Owner:	Merv & Kaye Slotnick
Year Estab:	1976
Comments:	The majority of the books in this two story shop are located on the upstairs level. The collection offers nothing out of the ordinary but the shop is worth a visit if you're in the area.

Douglas N. Harding Rare Books (ME53) 207-646-8785
Route 1
Mailing address: P.O. Box 184 04090

Collection:	General stock and ephemera.
# of Volumes:	100,000+
Specialties:	Maritime; local history; maps.
Hours:	July & August: Daily 9-9. Remainder of year: Daily 9-5.
Services:	Appraisals, search service, accepts want lists.
Travel:	I-95 to exit 2. Left off exit onto Route 109. At light, make left turn onto Route 1. Shop is about 1 mile ahead on right, just after post office. Map 10.
Credit Cards:	Yes
Owner:	Douglas N. Harding

Year Estab: 1982
Comments: Want a book? Name the subject and Harding's is as likely as any to have a copy - and in good condition. The store, which claims to have 100,000 volumes, does not exaggerate. Also, unlike large collections in barns that tend to be dusty and not always well organized, the books here are in excellent condition, meticulously organized and spaciously displayed. The owner operates a second store in Portland, ME.

Wiscasset

Barn Stages Bookshop (ME54)
U.S. Route 1
Mailing address: Pump Street Newcastle 04553

Collection: General stock.
# of Volumes: 18,000
Hours: Mid May-mid October: Monday-Friday 1-5.
Travel: One mile south of Wiscasset on U.S. Route 1, next to the Sea Basket restaurant. Map 8.
Credit Cards: No
Owner: Barbara W. Yedlin
Year Estab: 1992
Comments: A spacious well lit shop. Many of the books are library discards but there are some interesting finds. A theatre and music collection occupies a separate small room. Sales are limited to the general public only. The owner will not knowingly sell to dealers. The owner divides her time between this shop and shops in Newcastle and Damariscotta Mills.

Elliott Healy (ME55) 207-882-5446
Middle Street, P.O. Box 285 04578

Collection: General stock.
# of Volumes: 15,000
Specialties: Art; nature.
Hours: May 1-October 15: Daily 10-5. Rest of year by chance or appointment.
Travel: Off Route 1. Proceeding east, just before Wiscasset bridge. Map 8.

Credit Cards: Yes
Owner: Elliott Healy
Year Estab: 1989
Comments: This strong collection of quality books in excellent condition is divided between a tastefully decorated storefront shop and a garage like structure to the shop's rear. Books hunters are likely to find a treasure trove of books in all subjects. Moderately priced.

Woolwich

The Book Exchange (ME56) 207-442-8188
Route 1, Box 340 04579

Collection: General stock of hardcover and paperback and records.
# of Volumes: 10,000
Hours: Sunday-Thursday 10-6. Friday & Saturday 10-8.
Travel: On Route 1 just after Wiscasset bridge. Shop is on right. Map 8.
Credit Cards: Yes
Year Estab: 1988
Owner: David & Paula Rose
Comments: Although the collection here is predominately paperback, the shop does offer a limited but interesting selection of hardcover books with some rare items interspersed.

Arrowsic

Arrowsic Island Books & Prints 207-443-1510
Old Stage Road, HC 33 Box 230 04530

Collection: General stock.
# of Volumes: 1,500
Specialties: Literature; travel; Americana.
Hours: Owner is available most weekends April through October or by appointment.
Credit Cards: No
Owner: James E. Arsenault
Year Estab: 1988

Bar Harbor

Dunn & Powell Books 207-288-4665
The Hideaway 04609-1714

Collection: Specialty
# of Volumes: 15,000
Specialties: Mysteries
Services: Catalog
Credit Cards: Yes
Owner: Steve Powell & William Dunn
Year Estab: 1991
Comments: The business was formerly Dunn's Mysteries and Steve Powell Books. The business operates a second office in Meriden, CT. See Connecticut listing.

Bethel

Bethel Book Barn 207-824-3145
Main Street, Box 353 04217

Collection: General stock.
Specialties: History; biography; literature.
Credit Cards: No
Owner: Dan Cousens
Year Estab: 1981

Brewer

Maritime Book Shop 207-989-4227
P.O. Box 847 04412-0847 Fax: 207-947-4756

Collection: Speciality
# of Volumes: 1,000
Specialties: Maritime
Services: Appraisals, search service, catalog, accepts want lists.
Credit Cards: Yes
Owner: Jon B. Johansen
Year Estab: 1976

Brooklin

George & Patricia Fowler, Books 207-359-2070
Reach Road
Mailing address: HCR 63, Box 354 04616

Collection: Specialty
# of Volumes: 2,000
Specialties: Western Americana; storytelling; children's; modern literature.
Services: Appraisals, search service, catalog, accepts want lists.
Credit Cards: No
Owner: George & Patricia Fowler
Year Estab: 1987
Comments: Appointments to view stock are made only with dealers.

Brooks

Military History Bookshop 207-722-3620
P.O. Box 97 04921

Collection: Speciality
# of Volumes: 20,000
Specialties: Military; China; Far East.
Services: Catalog, appraisals, accepts want lists.
Credit Cards: No
Owner: Ray J. McGuire
Year Estab: 1960's

Brunswick

Cross Hill Books 207-729-8531
9 Noble Street
Mailing address: P.O. Box 798 04011

Collection:	Speciality
# of Volumes:	1,500
Specialties:	Maritime, including naval history, whaling, commercial fishing, sailing, yachting. All seas and ships.
Services:	Catalog, accepts want lists.
Credit Cards:	No
Owner:	William W. Hill
Year Estab:	1977

Charles Vincent Books 207-729-7854
1 Maple Street 04011

Collection:	General stock.
# of Volumes:	7,000-8,000
Hours:	By chance or appointment.
Services:	Appraisals, occasional lists.
Credit Cards:	No
Owner:	Charles Vincent
Year Estab:	1950

Walfield Thistle 207-443-3986
381 Bath Road 04011

Collection:	General stock (primarily non fiction).
# of Volumes:	8,000
Hours:	By chance or appointment.
Travel:	I-95 to exit 22. Take Route 1 north to Cook's Corner exit. Left turn onto Bath Road. Shop is 2 miles ahead on left just after cemetery on right. Shop housed in grey one story frame building with porch.
Credit Cards:	No
Owner:	Jean M. Thistle
Year Estab:	1950's
Comments:	A modest collection of books with no particular speciality. When we visited, the size of the collection was smaller than indicated above. The shop also sells collectibles.

Cape Elizabeth

Lombard Antiquarian Maps & Prints 207-799-1889
P.O. Box 281 04107

Collection:	Speciality
# of Volumes:	1,500
Specialties:	16th-19th century maps and charts of all world areas; botanical, architectural and natural history prints; early atlases, geographies; exploration and travel.
Services:	Illustrated catalog, appraisals, search service.
Credit Cards:	Yes
Owner:	Reginald & Sally Lombard
Year Estab:	1978

Dixmont

Ben-Loch Books 207-257-4768
RR #1, Box 1020 North Road 04932

Collection:	General stock.
# of Volumes:	4,000
Specialties:	Civil war; biography; literature; Americana; Jack London.
Hours:	By chance or appointment.
Services:	Accepts want lists.
Travel:	Exit 42 off I-95. Left onto Route 143. Proceed 3.6 miles. Right turn onto North Road for 1.6 miles. Shop is on right.
Credit Cards:	No
Owner:	Howard M. Foley
Year Estab:	1991
Comments:	Visiting this small out of the way shop is more like visiting friends in their country house. In addition to the books, the house features a bed and breakfast and a restaurant open on weekends. The collection, located on two floors, is modest in size but steadily growing. Whether you're interested in the Civil War or Jack London, the diversity of the titles are a book lover's dream come true with many titles one might never have known existed. The delightful B&B setting adds to the establishment's charm and uniqueness.

East Livermore

Alden Pratt, Books 207-897-6979
HC 60, Box 3375 04228

Collection:	Speciality
# of Volumes:	2,000
Specialties:	Local history; genealogy; Maine authors.
Services:	Mail order, catalog (genealogy only).
Credit Cards:	No
Owner:	Alden Pratt
Year Estab:	1982

Eliot

Books and Autographs 207-439-4739
287 Goodwin Road 03903

Collection:	Specialty
# of Volumes:	500-600 (books only)
Specialties:	20th century signed and first editions; autographs, letters, photographs with emphasis on performing arts, including opera, movies and theatre.
Services:	Catalog, accepts want lists.
Credit Cards:	Yes
Owner:	Harold Merry & Sherman Emery
Year Estab:	1983

Eustis

MacDonald's Military 207-297-2751
Coburn Gore 04936

Collection:	Speciality
# of Volumes:	2,000
Specialties:	Civil War (books, paper and photos).
Services:	Search service, catalog, accepts want lists.
Credit Cards:	No
Owner:	Thomas L. MacDonald
Year Estab:	1970

Farmington Falls

The Falls Book Barn 207-778-3429
Main Street, P.O. Box 58 04940

Collection:	General stock.
# of Volumes:	20,000
Hours:	By chance April-October and by appointment remainder of year.
Services:	Accepts want lists.
Travel:	3/10 mile from junction of Routes 2/27 and 41/156. Proceeding west, turn left onto Routes 41/156. Make first right. Barn is just ahead on left.
Credit Cards:	No
Owner:	Ethel Emerson
Year Estab:	1973
Comments:	A large well organized one story barn with clean, well kept reading copies in a friendly setting. The owner takes pride, as well she should, in her books.

Gardiner

Bunkhouse Books 207-582-2808
RFD 5A, Box 148 04345

Collection:	Limited general stock and specialty.
# of Volumes:	16,000
Specialties:	Maine fiction and non fiction; fishing.
Hours:	Although the shop is open Monday-Friday most afternoons, we advise calling ahead as the owner may be relocating in the future.
Services:	Appraisals, search service, accepts want lists, mail order.
Credit Cards:	No
Owner:	Issac Davis, Jr.
Year Estab:	1976
Comments:	When we visited, the collection appeared smaller than noted above.

Jay

River Oaks Books 207-897-3734
RFD 2, Box 5505 04239

Collection:	Vintage paperbacks and more modern paperbacks.

# of Volumes: 120,000+
Specialties: Mystery; science fiction.
Hours: By chance or appointment.
Services: Catalog, accepts want lists, mail/phone auctions of better vintage paperbacks.
Travel: Just off Route 140, approximately 1/4 mile from Route 4.
Credit Cards: Yes
Owner: Nick & Barbara Bogdon
Year Estab: 1984

Kennebunkport

A.L. Mabee Books 207-967-4152
RR 1, Box 933 04046

Collection: Speciality
# of Volumes: 500-1,000
Specialties: First edition children's and illustrated.
Services: Catalog, limited search service.
Credit Cards: Yes
Owner: Andrea Mabee
Year Estab: 1989

Manchester

Charles Robinson Rare Books 207-622-1885
P.O. Box 299 04351

Collection: Specialty
# of Volumes: 5,000
Specialties: Rare and fine books in many fields.
Services: Appraisals
Credit Cards: No
Owner: Charles Robinson
Year Estab: 1974

Mercer

Main(e)ly Books 207-474-3185
Route 2
Mailing address: 178 Madison Avenue Skowhegan 04976

Collection:	General stock, records, sheet music and used musical instruments.
# of Volumes:	10,000
Travel:	On Route 2 between New Sharon and Norridgewock. Proceeding west, shop is on left.
Credit Cards:	No
Owner:	Robert Chandler
Year Estab:	1980
Comments:	Although the owner categorizes his shop as "by appointment only," we found the shop open when we were passing by. We noted a good selection dealing with show business. The books are moderately priced. The shop is located near several other "by chance or appointment" shops with sizeable general collections.

Morrill

Seven Roads 207-342-4132
RR 1, Box 632 04952

Collection:	Speciality
# of Volumes:	"Small"
Specialties:	Classical studies; literature; philosophy; psychology; religion; music; first editions; scholarly.
Services:	Catalog, accepts want lists.
Credit Cards:	No
Owner:	Robert & Olympia Stitt
Year Estab:	1984

Newburgh

Gary W. Woolson, Bookseller 207-234-4931
Route 9
Mailing address: RFD 1, Box 1576 Hampden 04444

Collection:	Specialty books, maps, prints and paintings.
# of Volumes:	10,000

Specialties: Art; architecture literature; Maine; Americana; horticulture; natural history; Civil War; maritime; maps.
Services: Appraisals, catalog.
Credit Cards: No
Owner: Gary W. Woolson
Year Estab: 1967

Newport

Books Bought & Sold 207-368-5110
RFD 2, Box 3200 04953

Collection: Specialty
# of Volumes: 5,000
Specialties: Maine; hunting; guns.
Services: Accepts want lists, mail order.
Credit Cards: No
Owner: Jerry Robichaud
Year Estab: 1986

Norridgewock

Snowbound Books 207-634-4398
River Road, P.O. Box 458 04957

Collection: General stock, magazines and some paperbacks.
# of Volumes: 50,000
Specialties: Children's; children's series; military; Maine; women's studies.
Services: Search service, accepts want lists, catalog.
Travel: From Route 2, take Routes 7 & 201A north toward Madison. After crossing bridge take immediate right at end of bridge. Shop is 4th house from bridge on river side.
Credit Cards: No
Owner: Nancy Wright & Marla Bottesch
Year Estab: 1981
Comments: Located in a tightly packed two story barn, this shop contains some hard to find items generally in good condition and in the moderate to high price range. Additional books are stored in the owner's house. In addition to the specialties listed above, we noted a large mystery selection. Most of the books are priced after the buyer picks them.

North Monmouth

Joyce B. Keeler-Books 207-933-9088
RR #1, Box 1495, Wilson Pond Road 04265

Collection: General stock.
# of Volumes: 40,000
Specialties: Children's; Americana; science fiction; fantasy; hunting; fishing; military; natural history; Maine.
Services: Appraisals, search service, accepts want lists, catalog.
Travel: Turn north off Route 202 (about 10 miles west of Augusta) onto Main Street. At end of street, make right onto Wilson Pond Road and proceed one block. Farm is on left across from black mailbox with numbers "1495."
Credit Cards: No
Owner: Joyce B. Keeler

North Vassalboro

Bancroft Books 207-968-2495
RFD 1, Box 1680 04962

Collection: General stock.
# of Volumes: 5,000
Specialties: Literature; fiction; mystery.
Hours: By chance or appointment.
Services: Mail order, accepts want lists.
Credit Cards: No
Owner: Tom Bancroft
Year Estab: 1984

Northeast Harbor

Wikhegan Books 207-276-5079
Main Street
Mailing address: P.O. Box 370 Mt. Desert 04660

Collection: General stock and ephemera.
# of Volumes: 3,000-5,000
Specialties: Decorative and fine arts; maritime; women's studies; cookery; nature; Indians; travel; poetry.
Hours: By chance or appointment.

Services: Search service, catalog, accepts want lists.
Travel: Surrounded by Acadia National Park on Mount Desert Island.
Credit Cards: Yes
Owner: J. Fuerst
Year Estab: Late 1960's

Northport

Prescott Hill Books 207-338-6346
Prescott Hill Road
Mailing address: R.R. 2, Box 707 Belfast 04915

Collection: General stock.
# of Volumes: 12,000+
Specialties: Biography; history; first edition fiction; cookbooks.
Services: Mail order.
Credit Cards: Yes
Owner: Ron & Shirley Jarvella
Year Estab: 1992

Poland Spring

Ciderpress Bookstore 207-998-4338
Cleve Tripp Road, RFD 1 04274

Collection: General stock.
# of Volumes: 5,000-10,000
Specialties: Literature; science; history; philosophy; natural history; women.
Hours: By chance or appointment March 15-December 15 only.
Owner: Virginia Chuts

Portland

Flynn Books 207-772-2685
466 Ocean Avenue 04103

Collection: General stock.
# of Volumes: 10,000
Specialties: Americana; western Americana; New England; Maine; fine press books.

Services: Mail order, appraisals, accepts want lists.
Credit Cards: No
Owner: Robert & Anna Flynn
Year Estab: 1975

Saco

F.P. Wood, Books 207-282-2278
48 Ferry Road 04072

Collection: General stock.
# of Volumes: 10,000
Specialties: Maine; Americana; 19th century literature; shakers and communal and utopian literature.
Hours: By chance or appointment.
Services: Catalog, appraisals, search service, accepts want lists.
Credit Cards: No
Owner: Frank Wood
Year Estab: 1980

Sanford

The Book Addict 207-324-2243
Pine Tree Drive, Box 1281 04073

Collection: Speciality
# of Volumes: 5,000-7,000
Specialties: Adventure; biography; history; nature; sports; fiction.
Services: Search service, accepts want lists, mail order.
Credit Cards: No
Owner: David H. Foshey
Year Estab: 1976

Springvale

Harland Eastman-Books 207-324-2797
66 Main Street
Mailing address: P.O. Box 276 04083

Collection: General stock.
# of Volumes: 8,000
Specialties: Maine history and authors; children's.

Hours: By chance or appointment.
Services: Appraisals, accepts want lists.
Credit Cards: No
Owner: Harland H. Eastman
Year Estab: 1979

Wells

A. David Paulhus, Rare Books 207-646-7022
Burnt Mill Road, P.O. Box 501 04090

Collection: Specialty and small general stock.
# of Volumes: 6,000
Specialties: Early imprints; leather sets; illustrated children's; art.
Services: Appraisals, catalog, accepts want lists.
Credit Cards: No
Owner: A. David Paulhus
Year Estab: 1970

West Bath

F. Barrie Freeman-Rare Books 207-442-8452
Quaker Point Farm, RFD 1, Box 688 04530

Collection: Specialty
# of Volumes: Under 200
Specialties: Rare Americana; western Americana.
Services: Accepts want lists, mail order.
Credit Cards: No
Owner: F. Barrie Freeman
Year Estab: 1969

West Lebanon

Otter Brook Books 207-658-7996
Mailing address: P.O. Box 890 Milton, NH 03851

Collection: General stock.
# of Volumes: 2,000
Specialties: Natural history; forestry; agriculture; north country life; natural resources; conservation.
Services: Search service, mail order, accepts want lists, catalog planned.

Credit Cards:	No
Owner:	Gary Getchell
Year Estab:	1990
Comments:	In addition to the traditional book collector market, the owner says he is especially interested in working with biologists, conservationists and foresters.

Yarmouth

Sumner & Stillman 207-846-6070
P.O. Box 973 04096

Collection:	Speciality
# of Volumes:	1,000
Specialties:	First editions of 19th century authors.
Services:	Catalogs
Credit Cards:	Yes
Owner:	Richard S. Loomis, Jr.
Year Estab:	1980

York

Samuel Weiser Books 207-363-7253
P.O. Box 612 03910 Fax: 207-363-5799

Collection:	Specialty
# of Volumes:	15,000
Specialties:	Archaeology; folklore; mythology; mysticisim; Eastern and Western esoteric traditions; occult sciences; alternative health and healing; theology; philosophy.
Services:	Appraisals, accepts want lists, mail order.
Credit Cards:	Yes
Owner:	Donald Weiser

Attic Owl Books 207-778-2006
RFD 1, Box 1802 New Sharon 04955

Collection:	Speciality
# of Volumes:	3,500
Specialties:	Philosophy (rare and out-of-print).
Services:	Catalog, accepts want lists.
Credit Cards:	Yes
Owner:	William L. Reid
Year Estab:	1986

Bobrovnikoff Books 207-733-4773
Route 2, Box 5130 Lubec 04652

Collection:	General stock.
# of Volumes:	2,000
Services:	Search service, accepts want lists.
Credit Cards:	No
Owner:	Stephen P. Bobrovnikoff
Year Estab:	1967

Nathan Copeland, Bookseller 207-773-3647
72 Groveside Road Portland 04102

Collection:	Speciality
# of Volumes:	2,000
Specialties:	Maine history; maritime; World War II; travel.
Services:	Accepts want lists.
Credit Cards:	No
Owner:	Nathan Copeland
Year Estab:	1962

Brian W. Howard, Books 207-324-6471
P.O. Box 871 Sanford 04073

Collection:	Speciality
# of Volumes:	250+
Specialties:	Maine
Services:	Accepts want lists.
Credit Cards:	No
Owner:	Brian W. Howard
Year Estab:	1989

Nimue Books and Prints 207-947-8016
P.O. Box 325 Orono 04473

Collection: Specialty books, prints and ephemera.
# of Volumes: 2,000
Specialties: Natural history; exploration; early travel guides and baedekers; New England.
Services: Irregular catalog, search service, accepts want lists.
Credit Cards: No
Owner: Edward & Deborah Thompson

Grace Perkinson - Antiquarian Books 207-348-6034
P.O. Box 7 Deer Isle 04627

Collection: General stock.
# of Volumes: 5,000
Specialties: Literature; poetry; philosophy; history; religion.
Services: Appraisals, search service, accepts want lists.
Credit Cards: No
Owner: Grace Perkinson
Year Estab: 1978

Quill and Stylus 207-474-3403
329 Water Street Skowhegan 04976

Collection: Specialty
# of Volumes: 30,000+
Specialties: Americana (with emphasis on non fiction).
Services: Catalog, accepts want lists.
Credit Cards: No
Owner: Frank & Yvette Curran
Year Estab: 1974

Weyhe Art Books 207-288-4281
P.O. Box 217 Mount Desert 04660

Collection: Specialty
# of Volumes: 100,000
Specialties: Art; architecture; decorative arts.
Services: Catalog, appraisals, search service, accepts want lists.
Credit Cards: No
Owner: Deborah Kiley
Year Estab: 1924

Antique Dealers

Auld Acquaintance 207-622-5527
At Dealers Choice, 108 Water Street Hallowell

James H. LeFurgy Antiques & Books 207-623-1771
168 Water Street Hallowell

My Wife's Antiques 207-926-3302
Route 231 P.O. Box 108 New Gloucester

Under Cover Flea Market 207-783-3292
Route 26 Oxford

Wagon Wheel Antiques 207-998-4261
Route 26 Oxford

A wealth of treasures

Massachusetts

Alphabetical Listing By Dealer

Alphabetical Listing By Location

Location	Dealer	Page
Accord	Gidley Geographic	220
Acton	Henry Deeks	185
Alford	George Robert Minkoff, Inc.	185
Amherst	Atticus/Albion Used Books	121
	Amherst Antiquarian Maps	185
	Book Marks	121
	Valley Books	122
Andover	Alphabet Books & Antiques	122
	Andover Books & Prints	123
Arlington	Arlington Books	123
	Scientia Books	186
Ashfield	Yesterday's Books	124
Assonet	Osee H. Brady Books	186
Auburn	Kenneth Andersen	218
Avon	Bayskater Books	219
Bedford	Dunham's Book Store	125
Belmont	Payson Hall Book Guild	125
Bernardston	Astrtonomy Books, Paul W. Luther	186
	Bernardston Books	187
Beverly	Jean S. McKenna, Books	187
Boston	Ars Libri, Ltd.	126
	Avenue Victor Hugo Bookshop	126
	Thomas G. Boss Fine Books	127
	Boston Book Annex	127
	Boston Book Company	129
	Brattle Book Shop	129
	Bromer Booksellers, Inc.	130
	The Maury A. Bromsen Co.	187
	Buddenbrooks, Inc.	130
	Childs Gallery	131
	Choreographica	131
	Goodspeed's Book Shop, Inc.	131
	Priscilla Juvelis, Inc.	188
	The Nostalgia Factory	132
	David L. O'Neal, Antiquarian Booksellers	132
	Pepper and Stern Rare Books, Inc.	132
	Spenser's Mystery Bookshop	133

Amherst

Atticus/Albion Used Books (MA1) 413-256-1547
8 Main Street 01002

Collection	General stock of new and used hardcover and paperback.
# of Volumes:	10,000
Specialties:	Scholarly books.
Hours:	Monday-Saturday 9-11 PM. Sunday 11-8 PM.
Travel:	Route 9 exit off I-91. Proceed east for about 7 miles. Turn left at Amherst College lights. Shop is located in the heart of downtown Amherst. Map 16.
Credit Cards:	Yes
Owner:	Charles Nagarro
Year Estab:	1989
Comments:	The used books are located on the lower level of this otherwise new book shop. Most of the titles are of more recent origin and reflect the community's academic focus.

Book Marks (MA2) 413-549-6136
1 East Pleasant Street at Carriage Shops 01002

Collection:	Specialty
# of Volumes:	9,000
Specialties:	Emily Dickinson; literature; fiction; poetry and criticism; music; art.
Hours:	Monday-Saturday 10-5.
Travel:	Route 9 off I-91. Proceed east for about 7 miles. Turn left at Amherst College lights. Shop is in heart of downtown Amherst. Map 16.
Credit Cards:	No
Owner:	Frederick G. Marks
Year Estab:	1982
Comments:	A second floor shop located in a shopping center. The owner describes his collection as being more representative of the academic world than a "general shop," i.e, while there are no mysteries, cookbooks or science fiction, there is an ample stock of history, art and literature.

Valley Books (MA3) 413-256-1508
199 North Pleasant Street 01002 Fax: 413-253-7475

Collection: General stock of hardcover and paperback and ephemera.
# of Volumes: 35,000
Specialties: Literature; sports; popular culture; history; biography.
Hours: Monday-Friday 10:30-5:30. Saturday 10-5. Sunday 12-5.
Services: Appraisals, search service, catalog, accepts want lists, mail order.
Travel: Route 9 exit off I-91. Proceed east for about 7 miles. Turn left at Amherst College lights. Shop is on right after second traffic light. Map 16.
Credit Cards: Yes
Owner: Larry & Charmagne Pruner
Year Estab: 1975
Comments: A typical university town used book shop with the majority of the titles related to academia. The books are located on two levels.

Andover

Alphabet Books & Antiques (MA4) 508-475-0269
68 Park Street 01810 508-475-1582

Collection: General stock, prints and antiques.
# of Volumes: 6,000
Specialties: History; Irish literature; Celtic history; first editions.
Hours: Tuesday-Saturday 10-5. Sunday (Thanksgiving-Christmas only) 12-5.
Travel: Route 28 south from I-495 to downtown Andover. Shop is 1 1/2 blocks east of Main Street (Route 28). Park Street is adjacent to Old Town Hall. Map 12.
Credit Cards: No
Owner: Brenden Roche
Year Estab: 1988
Comments: A tiny shop, up one flight, with some quality books. If you're browsing, it shouldn't take more than 5-10 minutes to read almost every title. Only because this shop and its neighbor are located side by side would the trip to Andover be worth the time, unless, that is, you're interested in one of the shop's specialty areas.

Andover Books & Prints (MA5) 508-475-1645
68 Park Street 01810

Collection: General stock and prints.
# of Volumes: 10,000
Specialties: Garden history; herbs; folklore; New England; cats and catlore; fiction; poetry; art; antiques.
Hours: Monday-Friday 12-5. Saturday 10-5. September-May: Sunday 1-4 and by appointment.
Services: Appraisals, search service, quarterly newsletter.
Travel: Route 28 south from I-495 to downtown Andover. Shop is 1 1/2 blocks east of Main Street (Route 28). Park Street is adjacent to Old Town Hall. Map 12.
Credit Cards: Yes
Owner: V. David Rodger
Year Estab: 1978
Comments: Upstairs, and upstairs again, this bi-level shop contains a limited general stock, plus some interesting specialty items. The books are attractively displayed and most are in good condition. Coffee and tea are usually available. The owner sponsors literary teas during the school year. Gardening enthusiasts should enjoy visiting the bookshop's garden.

Arlington

Arlington Books (MA6) 617-643-4473
212 Massachusetts Avenue 02174

Collection: General stock.
# of Volumes: 150,000
Specialties: Music; theology; art; children's; military history; foreign language; foreign literature; poetry; cooking.
Hours: Sunday-Wednesday 10-5. Thursday 10-8. Friday 10-2.
Services: Accepts want lists, mail order.
Travel: Route 2 exit from I-95/128 towards Cambridge. At Lake Street exit, bear right and proceed 1/2 mile to Massachusetts Avenue. Turn left. Shop is halfway up street on left. From Harvard University, proceed 2 1/2 miles north on Massachusetts Avenue. Map 12.
Credit Cards: No

Owner: Howard Feldstein
Year Estab: 1989
Comments: Whether you're a specialist or just someone who cares for books, plan to spend at least an hour to half a day exploring the nooks and crannies of this extraordinary bi-level shop. From the outside, one gets the impression of a small shop with a limited stock. Once you enter, though, you'll find yourself lost more than once in a literal maze of bookshelves arranged to use every last inch of space as effectively as possible. While there is some inconsistency in terms of how the books are shelved (perhaps books misplaced by careless browsers), and in some cases, there may be more than one section of the same category of books, the number of different categories is vast. We saw common books, unusual books and rare books. If you can put up with the clutter and don't mind looking for books behind books or searching for a step ladder to reach the top shelves, you might turn up some really wonderful finds. Reasonably priced.

Ashfield

Yesterday's Books (MA7) 413-628-3249
Baptist Corner Road 01330

Collection: General stock.
# of Volumes: 2,000
Hours: Daily 9-5.
Services: Mail order.
Travel: 1/4 mile off Route 116. Look for a sign on the right and a low monument on the left. Map 16.
Credit Cards: No
Owner: Clayton & Ruth Craft
Year Estab: 1972
Comments: This small collection, located in a private home, focuses on fiction, children's books, hymnals and New Englandiana. The owners practice a "love thy neighbor" philosophy in that even when they're not at home, the shop is still open. Book hunters can browse through the collection and if they find something of interest, leave the proper payment on a tray.

Bedford

Dunham's Book Store (MA8) 617-275-9140
50 Great Road
Mailing address: 13 School Avenue 01730

Collection:	General stock.
# of Volumes:	25,000
Hours:	Wednesday-Saturday 11-5. Closed last 2 weeks of August and 1st week of September.
Travel:	3 miles south of Concord exit off Route 3 or exit 31 off I-95/128. Shop located on right on Route 4/125/62, 1/10 mile west of Bedford Center and about 2 1/2 miles west of Route 128 on Route 4. Map 12.
Credit Cards:	No
Owner:	Grace & Carroll Dunham
Year Estab:	1960
Comments:	A small, compact, well kept shop lined with fairly recent but nonetheless interesting out-of-print books. Although the owners do not list any specialty areas, we noted strong sections in cooking, horses, hunting and electronics. Some paperbacks in front. While the shop stocks some 25,000 volumes, the owners have an additional 150,000 titles in storage. A generous supply of stools makes browsing the lower shelves easier and more comfortable.

Belmont

Payson Hall Book Guild (MA9) 617-484-2020
80 Trapelo Road 02178

Collection:	General stock.
# of Volumes:	10,000
Specialties:	Modern first editions; Irish; New England; Americana; children's; art; architecture.
Hours:	Tuesday-Friday 12-5. Saturday 10-4.
Services:	Appraisals, search service, accepts wants lists, auctions.
Travel:	Trapelo Road, Belmont exit off Route 128. Alternate directions: Exit 59 (Belmont Center) off Route 6. Right at exit and proceed to end of Pleasant Street. Left onto Trapelo Road. Shop is about 1 mile ahead on right. Map 12.

Credit Cards: No
Owner: Clare M. Murphy
Year Estab: 1902
Comments: A storefront group shop displaying a mixture of common books, some rather rare items and a few higher priced gems from 18 different dealers. Definitely worth a visit. As with other group shops, if the book hunter has a specific interest, that interest may be duplicated in several sections, requiring the visitor to spend more time then would ordinarily be the case in a single dealer shop.

Boston

Ars Libri, Ltd. (MA10) 617-357-5212
560 Harrison Avenue 02118

Collection: Specialty
# of Volumes: 60,000
Specialties: Fine art, including out-of-print and rare.
Hours: Monday-Friday 9-6. Saturday 11-5.
Services: Catalog, appraisals, accepts want lists.
Travel: Located in the south end of Boston. Best to call for directions.
Credit Cards: No
Owner: Elmar W. Seibel
Year Estab: 1977

Avenue Victor Hugo Bookshop (MA11) 617-266-7746
339 Newbury Street 02115

Collection: General stock of used and new books, old magazines and pulps.
# of Volumes: 50,000+
Specialties: Science fiction; collectibles; Americana; pulps; westerns.
Hours: Monday-Friday 9-9. Saturday 10-8. Sunday 12-8.
Services: Search service, accepts want lists, mail order.
Travel: Map 11.
Credit Cards: Yes
Owner: Vincent McCaffrey
Year Estab: 1972

Comments: A street level shop that offers a unique collection that should not be missed. The books are in generally excellent condition and in our opinion are slightly overpriced.

Thomas G. Boss Fine Books (MA12) 617-421-1880
355 Boylston Street 02116 Fax: 617-536-7072

Collection: Speciality
# of Volumes: 5,000
Specialties: Fine bindings; press books; illustrated; art nouveau; arts and crafts; art deco; bookplates; books about books.
Hours: Monday-Saturday 10-5.
Services: Appraisals, catalog, accepts want lists.
Travel: Map 11.
Credit Cards: Yes
Owner: Thomas G. Boss
Year Estab: 1974
Comments: The shop's name says it all: fine books. The owner claims to have the largest U.S. stock of books of the 1890's and of bookplates of all eras. The shop shares quarters with another dealer in fine books, giving book hunters an opportunity to visit two quality stores at the same time.

Boston Book Annex (MA13) 617-266-1090
906 Beacon Street 02115

Collection: General stock.
# of Volumes: 60,000
Hours: Monday-Saturday 10-10. Sunday 12-10.
Travel: About one mile from the Back Bay section of Boston, at the corner of Beacon and Park Drive. Map 11.
Credit Cards: Yes
Owner: Helen Kelly
Comments: Somewhat off by itself, this shop offers a good general stock of moderately priced mostly out-of-print hardcover books and paperbacks. A fun place to browse. Although the owner did not list any specialties, we noted a strong film section. First editions and antiquarian books are available at the owner's Centre Street location. See next listing.

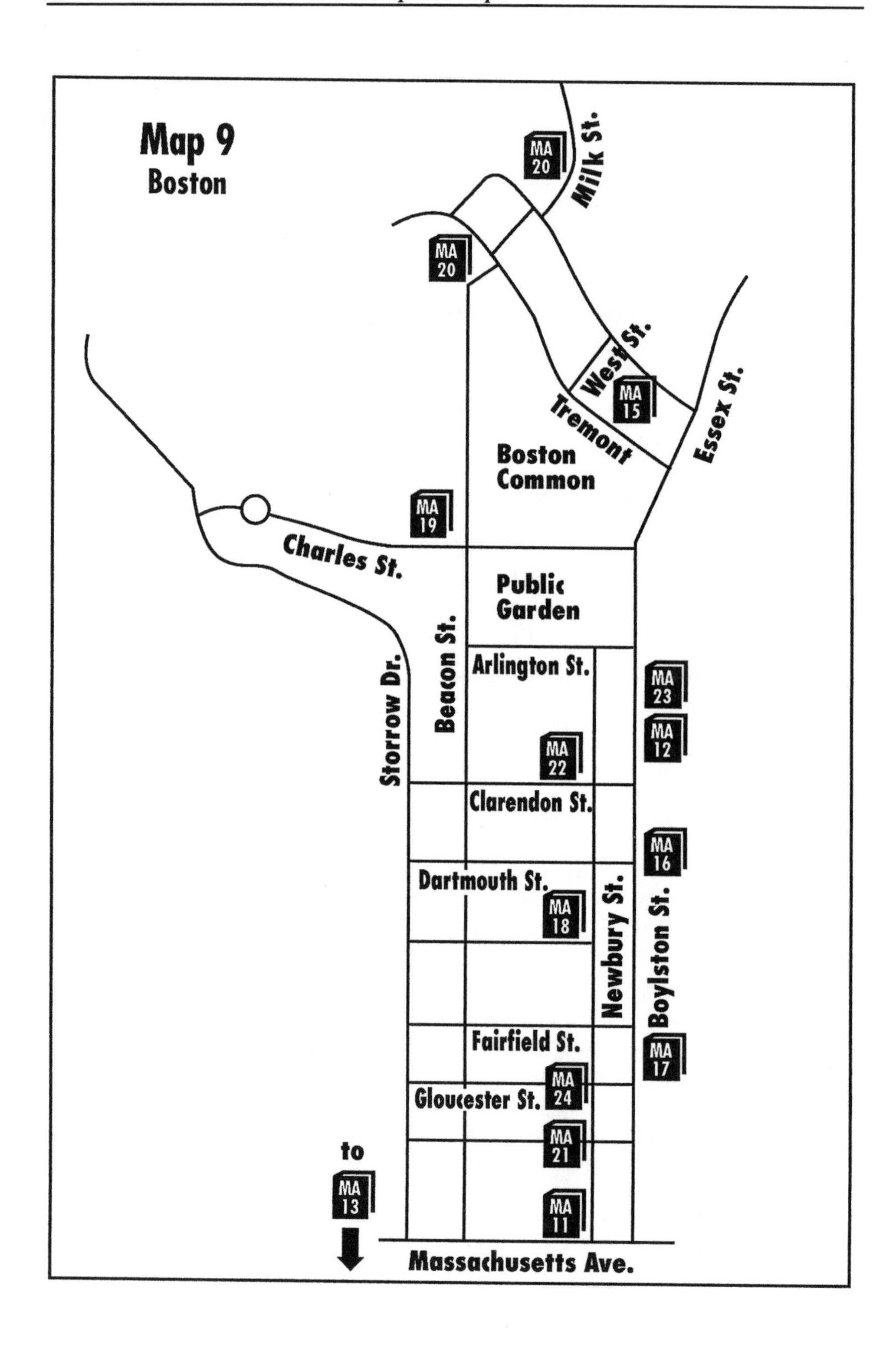

Map 9
Boston
MA 20
Milk St.
MA 20
West St.
MA 15
Tremont
Essex St.
Boston Common
MA 19
Charles St.
Public Garden
Beacon St.
Storrow Dr.
Arlington St.
MA 23
MA 12
MA 22
Clarendon St.
MA 16
Dartmouth St.
MA 18
Newbury St.
Boylston St.
Fairfield St.
MA 17
MA 24
Gloucester St.
MA 21
to
MA 13
MA 11
Massachusetts Ave.

Boston Book Company (MA14) 617-522-2100
705 Centre Street 02130 Fax: 617-522-9359

Collection:	General stock.
# of Volumes:	60,000
Specialties:	Japan; Korea; wood block print books; American and British first editions; sets; general antiquarian.
Hours:	Monday-Saturday 10-5.
Services:	Appraisals, search service, catalog, accepts want lists, binding and restoration.
Travel:	Route 1 south (Riverway) to Pond Street. Left on Pond. Right on Centre. Shop is 2 blocks ahead on right.
Credit Cards:	Yes
Owner:	Helen Kelly
Year Estab:	1979
Comments:	Located one flight up, this shop stocks a very well organized and computerized collection of books in pristine condition. The owner says she has the largest selection of modern first editions in New England. Used and out-of-print books are available at the shop's annex on Beacon Street.

Brattle Book Shop (MA15) 800-447-9595
9 West Street 02111 Fax: 617-338-1467

Collection:	General stock, magazines and ephemera.
# of Volumes:	200,000
Hours:	Monday-Saturday 9-5:30.
Services:	Appraisals, accepts want lists.
Travel:	1 block from Jordan Marsh and Filenes. Map 11.
Credit Cards:	Yes
Owner:	Kenneth Gloss
Year Estab:	1825
Comments:	A Boston fixture since 1825, this shop offers an extremely well organized general stock with no clearly identified speciality areas. However, we did note a large motion picture section when we visited. Newer used and out-of-print books are located on the first two floors with older and rarer books and a new arrivals section on the third floor. Prices range from $1.00 "run of the mill" reading copies to $100,000 collectibles. A fun place to browse with a well earned reputation for quality.

Bromer Booksellers, Inc. (MA16 617-247-2818
607 Boylston Street 02116 Fax: 617-247-2975

Collection:	Speciality
# of Volumes:	4,000
Specialties:	First editions; illustrated; private press; children's; miniature books; fine and artist bindings; decorative arts.
Hours:	Monday-Friday 9:30-5:30. Saturday 9-5.
Services:	Catalog.
Travel:	Map 11.
Credit Cards:	Yes
Owner:	Anne C. & David J. Bromer
Year Estab:	1965
Comments:	A genuine antiquarian shop located on the second floor of an office building. If your pocket book can support your tastes, this is the place for you. If you're simply interested in out-of-print or used books, don't bother. This isn't a shop for browsers.

Buddenbrooks, Inc. (MA17) 617-536-4433
753 Boylston Street 02116 Fax: 617-267-1118

Collection:	General stock.
# of Volumes:	6,000 (rare and antiquarian)
Specialties:	Literature; rare books; early printing; illustrated; voyages; travel; exploration; hunting; fishing; sports; fine bindings; library sets.
Hours:	Monday-Friday 8-11:30 PM. Saturday & Sunday 9-11:30 PM.
Services:	Appraisals, search service, catalog, accepts want lists.
Travel:	Map 11.
Credit Cards:	Yes
Owner:	M. Weinkle
Year Estab:	1975
Comments:	Primarily a new book store, most of the used and antiquarian books in this street level shop are kept in locked glass cases and are not readily accessible for browsing.

Childs Gallery (MA18) 617-266-1108
169 Newbury Street 02116 Fax: 617-266-2381

Collection:	Speciality
Specialties:	Illustrations for fine edition books; fine art.
Hours:	Tuesday-Friday 9-6. Monday & Saturday 10-5.
Travel:	Map 11.
Credit Cards:	Yes
Owner:	D. Roger Howlett
Year Estab:	1937

Choreographica (MA19) 617-227-4780
82 Charles Street 02114

Collection:	Speciality
# of Volumes:	5,000
Specialties:	Performing arts with a strong emphasis on dance, music, antiques and fine art.
Hours:	Monday-Saturday 9-5. Sunday 9-4.
Services:	Accepts want lists.
Travel:	Back Bay section of Boston between Pitney and Mt. Vernon Streets. Map 11.
Credit Cards:	Yes
Owner:	Ernest Morrell
Year Estab:	1965
Comments:	A small, crowded basement shop in the heart of Boston's Charles Street antique row. Worth a visit if you're interested in any of the shop's specialties.

Goodspeed's Book Shop, Inc. (MA20) 617-523-5970
7 Beacon Street & 2 Milk Street 02134

Collection:	General stock, ephemera and autographs.
Specialties:	Rare books; Americana; genealogies.
Hours:	Monday-Friday 9-5. Saturday 10-3. Closed Saturday during July & August.
Travel:	Map 11.
Owner:	George T. Goodspeed

The Nostalgia Factory (MA21) 617-236-8754
324 Newbury Street 02115

Collection:	Vintage paperbacks and ephemera.
# of Volumes:	2,000
Hours:	Monday-Saturday 10-7. Sunday 11-6.
Services:	Appraisals.
Travel:	Massachusetts Avenue exit from Route 3/93. Proceed north on Massachusetts Avenue to Newbury St. Map 11.
Credit Cards:	Yes
Owner:	Rudy Franchi
Year Estab:	1970
Comments:	Primarily an ephemera shop with a limited (less than 2,000 volumes) selection of hardcover and paperbacks.

David L. O'Neal, Antiquarian Booksellers (MA22) 617-266-5790
234 Clarendon Street 02116 Fax: 617-266-1089

Collection:	General stock.
# of Volumes:	5,000
Specialties:	15th-19th century books; fine leather sets and bindings; first editions; private press books; printing history; literature; Americana.
Hours:	Monday-Friday 9-5. Most Saturdays 10-4.
Services:	Appraisals, catalog, accepts want lists.
Travel:	Map 11.
Credit Cards:	Yes
Owner:	David & Mary O'Neal
Year Estab:	1968

Pepper and Stern Rare Books, Inc. (MA23 617-421-1880
355 Boylston Street 02116 Fax: 617-536-7072

Collection:	Speciality
# of Volumes:	2,000-3,000
Specialties:	American and English first editions (mostly 20th century, some 19th century); mystery; detective; Sherlock Holmes; autographed and signed copies; rare cinema.
Hours:	Monday-Saturday 10-5.
Services:	Catalog, accepts want lists.
Travel:	Map 11.
Credit Cards:	Yes

Owner:	Peter L. Stern
Comments:	A shop for the discriminating buyer interested in rare first editions of some very popular authors. The books are in excellent condition. The shop shares quarters with another fine book dealer, giving book hunters an opportunity to visit two quality shops at one time.

Spenser's Mystery Bookshop (MA24) 617-262-0880
314 Newbury Street 02115

Collection:	Specialty new and used hardcover and paperback.
# of Volumes:	12,000
Specialties:	Mysteries
Hours:	Monday-Saturday 10:30-5:30.
Travel:	Massachusetts Avenue exit from I-93. Proceed north on Massachusetts Avenue to Newbury Street. Map 11.
Credit Cards:	Yes
Owner:	Andrew Thurnauer
Year Estab:	1983
Comments:	For mystery fans, this shop offers a fine selection of reasonably priced books. The majority of the titles are new, however. Review copies of new mysteries are available at a discount price.

Brewster

Barbara Grant Antiques & Books (MA25) 508-896-7198
1793 Main Street
Mailing address: P.O. Box 1223 02631

Collection:	General stock.
# of Volumes:	10,000
Specialties:	Cape Cod; New England.
Hours:	May 1-October 30: Daily 10-5. Remainder of year by appointment.
Services:	Search service, accepts want lists, mail order.
Travel:	On Route 6A, between Routes 137 & 124. Map 14.
Credit Cards:	No
Owner:	Barbara Grant
Year Estab:	1980
Comments:	A combination antique/collectibles and used book shop with a collection of quite ordinary books. In our opinion, the size of the collection appears somewhat overstated.

The Punkhorn Bookshop (MA26) 508-896-2114
672 Main Street 02631

Collection:	General stock.
# of Volumes:	25,000
Specialties:	Art; antiques; literature; prints; natural history.
Hours:	Daily except Mondays 10-5 and by appointment.
Services:	Appraisals, search service, accepts want lists, mail order.
Travel:	Exit 9 off Route 6. Make left onto Route 134 and proceed for 3-4 miles to first stoplight (Shell gasoline station). Make right at light onto Route 6A. Shop is on right, about 1 mile after the Brewster/Dennis town line sign. Map 14.
Credit Cards:	No
Owner:	David L. Luebke
Year Estab:	1986
Comments:	Access to this spacious and meticulously cared for shop, located in the lower rear portion of the owner's home, is from a flight of stairs off the parking lot. The collection represents every area. The books are in excellent condition and are lovingly shelved and clearly marked. We saw several rare and unusual items that should tempt the true book afficionado. A small children's corner should help occupy the youngsters while their parents are browsing. A shop not to be missed both for its collection and ambience.

Brookline

Brandeis Book Stall (MA27) 617-731-0208
12 Sewall Avenue 02146

Collection:	General stock or hardcover and paperback.
# of Volumes:	5,000
Hours:	Monday-Saturday 10-5. Thursday till 9.
Services:	Accepts want lists.
Travel:	Close to Coolidge Corner in Brookline (where Harvard and Beacon Streets cross). Map 12.
Credit Cards:	No
Owner:	Operated by Brandeis women alumni.
Year Estab:	1985
Comments:	Located in the basement of a three story red brick building, this collection comes strictly from donations — you never know what you'll find.

Brookline Village Bookshop (MA28) 617-734-3519
23 Harvard Street 02146 Fax: 617-734-3519

Collection:	General stock.
# of Volumes:	50,000
Specialties:	History; literature; maritime; children's; art; cookbooks; railroads.
Hours:	Monday-Saturday 10-6. Thursday till 9.
Services:	Appraisals, search service, catalog, accepts want lists.
Travel:	Two blocks north of Route 9. First block is Washington Street. Second is Harvard. Map 12.
Credit Cards:	Yes
Owner:	James Lawton
Year Estab:	1981
Comments:	The owner of this storefront shop located on a busy thoroughfare makes the most of his limited space. The result, however, is a cramped setting that can be intimidating to the book lover wishing to browse leisurely. The books are of fairly recent vintage and are mostly in good condition.

Cambridge

Robin Bledsoe, Bookseller (MA29) 617-576-3634
1640 Massachusetts Avenue (Rear) 02138 Fax: 617-661-2445

Collection:	Speciality
# of Volumes:	3,000
Specialties:	Horses and all equestrian activities (new, imported, and used); scholarly and chiefly out-of-print books dealing with art history; classical archaeology; architecture; photography; landscape design; graphic design.
Hours:	Tuesday-Saturday 11-6 or by appointment.
Services:	Selective search service, catalog, accepts want lists.
Travel:	Four blocks from Harvard Square. The entrance to the book shop is located behind the stores. Look for the large blue "1640" banner and follow the garden path at the side of the building. Map 13.
Credit Cards:	Yes
Owner:	Robin Bledsoe
Year Estab:	1973
Comments:	One of largest stocks of equestrian books in the United States. The owner shares quarters with another used book dealer in the dimly lit basement of a private house.

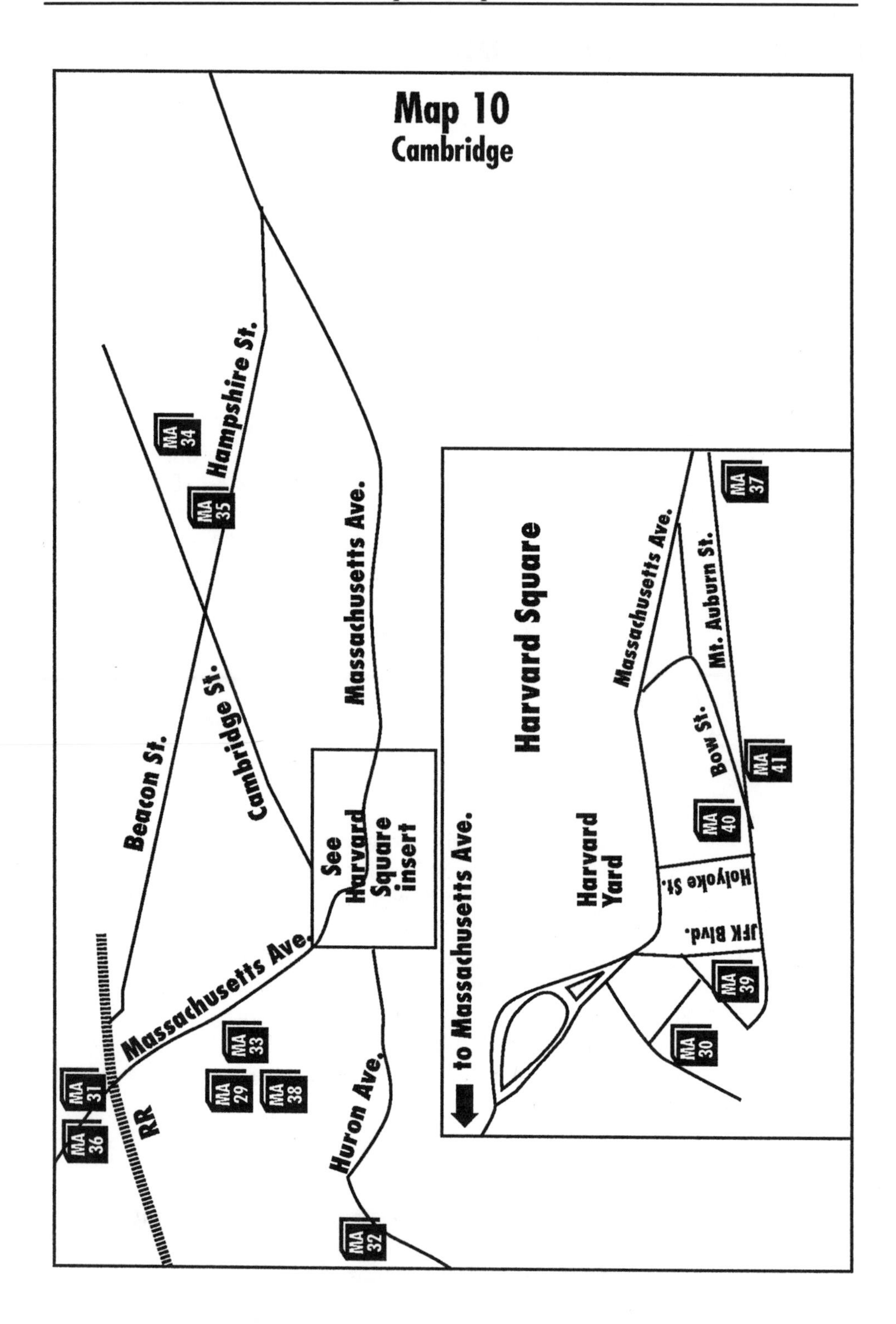
Map 10
Cambridge
Hampshire St.
Massachusetts Ave.
Beacon St.
Cambridge St.
See Harvard Square insert
Massachusetts Ave.
RR
Huron Ave.
MA 34
MA 35
MA 33
MA 29
MA 38
MA 31
MA 36
MA 32
Harvard Square
Massachusetts Ave.
Mt. Auburn St.
Bow St.
Harvard Yard
Holyoke St.
JFK Blvd.
to Massachusetts Ave.
MA 37
MA 41
MA 40
MA 39
MA 30

The Book Case (MA30) 617-876-0832
42 Church Street 02138

Collection:	General stock.
# of Volumes:	100,000+
Hours:	Monday-Saturday 10:30-5:30.
Services:	Accepts want lists.
Travel:	Near Harvard Square. Map 13.
Credit Cards:	No
Owner:	Robert Wanda & Colman Johnson
Year Estab:	1965

The Bookcellar Cafe (MA31) 617-864-9625
1971 Massachusetts Avenue 02140

Collection:	General stock of mostly used and some new books and new magazines.
# of Volumes:	25,000
Hours:	Daily 12-10 PM.
Services:	Search service, accepts want lists, mail order.
Travel:	Tufts Avenue exit from Route 2. Cafe is 1 mile down Massachusetts Avenue in basement of a red brick building that houses a stationery/art supply store. Map 13.
Credit Cards:	No
Year Estab:	1991
Comments:	A good selection of mostly used books in a basement setting that's easy to miss. Look for a sandwich style sign against the railing on the sidewalk. In addition to the books and refreshments, the shop/cafe sponsors special evening literary and music programs. If possible, an evening visit is suggested to get the full flavor of the cafe.

Bryn Mawr Book Store (MA32) 617-661-1770
373 Huron Avenue 02138

Collection:	General stock.
Hours:	Monday-Saturday 10-5; Shorter hours in August.
Services:	Catalog.
Travel:	From Route 2 (Alewife Brook Parkway) going east into Boston, turn left onto Huron and proceed 1/4 mile. Shop is on left at corner of Standish Street. Map 13.
Credit Cards:	No

Owner:	Anne Dane (Manager)
Year Estab:	1972

Canterbury's Book Shop (MA33) 617-864-9396
1675 Massachusetts Avenue 02138

Collection:	General stock.
# of Volumes:	30,000
Specialties:	American and English literature; fiction of all periods.
Hours:	Monday-Saturday 11-6. Sunday 12-5. Some evenings till 10.
Services:	Appraisals, accepts want lists.
Travel:	Several blocks north of Harvard Square. Map 13.
Credit Cards:	Yes
Owner:	Normam B. & Ernest Starr
Year Estab:	1991 (See Comments)
Comments:	The two rear rooms of this well organized shop are devoted exclusively to American and British literature. The shop's general collection, including some scholarly books and paperbacks and a new arrivals section are located in the front room. The entrance to the shop is up a few steps. The books are in mixed condition and are very reasonably priced. Before relocating in Cambridge, the owners operated the Starr Book Company in the Boston area for 50 years. The owners have an additional 200,000 volumes in storage.

Hampshire Books (MA34) 617-547-8095
157 Hampshire Street 02139

Collection:	General stock.
Specialties:	Art; architecture; Celtic; antiques.
Hours:	Wednesday-Sunday 11-5.
Services:	Appraisals, search service, accepts want lists.
Travel:	Allston/Cambridge exit off Mass Pike. Proceed toward Cambridge on Prospect Street. At Hampshire, make right turn. Map 13.
Credit Cards:	No
Owner:	Frank Crowley
Year Estab:	1987

House of Sarah Books (MA35) 617-547-3447
225 Hampshire Street 02139

Collection:	General stock.
# of Volumes:	7,000
Specialties:	Women in religion.
Hours:	Tuesday-Saturday 11-6. Thursday till 7. Sunday 12-5.
Services:	Search service, catalog, accepts want lists, book repairs.
Travel:	Inman Square section of Cambridge. I-93 to McGrath Highway to Cambridge Street. Shop is at intersection of Hampshire and Cambridge Streets. Map 13.
Credit Cards:	Yes
Owner:	Mary Tardiff
Year Estab:	1990
Comments:	A bi-level storefront shop that offers a little bit of everything. The general stock and a small children's corner are located on the first floor. The shop's specialty collection and paperbacks are located in two upstairs rooms. The books are in immaculate condition.

Kate's Mystery Books (MA36) 617-491-2660
2211 Massachusetts Avenue 02140

Collection:	Specialty new and used hardcover and paperback.
# of Volumes:	500+ (used)
Specialties:	Mysteries
Hours:	Monday-Wednesday 12-6. Thursday 12-8. Friday 12-7. Saturday 11-5. Sunday 1-5.
Travel:	Cambridge exit off Mass Pike. Proceed on Massachusetts Avenue to Porter Square. Look for an orange and black Victorian style house. Map 13.
Credit Cards:	Yes
Owner:	Kate Mattes
Year Estab:	1983
Comments:	Used book collection is primarily paperback.

McIntyre & Moore Booksellers (MA37) 617-491-0662
8 Mount Auburn Street 02138

Collection:	General stock of used and some new books.

# of Volumes:	50,000
Specialties:	Philosophy; theology; ancient and medieval history; art; architecture; photography; philosophy of science; advanced mathematics; physics; chess; anthropology.
Hours:	Monday-Saturday 10-10. Sunday 12-10.
Travel:	Near Harvard Square. Map 13.
Credit Cards:	Yes
Owner:	Daniel Moore & Michael McIntyre
Year Estab:	1983
Comments:	Almost like two stores in one, this shop is divided into two distinct halves. While one side of the shop stocks scholarly books in all fields, the other side features mysteries, science fiction and other general subjects. The entrance is down a few steps.

H. L. Mendelsohn, Fine European Books (MA38) 617-576-3634
1640 Massachusetts Avenue (Rear) 02138

Collection:	Speciality
# of Volumes:	1,000
Specialties:	Decorative arts (especially in Europe); architecture; city planning, landscape design.
Hours:	Tuesday-Saturday 11-6.
Services:	Catalog, accepts want lists.
Travel:	Four blocks from Harvard Square. The entrance to the book shop is located behind the stores. Look for the large blue "1640" banner and follow the garden path at the side of the building. Map 13.
Credit Cards:	No
Owner:	Harvey L. Mendelsohn
Year Estab:	1981
Comments:	A fine collection of specialty books in the dimly lit basement of a private house. The owner shares quarters with another specialty used book dealer.

Pandemonium Books & Games (MA39) 617-547-3721
8 JFK Street, 2nd Floor 02138

Collection:	Specialty new and used hardcover and paperback.
# of Volumes:	2,000 (used)
Specialties:	Science fiction; horror; fantasy.
Hours:	Sunday & Wednesday 11-6. Other days 11-10 PM.

Travel: Map 13.
Credit Cards: Yes
Owner: Tyler Stewart
Year Estab: 1989
Comments: Approximately 10% of the used book collection is hardcover.

Pangloss Bookshop (MA40) 617-354-4003
65 Mount Auburn Street 02138

Collection: Specialty
# of Volumes: 50,000
Specialties: Scholarly books in the humanities and social sciences.
Hours: Daily except Sunday 10-7. Till 10 Thursday & Friday.
Services: Search service, accepts specific want lists.
Travel: Near Harvard Square. See map. Map 13.
Credit Cards: Yes
Owner: Herbert R. Hillman, Jr.
Year Estab: 1950
Comments: A shop for the academic book collector. The shop is presided over by a friendly owner who takes pride in serving the academic community and who is most willing to share his in depth knowledge of other area book dealers. The books are in excellent condition.

Starr Book Shop (MA41) 617-547-6864
29 Plympton Street 02138

Collection: General stock.
# of Volumes: 50,000+
Hours: Monday-Saturday 10-8. Sunday 12-6.
Travel: Near Harvard Square. Map 13.
Credit Cards: Yes
Owner: Cindy Jaycox

A well stocked shop with a small crowded room on the street level and a large basement. The collection consists primarily of scholarly titles and a large section of new review copies at 40%-50% off publisher's price. Additional books are in storage.

Chatham

Papyrus - Mostly Books (MA42) 508-945-2271
400 Main Street 02633

Collection:	General stock, ephemera, art gallery, antiques and collectibles.
# of Volumes:	3,000
Specialties:	Modern firsts; biography; American and British literature.
Hours:	Monday-Saturday 10-5. Sunday 12-5. January and February by appointment only.
Services:	Search service, accepts want lists.
Travel:	From Route 6 south, take exit 11 and make left turn onto Route 137 south. Stay on Route 137 till the end. Make left onto Route 28 and proceed into downtown Chatham. Stay on Main Street after the rotary. Map 14.
Credit Cards:	No
Owner:	Katharine Dalton
Year Estab:	1983
Comments:	A small shop in a multi shop setting with a modest collection not particularly strong in any one subject area. Don't overlook the bargain book section where we were able to pick up a book relating to our own field of interest quite inexpensively.

Yellow Umbrella Books (MA43) 508-945-0144
501 Main Street 02633

Collection:	Specialty
# of Volumes:	500+
Specialties:	Cape Cod; New England; maritime; classics; poetry; nature; Americana.
Hours:	Summer: Daily 9 AM-10 PM. Winter: 10-5.
Services:	Search service, accepts want lists.
Travel:	Exit 11 off Route 6. Proceed on Route 137 south to Route 128. Take Route 28 to Chatham Center. Map 14.
Credit Cards:	Yes
Owner:	Eric Linder
Year Estab:	1977
Comments:	A modest collection of used books located in the rear of this otherwise new book shop. With the exception of a large selection of books by regional author Joseph Lincoln, the

used book collection consists mostly of more contemporary titles. Don't expect any bargains, except perhaps for the special bargain table outside.

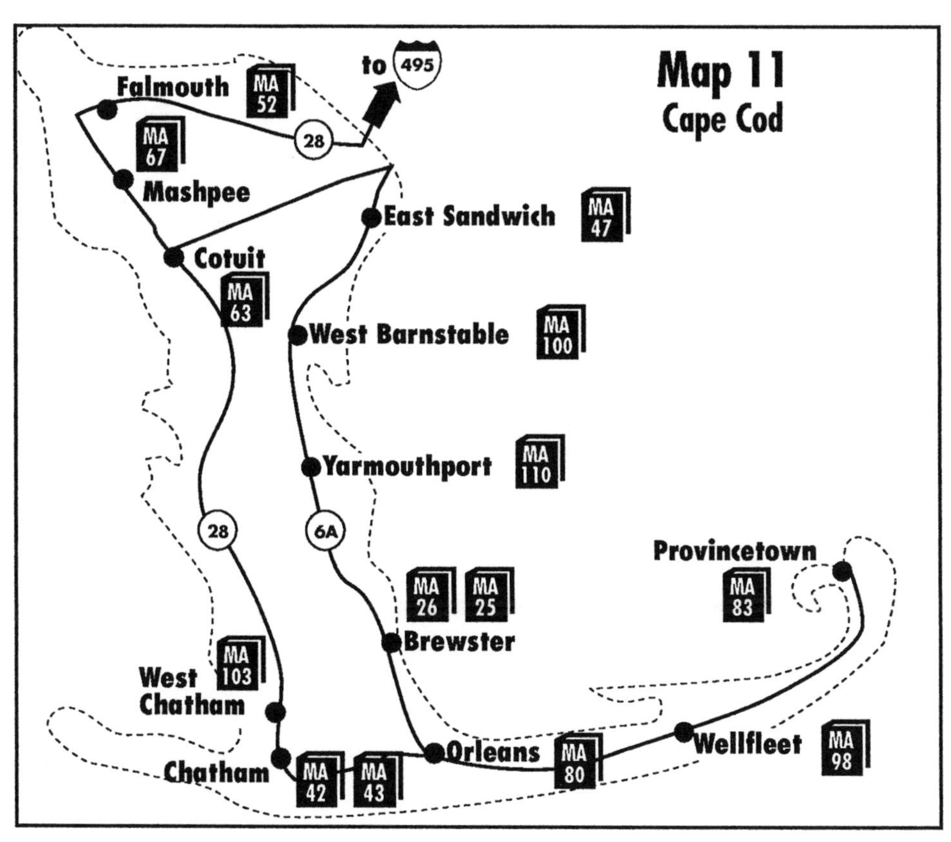

Concord

Barrow Bookstore (MA44) 508-369-6084
79 Main Street 01742

Collection: General stock.
# of Volumes: 12,000
Specialties: Concord authors; children's; history; rare out-of-print books.
Hours: Monday-Saturday 9:30-5. Sunday 12-5.
Services: Search service, accepts want lists, mail order.

Travel:	Route 128 to Route 2A west. Proceed to Main Street in Concord Center. Shop is located in rear courtyard. Look for an old fashioned wheel barrow with books on lawn in front of building. Map 12.
Credit Cards:	Yes
Owner:	Pamela Fenn
Year Estab:	1971
Comments:	A spaciously laid out street level shop offering more recent used books with most subjects represented but not in any depth. Some paperbacks. Comfortable seating area.

Books With A Past (MA45) 508-371-0180
17 Walden Street 01742

Collection:	General stock.
# of Volumes:	9,000
Specialties:	New England; transcendentalism; Concord authors.
Hours:	Monday-Saturday 10-5.
Services:	Search service, accepts want lists.
Travel:	Just off Main Street (Route 62) in center of town. Map 12.
Credit Cards:	No
Owner:	Anne Wanzer & Susan Tucker
Year Estab:	1981
Comments:	One flight up, this shop stocks a modest sized collection of books in good condition. All major subject categories are represented. Concord authors and books about Massachusetts and New England are located in a separate small room.

Cotuit

Isaiah Thomas Books & Prints (MA63) 508-428-2752
4632 Falmouth Road (Route 28) 02635

Collection:	General stock, prints and ephemera.
# of Volumes:	60,000
Specialties:	Miniature books; first editions.
Hours:	Summer: Daily 12-7. Rest of year: Tuesday-Saturday 10-5. Sunday 12-5.
Services:	Appraisals, search service, accepts want lists, lectures on book collecting.
Travel:	Located at junction of Routes 28 and 130. Map 14.

Credit Cards:	Yes
Owner:	Jim Visbeck
Year Estab:	1969
Comments:	A large shop located on the first floor of a white Victorian house with a large parking lot in front. Although the entrance is up a few steps, a ramp is available upon request. The shop offers a selection of moderately priced quality books. All subject areas are represented and some rare finds are to be had. In addition to the specialties noted above, the shop also has a strong collection of books on book collecting. A shop definitely worth visiting.

Duxbury

Wickham Books (MA46) 617-934-6955
285 St. George Street
Mailing address: P.O. Box 203 02331

Collection:	General stock and framed and unframed prints.
# of Volumes:	4,000
Specialties:	Children's; southeast Massachusetts; maritime; antiquarian prints.
Hours:	Tuesday-Saturday 10-5. Summer only: Also Sunday 1-5.
Services:	Search service, accepts want lists.
Travel:	Exit 11 off Route 3. Proceed east on Route 14 for 3 miles. Map 15.
Credit Cards:	No
Owner:	Miriam & Al Wickham
Year Estab:	1989
Comments:	Located in an historic seacoast village, this bi-level shop offers quality books on the first level with more common titles and children's books upstairs. Most subject areas are represented. The books are not inexpensive.

East Sandwich

Titcomb's Bookshop (MA47) 508-888-2331
432 Route 6A
Mailing address: P.O. Box 45 02537

Collection:	General stock of used and new books.
# of Volumes:	10,000

Specialties: Regional; genealogy; maritime; fishing; children's; decorative arts.
Hours: Monday-Saturday 10-5. Sunday 12-5.
Services: Appraisals, search service, accepts want lists, mail order.
Travel: Exit 3 from Route 6. Proceed north 1 mile, then east 1 mile on Route 6A. Look for statue of colonial man holding a book. Map 14.
Credit Cards: Yes
Owner: Ralph & Nancy Titcomb
Year Estab: 1970's
Comments: A shop designed for browsers. This spaciously laid out multi level shop is housed in a new barn like building attached to the owner's home. New books and most non fiction used books, including an interesting section on pirates, are located on the first floor, with fiction, poetry and biographies shelved upstairs. When we visited, a bargain mystery collection was located in the basement. Comfortable chairs are located throughout the shop.

Easthampton

Kenneth Schoen, Bookseller (MA48) 413-527-4780
1 Cottage Street 01027

Collection: General stock.
# of Volumes: 15,000
Specialties: Judaica; exile literature; the Holocaust; psychoanalysis; German literature; philosophy.
Hours: Monday-Friday 10-6 and by appointment.
Services: Appraisals, search service, catalog, accepts want lists.
Travel Exit 17B off I-91N and follow signs to Easthampton. From downtown Easthampton, turn onto Union Street and proceed to end. Shop is in a restored factory building on left. There is a direct entrance to the book shop to the left of the building's main entrance. Map 16.
Credit Cards: No
Owner: Kenneth Schoen
Year Estab: 1986
Comments: Located on the street level (level 2) of a former factory building, this shop has an amazing selection of books on anything remotely related to Judaica, i.e, religion, politics, art, literature, propaganda, etc. Whether you're a scholar

interested in the history of the Holocaust or simply someone who wants to find his or her religious roots, if the subject is in any way related to the Jewish people, the book is likely to be available here. And even if you don't find what you're looking for, you're sure to enjoy chatting with the owner. If you have the time, you might want to visit some of the artists and craftspeople in the building.

Essex

White Elephant Shop (MA49) 508-768-6901
32 Main Street (Route 133)

Collection: General stock, records and magazines.
# of Volumes: 1,500
Hours: Monday-Saturday 10-5. Sunday 12-5.
Travel: On Route 133 next to the Essex Shipbuilding Museum. Map 17.
Credit Cards: No
Owner: Tom Ellis & Rick Grobe
Comments: A combination antique/collectible and used book shop with a modest collection of books in most categories. The books aren't in the best of condition. Prices vary. Hardcover specials were available for 25 cents a copy.

Fall River

Bookhaven Bookstore (MA50) 508-679-0188
1749 North Main Street 02720

Collection: General stock and ephemera.
# of Volumes: 15,000
Specialties: Maritime; military; local history; New England; Lizzie Borden.
Hours: Daily 9-4:30.
Services: Appraisals, accepts want lists.
Travel: Route 79 north exit off I-95. From Route 79, turn onto North Main Street and proceed south for 1/4 mile. Map 15.
Credit Cards: No
Owner: Ralph A. Roberts
Year Estab: 1971
Comments: This storefront shop could benefit from both some tidying

up and some organization. The collection consists primarily of old books not always in the best of condition. Many of the shelves are not marked and books are not always shelved by category. With a little patience though, one might find something one is looking for. Books are inexpensively priced. According to the owner, one half the stock is turned over every few months.

Taste of Honey Bookstore (MA51) 508-679-8844
1755 North Main Street 02720 508-673-5258

Collection: General stock.
# of Volumes: 10,000
Hours: Wednesday-Saturday 10-4 or by appointment.
Services: Search service, accepts want lists.
Travel: Route 79 north exit off I-95. From Route 79, turn onto North Main Street and proceed south for 1/4 mile. Map 15.
Credit Cards: No
Owner: James F. McKenna
Year Estab: 1978
Comments: A small crowded shop with floor to ceiling shelves that appear almost ready to tip over. The collection is modest in size but worth a visit if you're in the area. Although not listed as a specialty, the shop does stock Lizzie Borden material.

Falmouth

Falmouth Bookshop (MA52) 508-540-6775
665 Main Street 02540

Collection: General stock and ephemera.
# of Volumes: 10,000
Hours: Monday, Tuesday, Friday 10-6. Saturday 11-5. Wednesday, Thursday, Sunday by chance.
Services: Appraisals, search service, accepts want lists, mail order.
Travel: On Route 28 in Falmouth Center. Map 14.
Credit Cards: No
Owner: Randall Hawkins
Year Estab: 1985
Comments: A small two story shop with a modest general stock. Some bargain books but not much to get excited about.

Florence

Bookends (MA53) 413-585-8667
93 Main Street
Mailing address: P.O. Box 60432 01060

Collection: General stock.
# of Volumes: 15,000
Specialties: Ireland; Latin America; biography; fiction; literary criticism; travel; natural history; poetry; music.
Hours: Tuesday-Saturday 10-5:30. Sunday 12-5.
Services: Accepts want lists.
Travel: Northampton exit off I-91. Proceed on Route 9 west to Northampton. Florence is 2.3 miles after downtown Northampton. Shop is located next to Miss Florence Diner. Map 16.
Credit Cards: No
Owner: Edward K. Shanahan
Year Estab: 1990
Comments: Easy to find, this book shop is located in a former three story private home. In addition to the specialties listed above, we observed a nice collection of books dealing with journalism, the media, New England and film. Most of the books are in very fine condition and each section has a reasonable depth of quality titles. There are comfortable leather armchairs in almost every room if you want to sit a while and thumb through a book you're considering purchasing. The coffee pot is always on which, in our view, is a sign that the owner truly welcomes book lovers. A children's corner is located on the first floor.

Framingham

Vintage Books (MA54) 508-875-7517
117 Concord Street 01701

Collection: General stock of hardcover and paperback.
# of Volumes: 40,000
Specialties: Quakers; religion; Americana; biography; fiction; self help; poetry.
Hours: Tuesday-Saturday 10-6. Friday till 9.

Services: Search service, catalog (Quakeriana).
Travel: Exit 13 off Mass Pike. Proceed on Route 30 west to Route 126 south. On Route 126, proceed 2 miles to downtown Framingham. Shop is on left between Woolworth's and Radio Shack. Map 12.
Credit Cards: Yes
Owner: Nancy & David Haines
Year Estab: 1988
Comments: A spacious layout and comfortable chairs (including two rocking chairs) makes browsing this bi-level storefront shop a delight. The collection is extremely well organized. A special showcase section features collectible books from specialty dealers. There's also a bargain table. Definitely worth a visit.

Franklin

Shire Book Shop (MA55) 508-528-5665
305 Union Street 02038

Collection: General stock
# of Volumes: 150,000+
Specialties: Art; photography; classics; biography; children's; history; science; early 20th century fiction.
Hours: Monday-Friday 10-8. Saturday 9-5. Sunday & holidays 12-5.
Services: Appraisals, search service, accepts want lists.
Travel: Exit 17 off I-495. Proceed on Route 140 south for 1 1/2 miles to Union Street (look for set of lights at cemetery). Right onto Union and proceed 1/4 mile to railroad tracks. Turn right at Shire sign and proceed to second building on site. Map 12.
Credit Cards: No
Owner: Jack Boland
Year Estab: 1982
Comments: Located on the first floor of a renovated turn of the century mill building, this is a shop in transition. The shop offers books and more books in a vast, well organized, warehouse like setting. Although a large number of the books are library discards of fairly common titles, the new owner is in the process of upgrading the stock. Hardcover and paperbacks are shelved together and the titles of better books in

the collection are available on computer. The owner has plans for several major interior changes, including a special children's section. Railroad buffs can enjoy watching and listening to the trains that pass in front of the shop on a regular basis. Worth a visit if you're in the area.

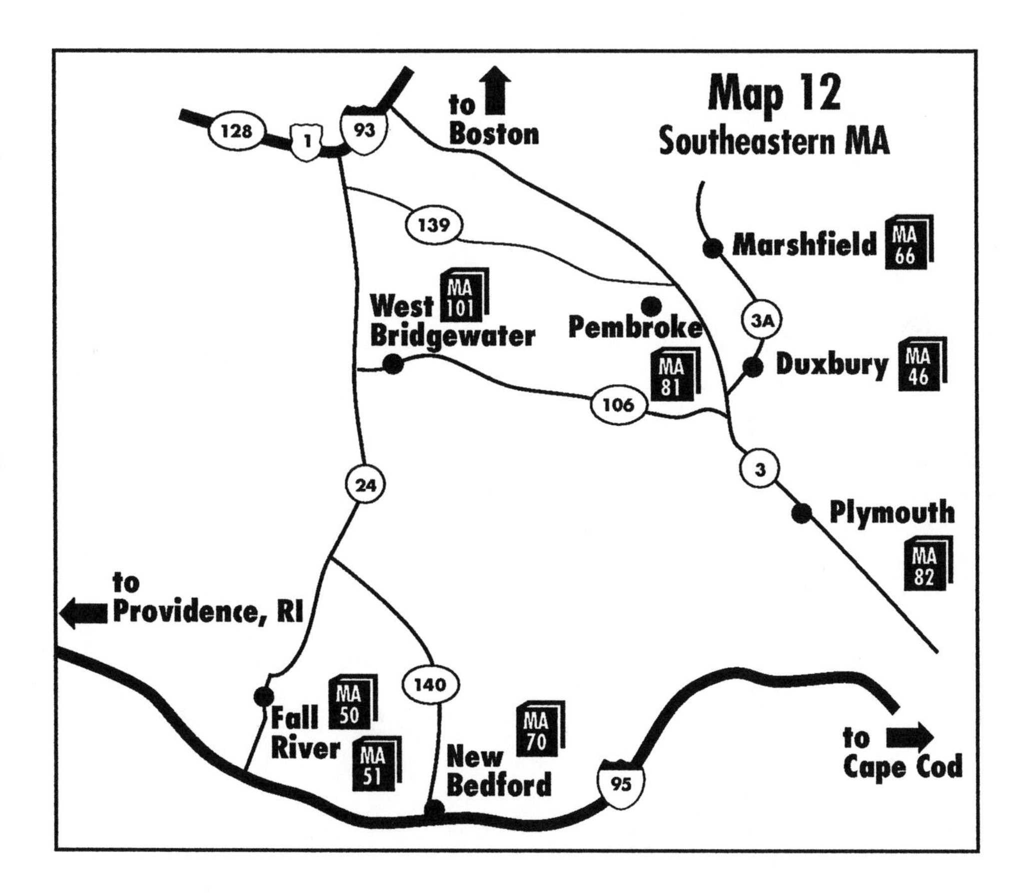

Gardner

Irene's Book Shop (MA113) 508-632-5574
49 West Broadway 01440

Collection:	General stock.
# of Volumes:	25,000
Hours:	Monday-Friday 1-5 but best to call ahead. Saturday & Sunday by appointment.
Services:	Appraisals, search service, catalog, accepts want lists.
Travel:	Map 12.
Credit Cards	No
Owner:	Irene M. Walet
Year Estab:	1967

Georgetown

Hawthorne Bookshop (MA90) 508-352-9923
1 East Main Street 01833

Collection:	General stock.
# of Volumes:	5,000
Specialties:	Classics; New England history; children's.
Hours:	Tuesday-Sunday 11-5.
Services:	Search service.
Travel:	Exit 53B (Route 97) off I-95. Proceed 3 miles into town. Shop is on the corner of East Main Street and Route 133 in a three story gray frame building with mauve shutters. Map 17.
Credit Cards:	No
Owner:	Barbara J. Whitmore
Year Estab:	1991
Comments:	A pleasant little shop, down one flight of stairs, with a mixed collection of hardcover and paperbacks and a special back room bargain section. Reasonably priced. Weary book hunters will enjoy the cozy sitting area in the middle of the shop and a chat with the owner who describes herself and her shop as being "user friendly." The shop takes its name from the owner's interest in the author of *The House of Seven Gables* and *The Scarlett Letter*.

Gloucester

The English Bookshop (MA56) 508-283-8981
22 Rocky Neck Avenue 01930

Collection:	General stock.
# of Volumes:	7,500+
Specialties:	Women; homelife before 1920; children's illustrated classics; Great Britain; commercial fishing.
Hours:	Tuesday-Saturday 2:30-6:30.
Services:	Search service, accepts want lists.
Travel:	In East Gloucester at end of Route 128. Map 17.
Credit Cards:	No
Owner:	Margaret M. Sibley
Year Estab:	1959

Ten Pound Island Book Co. (MA57) 508-283-5299
3 Center Street 01930

Collection:	Specialty
# of Volumes:	6,000
Specialties:	Maritime; coastal America; New England history; natural history.
Hours:	Monday-Saturday 12-5.
Services:	Appraisals, catalog.
Travel:	1st rotary after bridge off Route 128 north. Proceed on Washington Street to downtown Gloucester. Center Street is a one way street off Main Street. Map 17.
Credit Cards:	Yes
Owner:	Gregor Gibson
Year Estab:	1976
Comments:	If you're interested in the shop's specialties, you'll find a visit to this compact storefront shop worth your time.

Great Barrington

The Bookloft (MA58) 413-528-1521
Barrington Plaza (Route 7) 01230

Collection:	General stock of new and used books.
# of Volumes:	500-1,000 (used)
Specialties:	Hal Borland.

Hours:	Monday-Friday 9:30-9. Saturday 9:30-5:30. Sunday 12-5.
Services:	Appraisals, search service.
Travel:	On Route 7, north of downtown Great Barrington. Next to McDonalds. Map 16.
Credit Cards:	Yes
Owner:	Eric Wilska
Year Estab:	1974
Comments:	The used book section is to the rear of this mostly new book store. The collection is relatively small with sections in mystery, biography, Judaica and the works of local nature writer Hal Borland. The used books are a mix of hardcover (mostly recent volumes) and paperback.

Hugo Black's Bookshop (MA59) 413-528-4902
10 Dresser Avenue 01230

Collection:	General stock.
# of Volumes:	10,000
Hours:	Tuesday-Saturday 10-6. Sunday 1-5.
Services:	Accepts want lists.
Travel:	Route 7 to downtown Great Barrington. Shop is directly behind library. Map 16.
Credit Cards:	No
Owner:	Hugo Black
Year Estab:	1991
Comments:	This shop, located in the rear portion of a private home, may have a claustrophobic effect on some book hunters. A narrow hallway connects an entry area with three small rooms that are more the size of large closets. Each room contains books packed from floor to ceiling, and in many cases, books are shelved behind books. While Dashiell Hammett's Thin Man would have little trouble fitting around the shelves in the middle of each "room," all others beware. Although we were unable to discern a clear pattern of how the collection was organized, we did spot an emphasis on the beat generation as well as some other fine books.

Yellow House Books (MA60) 413-528-8227
252 Main Street 01230

Collection:	General stock.
# of Volumes:	5,000

Specialties:	Metaphysical; music; children's.
Hours:	Monday-Saturday 10:30-5:30.
Services:	Accepts want lists.
Travel:	Route 7 to downtown Great Barrington. Shop is next to the Great Barrington Savings Bank. Map 16.
Credit Cards:	No
Owner:	Bonnie & Bob Benson
Year Estab:	1991
Comments:	The owners of this relatively new store have made a conscious decision to stock their small two room shop with a carefully selected collection of more recent used books, all in fine condition. The books are attractively displayed for leisurely browsing. The entrance is up a few steps.

Greenfield

Federal Street Books (MA61) 413-772-6564
8 Federal Street 01301

Collection:	General stock.
# of Volumes:	50,000
Hours:	Monday-Saturday 9:30-5:30.
Services:	Appraisals, accepts want lists.
Travel:	Greenfield exit off I-91. Proceed into downtown Greenfield. Shop is at the corner of Federal Street (Routes 5/10) and Main Street. Map 16.
Credit Cards:	No
Owner:	Leo Cormier
Year Estab:	1981
Comments:	A storefront store with a large selection of mostly reading copies and some library discards. The collection is strong in fiction, with a smattering in most of the other categories typically found in a general stock. Very reasonably priced.

Holyoke

National Yiddish Book Center Annex (MA62) 413-536-0584
100 Lyman Street 01040

Collection:	Specialty
# of Volumes:	1 million+
Specialties:	Yiddish books in all subject areas; Yiddish sheet music.

Hours:	Monday-Friday 9-3:30, but best to call ahead.
Services:	Catalog, search service of Center's computerized collection, accepts want lists.
Travel:	Map 16.
Credit Cards:	Yes
Owner:	Olivier Szlos (Director)
Year Estab:	1980
Comments:	The largest international collection of Yiddish books. The Center also operates a gift shop that sells new Yiddish books and a library at 48 Woodbridge Street in South Hadley.

Malden

Black Orchid Books (MA64) 617-321-8966
661 Salem Street 02148

Collection:	Speciality
# of Volumes:	2,000
Specialties:	Investment/collector editions in science fiction; horror; mystery.
Hours:	Monday-Saturday except Wednesday 10-6. Sunday 12-5.
Services:	Appraisals, search service, catalog, newsletter.
Travel:	Route 1 south to Route 99. Right at second set of lights onto Salem Street. After next set of lights (Maplewood Square), look for parking. Shop is on left. Map 12.
Credit Cards:	Yes
Owner:	John Howard
Year Estab:	1989
Comments:	Located in the basement of a used paperback shop, the owner has attempted to create an atmosphere of the mysterious and supernatural by means of indirect lighting, recessed bookcases, and the presence of a large ceremonial table set with ornate wine goblets. The bookcases, however, display only a handful of books, most of which are limited or collector editons. There are few rare or older items. While fans of Arkam House books or authors from Lovecraft to Stephen King may find something here of interest, an examination of the owner's catalog may save them a visit.

Marblehead

Much Ado (MA65) 617-639-0400
7 Pleasant Street 01945

Collection:	General stock.
# of Volumes:	35,000
Specialties:	Literature; children's; children's illustrated; maritime; New England.
Hours:	Monday-Friday 9:30-5:30. Saturday 10-5:30. Sunday 11-5:30. Other times by appointment.
Services:	Appraisals, search service, accepts want lists. Publishes a newsletter featuring quizzes, quotes and information on new arrivals. Subscriptions cost $20/year and subscribers receive a 20% discount on purchases.
Travel:	Route 128 to Route 114. Stay on road through Marblehead. Shop is last building on left. From Boston: Route 1A to Route 127, through Lynn at Swampscott. Map 17.
Credit Cards:	Yes
Owner:	Nash Robbins
Comments:	One of the nicest shops we have visited, this two story shop offers a fine selection of quality books. In addition to the specialties listed above, we noted strong collections in mystery, film, fiction and travel. Younger book browers should enjoy the special children's nook located off by itself on the second floor. Moderately priced.

Marshfield

Lord Randall Bookshop (MA66) 617-837-1400
22 Main Street 02050

Collection:	General stock.
# of Volumes:	20,000
Specialties:	New England; local history; art; literature; children's.
Hours:	Tuesday-Saturday 11-5.
Services:	Appraisals, search service, accepts want lists, mail order.
Travel:	Route 3 to Route 139. Proceed on Route 139 east (to Marshfield) for 2 1/2 miles. At traffic light turn left. Shop, a gray shingled barn, is first building on right. Map 15.
Credit Cards:	No
Owner:	Gail Wills

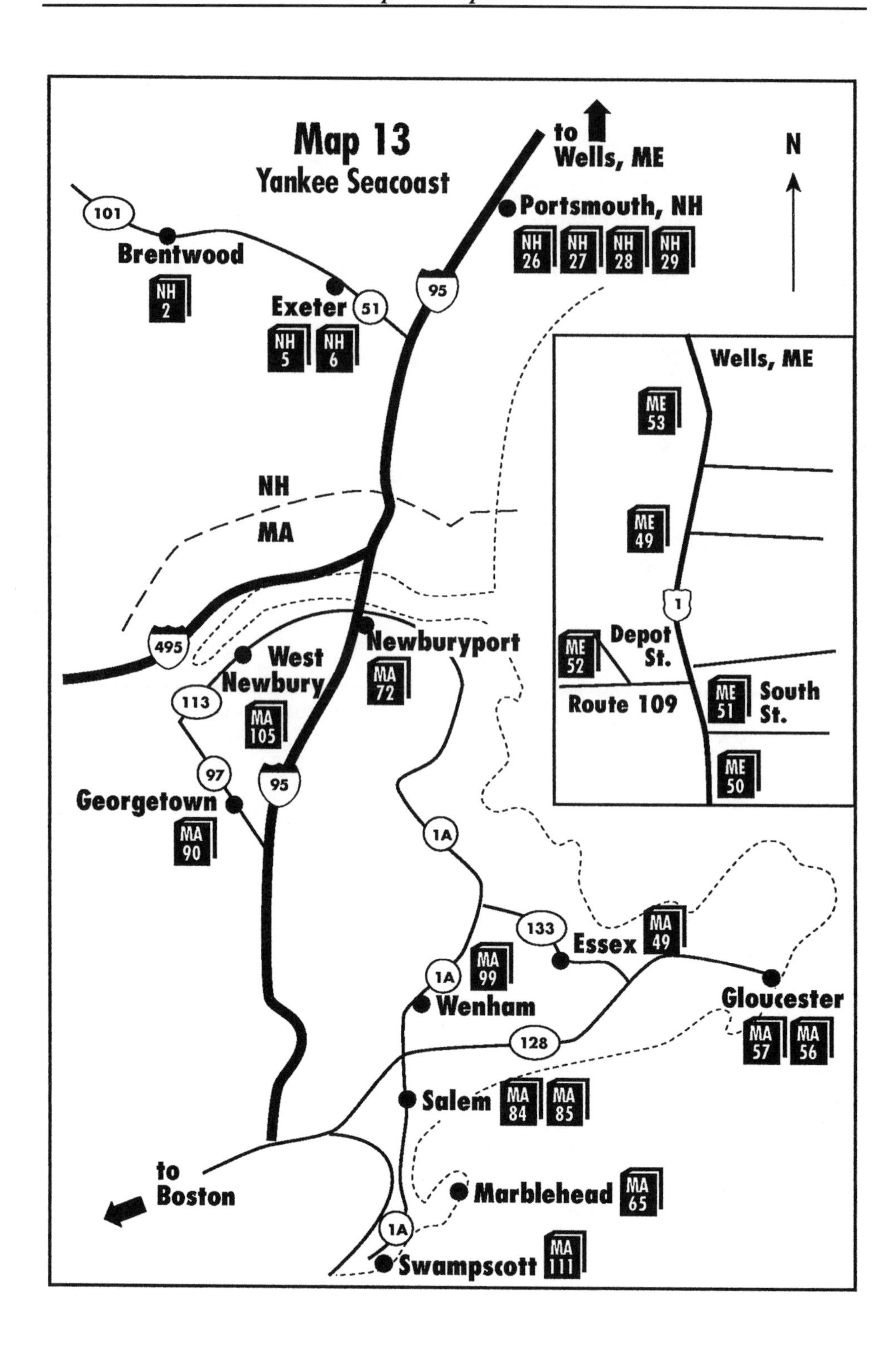
Map 13
Yankee Seacoast
to Wells, ME
N
Portsmouth, NH
NH 26
NH 27
NH 28
NH 29
101
Brentwood
NH 2
Exeter
51
NH 5
NH 6
95
Wells, ME
ME 53
ME 49
1
ME 52
Depot St.
Route 109
ME 51
South St.
ME 50
NH
MA
495
West Newbury
Newburyport
MA 72
113
MA 105
97
95
Georgetown
MA 90
1A
133
Essex
MA 49
MA 99
1A
Wenham
Gloucester
MA 57
MA 56
128
Salem
MA 84
MA 85
to Boston
Marblehead
MA 65
1A
Swampscott
MA 111

Year Estab:	1972
Comments:	A typical book barn atmosphere: somewhat dusty and dimly lit in sections. The books are old rather than rare and not necessarily in the best condition. Despite a modest amount of disarray, however, you may find some hidden treasures here. The collection is definately worth browsing.

Masphee

Cape Cod Book Center (MA67) 508-477-9903
Route 28, Box 1380 02649

Collection:	General stock of used and new books.
# of Volumes:	5,000-10,000
Specialties:	Nature; Cape Cod; fishing; hunting; mystery; new age.
Hours:	Monday-Friday 9-6. Saturday 9-5:30. Sunday 10-5.
Services:	Search service, accepts want lists.
Travel:	On Route 28, near Route 130. Map 14.
Credit Cards:	Yes
Owner:	Carole W. Aronson-Plummer
Year Estab:	1974
Comments:	The collection in this one story roadside shop consists primarily of more recent used books with few if any rare items. In addition to the specialties listed above, the shop is also strong in children's books and cookbooks.

Montague

The Book Mill (MA68) 413-367-9959
Greenfield Road 01351

Collection:	General stock.
# of Volumes:	50,000
Specialties:	Contemporary fiction; radical studies; academic.
Hours:	Daily 10-6 and most weekends till midnight.
Services:	Accepts want lists, catalog (radical studies only).
Travel:	Exit 24 off I-91. Follow Route 116 south to Sunderland center, then go left onto Route 47 north. Proceed for about 8 miles and go through Montague Center. After you pass the village green and a small bridge, the Mill will be on the left. Map 16.
Credit Cards:	Yes

Owner: David Lovelece & John Petrovato
Year Estab: 1989
Comments: A shop worth going out of your way for — both for its collection and its unusual setting and ambience. Located in a restored 1802 grist mill, the shop is at the end of a long winding road. Once your arrive, you can enjoy a refreshing snack in the shop's indoor cafe or on the outdoor patio overlooking the flowing river. The book collection is divided among three levels, one of which includes a single room devoted exclusively to art books. The books are very moderately priced. On weekends, the Mill hosts concerts and poetry readings. The facility can be rented for private parties.

Needham Heights

Whittemore's (MA69) 617-449-1500
3 Wexford Street 02194

Collection: Specialty
# of Volumes: 500-1,000
Specialties: Christianity
Hours: Monday-Saturday 9:30-5:30 and till 8:30 on Thursday and Friday.
Travel: Exit 19A off Route 128. Coming off exit, get into left lane and make first left (at Gulf Station) onto Wexford Street. Shop is the second building on right. Map 12.
Credit Cards: Yes
Year Estab: 1940's

New Bedford

Saltmarsh's (MA70) 508-997-0061
777 Purchase Street 02740 Fax: 508-996-0933

Collection: General stock.
# of Volumes: 40,000
Specialties: Lizzie Borden; Hetty Green.
Hours: Monday-Saturday 9:30-5.
Services: Search service, accepts want lists.

Travel: Exit 15 (Route 18) off I-195. Proceed to downtown. At third street, take right onto Union Street. Proceed to Purchase and make right onto Purchase. Shop is on left. Map 15.
Credit Cards: Yes
Owner: Robert J. Saltmarsh
Year Estab: 1864
Comments: In addition to used books, this 128 year old family owned store sells new books, stationery, toys and a potpourri of other items.

New Salem

The Common Reader Bookshop (MA71) 508-544-3002
8 Old Main Street 01355

Collection: General stock, ephemera and framed prints.
# of Volumes: 10,000
Specialties: Women.
Hours: May-October: Wednesday-Sunday 10-5.
Services: Search service, accepts want lists.
Travel: Located off Route 202. Map16.
Credit Cards: No
Owner: Doris Abramson & Dorothy Johnson
Year Estab: 1980
Comments: This lovely book shop is located in a former elementary school. The owners make excellent use of what used to be two classrooms and a connecting hallway. One large room is devoted to books by and about women (fiction, biography, woman's issues, etc.), as well as how-to books, cooking, children's books and some lovely antique items. The second room is devoted to general fiction, history, travel, etc. We also noted good sections on religion and New Englandiana. Both rooms are spaciously laid out for comfortable browsing. Our only regret about this shop is that book lovers can only visit it during the months of May-October: the old building is too expensive to heat during the winter.

Newburyport

Olde Port Book Shop (MA72) 518-462-0100
18 State Street 01950 800-870-1500

Collection:	General stock, prints and autographs.
# of Volumes:	15,000
Specialties:	Art; gardening; cooking; sports; literature; children's; military history.
Hours:	Monday-Saturday 10-5:30. Friday till 8. Sunday 12-5.
Services:	Appraisals, search service, accepts want lists.
Travel:	In the heart of downtown Newburyport. From Route 1A, make right onto Green and proceed to end of street. Then right onto Water and right onto State. Map 17.
Credit Cards:	Yes
Owner:	Phil Reynolds
Year Estab:	1991
Comments:	The owner of this immaculately cared for bi-level group shop displaying the wares of 17 used book dealers has tried, and succeeded, in duplicating the cozy atmosphere of a home library setting. The books are in excellent condition. As with other group shops, we suggest you leave yourself ample browsing time, especially if you're interested in a special area.

Newton

The Book Collector (MA73) 617-964-3599
375 Elliot St. 02164

Collection:	General stock.
# of Volumes:	30,000
Specialties:	Americana; New England history; literature.
Hours:	Monday-Saturday 10-5.
Services:	Appraisals, search service, accepts want lists, mail order.
Travel:	From Route 9 eastbound, take first exit after Route 128/I-95. At end of exit turn right and proceed up the hill. At top of hill turn right at stop sign onto Chestnut Street. Proceed down the hill to traffic light at Elliot Street. Turn right and proceed about 50 feet. Turn right into parking lot of Echo Bridge Office Park. "375" is on right side of building. Map 12.

Credit Cards:	No
Owner:	Theodore & Neil Berman
Year Estab:	1972
Comments:	Located on the lower level of a small office park, this shop offers a good sized collection of moderately priced previously read books. While the collection is well organized and the books are in good condition, there are few if any rarities here. Although the subject categories are marked on the shelves, the labels are easily overlooked.

North Orange

Armchair Books (MA74) 508-575-0424
107 Main Street 01364

Collection:	General stock.
# of Volumes:	10,000
Specialties:	Town histories.
Hours:	Generally Tuesday-Saturday 9-6 and Sunday & Monday 10-6, but best to call ahead.
Services:	Accepts want lists.
Travel:	Proceed on Route 2A through Orange. Make left turn at Wheeler Avenue (look for a North Orange sign on the right and the Silver Spur cocktail lounge on the left). Continue on Wheeler until you see the shop on the right. Map 16.
Credit Cards:	Yes
Owner:	Ed & Pat Rumrill
Year Estab:	1974
Comments:	The majority of the collection is housed in one small room of a private home and consists mainly of older ficton with a smattering of New Englandiana and some history. The owner's better books, including first editions, are not displayed in the open portion of the shop. The books are most reasonably priced. This is the kind of shop for book hunters who enjoy traveling rural roads to out of the way places. On our visit, the size of the collection appeared to be smaller than the 10,000 estimate given by the owner.

Northampton

Globe Bookshop (MA75) 413-584-0374
38 Pleasant Street 01060

Collection:	General stock of new and used hardcover and paperback.
# of Volumes:	40,000 (20,000 used)
Specialties:	Poetry; fiction; art.
Hours:	Monday-Saturday 9-9. Sunday 10-5.
Services:	Appraisals, search service.
Travel:	Exit 18 off I-91. At end of ramp, make left and proceed on Pleasant to downtown. Shop is just before Main Street on right. Map 16.
Credit Cards:	Yes
Owner:	Mark Brumberg
Year Estab:	1984
Comments:	A two story combination new and used book shop that shelves its new and used books next to each other by subject. The used titles are primarily of more recent vintage.

Haymarket Cafe (MA76) 413-586-9969
15 Ambler Lane 01060

Collection:	General stock.
# of Volumes:	7,000
Specialties:	Fiction; philosophy; radical studies.
Hours:	Tuesday-Sunday 9AM-midnight.
Travel:	Exit 18 off I-91. At end of ramp, make left and proceed to Main Street. Left onto Main, then right onto Crackerbarrel Alley. Shop is to the right at the end of the parking lot in the back of a building. Map 16.
Owner:	Peter & David Simpson
Year Estab:	1991
Comments:	This combination basement level book shop and cafe offers an interesting bohemian atmosphere that more mature book hunters may enjoy sampling, particuarly if they visit the shop at night. The collection includes a good selection of fiction in mixed condition. Unfortunately for serious book browsers, the lighting was poor in some areas. We also noted a display of radical newsletters and literature.

Lunaria-A Feminist Bookstore (MA77) 413-586-7851
90 King Street 01060

Collection:	Speciality used and new books.
# of Volumes:	10,000
Specialties:	Feminism; lesbianism; feminist music.
Hours:	Tuesday, Wednesday, Friday 10-6. Thursday 10-8. Saturday 10-5. Sunday 12-5.
Services:	Search service, catalog, accepts want lists.
Travel:	Exit 18 off I-91. At end of ramp, make left and proceed to Main Street in Northampton. After crossing Main Street, the road becomes King Street. Shop is 2 blocks ahead on left, across from a church. Map 16.
Credit Cards:	Yes
Owner:	Madelaine Zadik & Rose Maloof
Year Estab:	1988
Comments:	The used books are in the rear of this street level stop. The owners claim to have the largest selection of used feminist and lesbian materials in the country.

Old Book Store (MA78) 413-586-0576
32 Masonic Street 01060

Collection:	General stock of hardcover and paperback.
# of Volumes:	25,000
Hours:	Tuesday-Saturday 10-5.
Services:	Accepts want lists.
Travel:	Exit 18 off I-91. At end of ramp, make left and proceed to Main Street. Turn left onto Main and proceed to Masonic Street. Right onto Masonic. Shop is across from municipal parking lot. Map 16.
Credit Cards:	No
Owner:	H. Walz
Year Estab:	1958
Comments:	A small compact shop with an entrance down a few steps. The collection consists primarily of scholarly titles of interest to the academic community in the immediate area. We noted a strong collection of foreign language books.

Oak Bluffs

Book Den East (MA79) 508-693-3946
New York Avenue
Mailing address: P.O. Box 721 02557

Collection:	General stock.
# of Volumes:	20,000
Hours:	May-October: Monday-Saturday 10-5. Sunday 1-5. November-April: Thursday-Sunday 11-4.
Services:	Search service, accepts want lists.
Travel:	On main road between Oak Bluffs and Vineyard Haven, 1/2 mile from the Oak Bluffs ferry docks.
Credit Cards:	Yes
Owner:	Cynthia & Ivo Meisner
Year Estab:	1977
Comments:	The shop is located in a 19th century carriage barn.

Orleans

Haunted Book Shop (MA80) 508-255-3780
47 Main Street
Mailing address: P.O. Box 558 02653

Collection:	General stock.
# of Volumes:	10,000 +
Specialties:	Art; poetry; Heritage Press books; classical literature; New England.
Hours:	June 1-Labor Day: Monday-Saturday 9-7, Sunday 11-5. Remainder of year: Monday-Saturday 10-5.
Services:	Search service.
Travel:	Exit 12 off Route 6. Right turn onto Route 6A. Right at Main Street (second set of lights) and proceed 1/2 block. Shop is on the right. Map 14.
Credit Cards:	Yes
Owner:	Drucilla Meany
Year Estab:	1985
Comments:	This storefront shop in the heart of downtown Orleans offers a good, well organized collection in most categories. We found some items a bit pricey. A friendly dog is always on hand to greet customers and children.

Pembroke

Leslie J. Molyneaux, Bookseller(MA81) Shop: 617-826-2838
236 Water St. at N. River Antiques Center Home: 617-829-3624
Mailing address: 23 Water Street Hanover 02339

Collection:	Speciality
# of Volumes:	1,000+
Specialties:	Americana; maritime; ephemera, postcards.
Hours:	Monday-Saturday 11-5. Sunday 1-5.
Services:	Appraisals, search service, accept want lists, mail order.
Travel:	1 mile west of exit 12 off Route 3 on Route 139. Across from Garden World Nursery. Map 15.
Credit Cards:	Yes
Owner:	Leslie J. Molyneaux
Year Estab:	1991
Comments:	If your interest is in Massachusetts history, Americana, natural history or maritime books, stop and check the contents of this small but impressive collection located in a two story shop antique/collectibles shop. If you have any other interest, though, we advise you to skip this shop. Note: If you don't see what you're looking for, ask, as the owner has an additional stock of 5,000 books not available for public perusal.

Plymouth

The Yankee Book & Art Gallery(MA82) 508-747-2691
10 North Street 02360

Collection:	General stock.
# of Volumes:	6,000
Specialties:	Local history; Pilgrims; leather bindings; travel; exploration; Americana; art; manuscripts; poetry.
Hours:	Tuesday-Saturday 11-5. Sunday 12-4.
Services:	Appraisals, search service, accepts want lists.
Travel:	Exit 6 off Route 3. Make right onto Route 44, and a right at light. Make left on North Street. Map 15.
Credit Cards:	Yes
Owner:	Charles F. Purro
Year Estab:	1981

Comments:	Located in the Plymouth historic district, this shop offers a modest collection in terms of size but not quality. Most, but not all, subjects are represented and the books are in excellent condition. Slightly overpriced.

Provincetown

Bryant's (MA83) 508-487-0657
465 Commercial Street 02657

Collection:	Specialty
# of Volumes:	5,000-6,000
Specialties:	Commercial fishing. Stock is mostly government publications from the 19th century.
Hours:	June-September: Monday-Saturday 9-6. Remainder of year by appointment.
Services:	Appraisals, accepts want lists.
Travel:	Located on the shore. Map 14.
Credit Cards:	No
Owner:	George D. Bryant
Year Estab:	1837

Salem

Acorn Books (MA84 508-744-9522
205 Essex Street 01970

Collection:	General stock of hardcover and paperback.
# of Volumes:	25,000
Specialties:	History; philosophy; classical literature.
Hours:	Monday-Saturday 10-6. Sunday 12-6.
Services:	Search service, accepts want lists.
Travel:	Route 1A north into Salem. As you enter Salem, you will be on Hawthorne Boulevard. At the light (look for a hotel), make a left onto Essex Street and proceed till you can't go any further. Make a right onto Washington Street. The municipal garage will be ahead on your left. The shop is in the pedestrian mall. Map 17.
Credit Cards:	No
Owner:	Arthur W. DeSousa

Comments: Spaciously laid out for leisurely browsing, this street level store offers mostly moderately priced reading copies and some scholarly books and classics. A special new arrivals section is located in the front of the store and a bargain section occupies one of the rear rooms.

The Old Book Shop (MA85) 508-744-4193
296 Essex Street 01970

Collection: General stock.
# of Volumes: 10,000
Hours: Monday-Friday 10:30-4. Saturday 9:30-5. Sunday 12-3.
Travel: Route 1A north into Salem. From Hawthorne Blvd. make a left onto Essex Street at the light (look for a hotel). Map 17.
Credit Cards: No
Comments: This is a small crowded storefront shop where unfortunately some bookcases block or restrict access to others. The lighting in the rear portion of the store is poor. The books, in mixed condition with some quite old, are not always shelved by subject and some subject areas were not labeled. Some finds but few bargains. The owner, who has been in business a long time, has a personality all his own.

Sheffield

Berkshire Used Books (MA86) 413-229-0122
510 South Main Street (Route 7) 01257

Collection: General stock and matted magazine covers.
# of Volumes: 8,000-10,000
Specialties: Literature; first editions; children's; cooking; sports; railroads; travel; history; military.
Hours: April-December: Thursday-Monday 11-6. January-March: Most weekends and by chance or appointment.
Services: Accepts want lists.
Travel: On Route 7, 2 miles from Connecticut border and 1 mile south of village. Next to Fellerman Glass Works. Map 16.
Credit Cards: No
Owner: Esther & David Kininmonth
Year Estab: 1992
Comments: Both floors of this new two story red frame building are spaciously laid out with plenty of space between the book-

shelves for leisurely browsing. The preponderance of the collection fits into the more recently used category, with some older and even a few rarer items interspersed. All the books are in fine condition and well cared for. The shop is located near several antique shops for the convenience of travelers who like to combine book and antique browsing.

Shelburne Falls

Boswell's Books (MA87) 413-625-9362
1 State Street 01370

Collection: General stock of new and used books.
# of Volumes: 5,000 (combined)
Hours: Daily, but call ahead as hours vary. Thursdays open till 7.
Services: Appraisals, accepts want lists.
Travel: Route 2A to Shelburne Falls. Shop is at corner, directly across from bridge. Map 16.
Credit Cards: Yes
Owner: Anne Plunkett
Year Estab: 1986
Comments: A quaint shop located in the heart of the village. The shop combines both new and used books, shelving them together by subject. The books are priced to sell.

Somerville

Zembia Books (MA88) 617-625-6640
93 Holland Street 02144

Collection: General stock.
# of Volumes: 10,000+
Specialties: Literary criticism; film; popular culture; multi cultural studies; fine art.
Hours: Tuesday-Sunday. Call for hours.
Travel: From intersection of Route 16 and Masschusetts Avenue: Proceed south on Masschusetts. Left onto Cameron Avenue, then right onto Holland Street. Shop is on left. Shop is near public transporation (Davis Square stop). Map 12.
Credit Cards: Yes
Owner: Judith Tingley
Year Estab: 1986

South Egremont

Bruce & Susan Gventer: "Books" (MA89) 413-528-2327
Tyrell Road
Mailing address: P.O. Box 298 01258

Collection: General stock.
# of Volumes: 20,000
Specialties: Americana; art; bindings; 19th century color plate books; costume and fashion; illustrated; imprints; medieval manuscript pages.
Hours: Wednesday-Sunday 10:30-5.
Services: Accepts want lists.
Travel: Tyrrell Road is off Route 23, across from John Andrews Restaurant and 1 mile east of Hillsdale, NY or 2 1/2 miles west of the South Egremont post office. Map 16.
Credit Cards: No
Owner: Bruce & Susan Gventer
Year Estab: 1980
Comments: A one story barn like structure that houses a mixed collection of interesting used books, older volumes that have "been around" and more recent titles. Prices are reasonable. The owners provide free reading copies of worn books.

South Otis

Otis Country Fare (MA91) 413-269-4047
Route 8 01253

Collection: General stock.
# of Volumes: 6,000
Hours: Tuesday-Friday 11-5. Saturday and Sunday 10-5.
Services: Accepts want lists; search service, mail order.
Travel: 1/3 mile south of junction of Routes 23 & 8. Shop is on right. Map 16.
Credit Cards: No
Owner: Frances MacArthur
Year Estab: 1987

Southampton

Heritage Books (MA92) 413-527-6200
College Highway (Route 10)
Mailing address: P.O. Box 48 01073

Collection: General stock and ephemera.
# of Volumes: 7,500
Specialties: Children's; mystery; fiction; vintage paperbacks.
Hours: Monday-Friday 9:30-4:30.
Services: Search service, accepts want lists, mail order.
Travel: Exit 3 off Mass Pike. Proceed on Route 10 north for about 6 miles. Shop is on corner of Route 10 and Clark Street. Look for a two story, dark brown building. Map 16.
Credit Cards: No
Owner: Rosemarie Coombs
Year Estab: 1987
Comments: The collection is in an attractive two story shop with a loft area overlooking a ground floor foyer. The fiction section, located upstairs, combines both newer titles and books that have been out of print for several generations. If you arrive during lunch time and find the shop closed, ring the bell as the owner may be in the adjoining surveyor's office. If you're looking for ways to store ephemera, you'll want to check out the owner's creative use of old wine crates.

Springfield

Johnson's (MA93) 413-732-6222
1379 Main Street 01103
Fax: 413-736-7762

Collection: General stock, records and magazines.
# of Volumes: 75,000+
Specialties: Local history; New England; *Life* ; *National Geographic.*
Hours: Monday-Saturday 9:30-5:30. Thursday till 8.
Services: Search service.
Travel: Springfield Center exit off I-91. Store is one block from exit. Street parking may be a problem but there's a municipal lot just two blocks away. Map 16.
Credit Cards: Yes
Owner: Paul, Peter & Charles Johnson

Year Estab: 1893

Comments: Don't be fooled by the fact that Johnson's is a shop that sells new books as well as a fine selection of greeting cards, stationery and gifts. Visitors willing to climb a flight of stairs in a second building to the rear of the first building will find a large room dedicated only to used books. In addition to review copies of recent publications (all generously discounted), there are shelves and shelves of older and frequently hard to find items. The collection is well organized and most categories are represented. The books are reasonably priced.

Redbrick Books (MA94) 413-732-2213
797 Page Boulevard 01104

Collection: General stock of mostly paperbacks with some hardcover.
# of Volumes: 22,000
Specialties: Children's.
Hours: Monday-Saturday 10-5.
Services: Accepts want lists.
Travel: East Springfield exit off I-291. Map 16.
Credit Cards: No
Owner: Marcia J. Fuller
Year Estab: 1981
Comments: We don't recommend your going out of your way to visit this shop. While the store does have a small collection of used hardcover books, the stock is predominately paperback.

Sterling

Sterling Bookstore (MA95) 508-422-6897
Route 12 North 01564

Collection: General stock and ephemera.
# of Volumes: 50,000
Specialties: Local history; science; comics; old magazines.
Hours: Friday 6-9 PM. Saturday 10-7. Sunday 11-7.
Services: Appraisals.
Travel: Exit 6 south of I-190. 1/4 mile from exit. Look for stand alone building with large sign, "Books." Map 12.
Credit Cards: No
Owner: Hopfmann Enterprises
Year Estab: 1954

Comments: This one story building, located along a major road, offers older books, not always in the best of condition. If you're looking for titles representing bygone days, there's a good likelihood you'll find them here. When we visited the shop, the size of the collection appeared to be smaller than the 50,000 estimate given by the owner.

Stow

Yankee Packet Books (MA112) 508-897-1746
531 Great Road 01775

Collection: General stock.
# of Volumes: 10,000
Specialties: Americana; American history; architecture; books on books; natural history; maritime; philosophy; religion; travel.
Hours: Thursday-Saturday 10-5. Sunday 1-5. Other times by appointment.
Services: Appraisals, search service.
Travel: Exit 27 east off I-495. Proceed 4 miles east on Route 117. Watch for sign on left "Old Books And Prints." Map 12.
Credit Cards: No
Owner: John R. Dudley
Year Estab: 1981
Comments: This well kept, attractively decorated barn is located to the rear of the owner's home. The collection is nicely displayed for browsing with few areas represented in any great depth. We noted several older volumes. Reasonably priced.

Sudbury

Bearly Read Books, Inc. (MA97) 508-443-4034
320 Boston Post Road (Route 20) 01776

Collection: General stock of hardcover and paperback.
# of Volumes: 25,000
Specialties: Military history; local history; science fiction; children's; aviation; maritime; mysteries; classics.
Hours: Monday-Wednesday 10-6. Thursday & Friday 10-8. Saturday 10-5. Sunday 12-5.
Services: Search service, accepts want lists.

Travel:	From Route 128, take Route 20 west for about 7 miles. Shop is in a large red building with a porch on the right. Map 12.
Credit Cards:	Yes
Owner:	David Van Buskirk
Year Estab:	1989
Comments:	Several cats, an array of stuffed bears and friendly owners (not necessarily in that order) add to the pleasant atmosphere in this three year old shop. The collection consists primarily of newer used books with a few older items. Reasonably priced. The entrance is up a few steps.

Swampscott

Book Stall (MA111) 617-599-2223
Humphrey Street 01907

Collection:	General stock of hardcover and paperback.
# of Volumes:	5,000
Hours:	Monday-Saturday 9-6. Summer only: also Sunday 10-3.
Travel:	Route 1A to center of town. Shop is across from Cap'n Jack's Inn. Map 17.
Credit Cards:	No
Year Estab:	1992
Comments:	A small, street level shop with a limited selection of mostly popular titles. Worth a visit only if you're in the area.

Wellfleet

Herridge Books (MA98) 508-349-1323
East Main Street
Mailing address: P.O. Box 795 02667

Collection:	General stock of hardcover and paperback.
Hours:	Memorial Day-Columbus Day: Daily 10-6 and till 10 Thursday, Friday, Saturday. Columbus Day-Christmas: Thursday-Sunday 10-6. Remainder of year by appointment.
Services:	Search service, accepts want lists.
Travel:	Route 6 to Wellfleet. Shop is at corner or Main and Commercial. Map 14.
Credit Cards:	No

Owner: Peter C. Hiller
Year Estab: 1991
Comments: Owner estimates that stock is half hardcover, half paper.

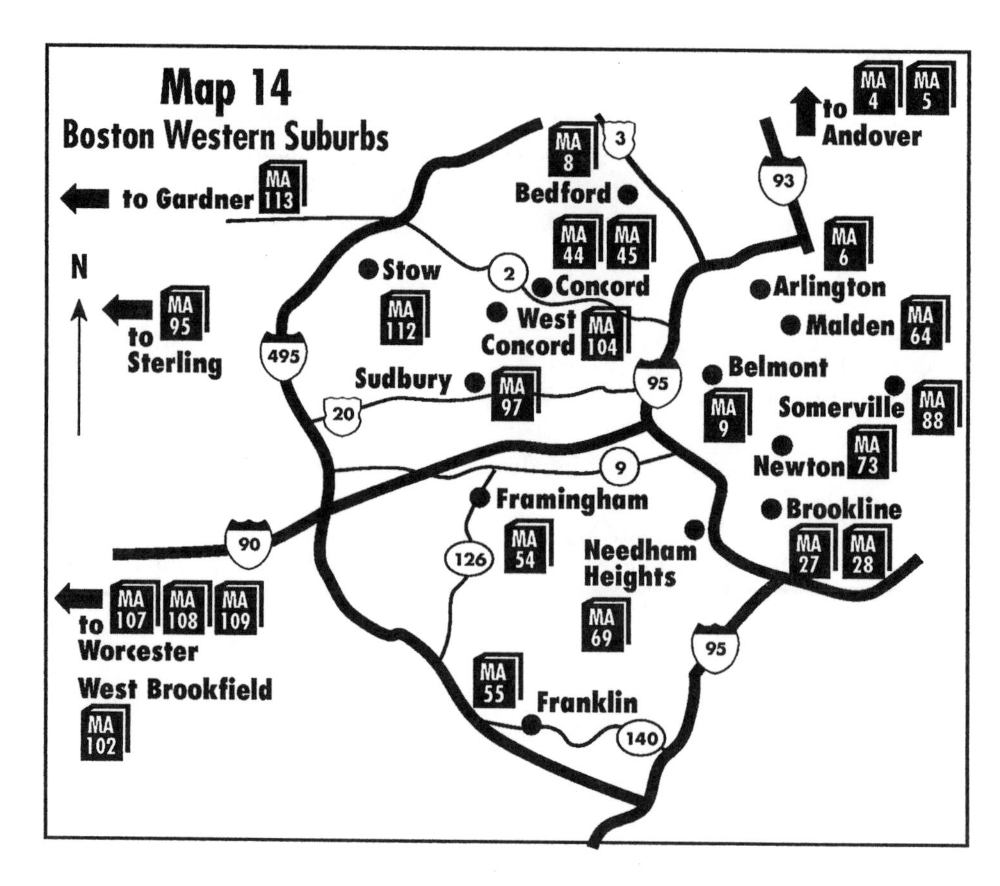

Wenham

Aachen Books (MA99) 508-468-4066
300 Main Street (Route 1A)
Mailing address: P.O. Box 2081 So. Hamilton 01982

Collection: General stock.
# of Volumes: 5,000
Specialties: Military; maritime; hunting; fishing; Americana.
Hours: Wednesday-Friday 12-9. Saturday & Sunday 12-6.
Services: Appraisals, search service, catalog.

Hours: Tuesday, Wednesday, Friday, Saturday 12-5.
Services: Accepts want lists.
Travel: On Route 1A, approximately 4 miles north of intersection of Route 128 and Route 1A (exit 20 from Route 128). Map 17.
Credit Cards: No
Owner: Cheever Cressy
Year Estab: 1990
Comments: The shop is located on the second floor of a cluster of new shops. The collection is a potpourri of volumes running a wide gamet of subjects. Most of the titles are interesting; few are common. The owner takes great pride in his selection of stock, and in our opinion, his pride is well deserved. Moderately priced.

West Barnstable

Columbia Trading Co. Nautical Books (MA100) 508-362-8966
504 Main Street (Route 6A) 02668 Fax: 508-362-3551

Collection: Speciality
# of Volumes: 10,000+
Specialties: Maritime: every aspect of the sea, including fiction and 10,000 periodicals.
Hours: Monday-Saturday 9-5.
Services: Appraisals, search serivce, catalog, accepts want lists.
Travel: Exit 5 from Route 6. Left off ramp onto Route 149. Left onto 6A and proceed south for 9/10 of a mile. Shop is on right at corner of Meadow Lane. Map 14.
Credit Cards: No
Owner: Bob & Ed Glick
Year Estab: 1983
Comments: If this is your area of interest, this shop has it all. The shop is located on the ground floor level of the owner's home and is decorated with nautical antiques and prints.

West Bridgewater

The Book Store (MA101) 508-588-4774
222 North Main Street 02379-1273

Collection: General stock.
# of Volumes: 100,000

Specialties: Fantasy; horror; local history.
Travel: Exit Route 106 (West Bridgewater) from Route 24. At intersection of Routes 28 & 106 turn left. Shop is 6/10 mile from intersection, on left in a one story "L" shaped building with green wood siding. Map 15.
Credit Cards: Yes
Owner: David E. Johnson
Year Estab: 1972
Comments: A huge collection of extremely well organized books more for the general reader and book lover than the scholar. While the shop offers a nice selection in most areas, in addition to the specialty areas listed above, we noted particularly strong collections in mystery, entertainment and contemporary fiction. Very reasonably priced. The aisles are a bit cramped and many have stacks of books in front of the shelves, but if you have patience, there's a good chance you'll find something of interest. The owner's goal: "We want you to take a lot home with you."

West Brookfield

Book Bear (MA102) 508-867-8705
86 West Main Street (Route 9)
Mailing address: P.O. Box 663 01585

Collection: General stock.
# of Volumes: 60,000-70,000
Specialties: Psychology (20,000 volumes); anthropology; occult; science; technical.
Hours: Daily 10-6.
Services: Appraisals, search service, catalog (psychology and psychiatry only), accepts want lists.
Travel: On Route 9, 7/10 of a mile west of the center of town. From Sturbridge exit of Mass Pike, go 2 miles west on Route 20, then north 7 miles on Route 148 and 4 miles on Route 9. Map 12.
Credit Cards: No
Owner: Al Navitski
Year Estab: 1979
Comments: This substantial collection is housed in a two story former private residence. In addition to the specialities noted above, we observed a large religion section. After browsing

through the collection, we concur with the owner when he says, "We see ourselves as a country bookshop with a quite general stock of good used books. We turn up a few rare books but they are not our focus. We consider our prices moderate."

West Chatham

B & B's Book Nook (MA103) 508-945-4265
1300 Main St. (Wayne's Antique Center) 02659

Collection: General stock.
# of Volumes: 5,000
Specialties: Cape Cod
Hours: Wednesday-Sunday 12-5.
Travel: Map 14.
Credit Cards: No
Owner: I. Thomas Buckley
Comments: The collection is located in a single room in an antiques/ collectible center.

West Concord

Books Again (MA104) 508-369-1688
79 Commonwealth Avenue 01742

Collection: General stock of hardcover and paperback books, records and sheet music.
# of Volumes: 16,000+
Hours: Monday-Thursday 10-7. Friday 10-8. Saturday 10-5. Sunday between Labor Day & July 4: 1-6.
Services: Appraisals, search service, catalog, accepts want lists.
Travel: Route 2 to Route 62 west. Bear right at second set of lights. Proceed across tracks. Shop is the second store on left opposite post office. Map 12.
Credit Cards: Yes
Owner: Allan R. & Marie E. Dunham
Year Estab: 1988
Comments: A storefront location in the center of town with ample room between bookcases, comfortable chairs and stools to help browsers reach the lower shelves without bending. The collection consists primarily of more recently used books with

a few older volumes scattered among the shelves. Very reasonably priced. Bargains to be had.

West Newbury

The Joy Of Books (MA105) 508-363-2343
320 Main Street (Route 113) 01985

Collection:	General stock.
# of Volumes:	3,000-5,000
Hours:	Monday-Saturday 10:30-4:30.
Travel:	Located directly on Route 113, a short distance west of I-95. Map 17.
Credit Cards:	No
Owner:	Russ Joy
Comments:	A modest collection of quality books, mostly in good condition. We found some items a bit pricey.

Whately

Whately Antiquarian Book Center (MA106) 413-247-3272
13 West Street (Route 5)
Mailing address: P.O. Box 155 Conway 03141

Collection:	General stock.
# of Volumes:	15,000
Specialties:	Americana; technical; art; photography; literary first editions; mystery; fantasy; religion; social reform; hunting; fishing; local history; military.
Hours:	Monday-Saturday, except Wednesday, 10-5:30. Sunday 12-5.
Services:	Appraisals, search service, accepts want lists.
Travel:	From south: exit 22 off I-91. Proceed north on Route 5 for 1 1/2 miles. Shop is in brick schoolhouse on left. From north. exit 26 off I-91. Proceed south on Route 5 for 1 1/2 miles. School house is on right. Map 16.
Credit Cards:	No
Owner:	Tom LaBelle & Eugene Povirk
Year Estab:	1991
Comments:	This group shop of over 50 dealers offers a good sized collection with some prime items. The shop has something for everyone and there's hardly a subject we did not see repre-

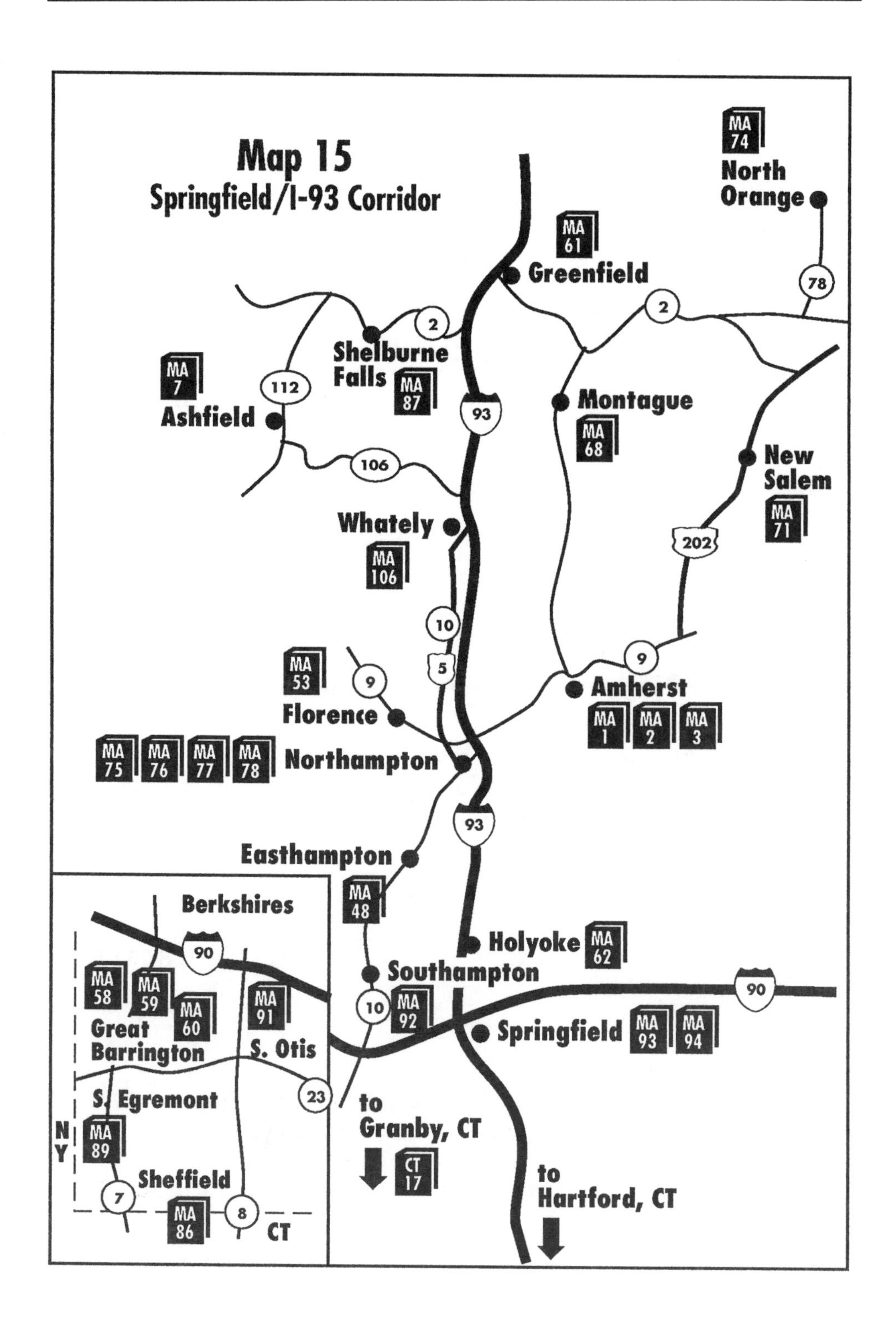

Map 15
Springfield/I-93 Corridor
MA 74
North Orange
MA 61
Greenfield
78
2
2
Shelburne Falls
MA 87
MA 7
112
Ashfield
93
Montague
MA 68
106
New Salem
MA 71
Whately
MA 106
202
10
MA 53
9
5
9
Amherst
MA 1
MA 2
MA 3
Florence
MA 75
MA 76
MA 77
MA 78
Northampton
93
Easthampton
MA 48
Berkshires
90
Holyoke
MA 62
Southampton
90
MA 58
MA 59
MA 60
MA 91
10
MA 92
Springfield
MA 93
MA 94
Great Barrington
S. Otis
23
S. Egremont
to Granby, CT
NY
MA 89
CT 17
Sheffield
to Hartford, CT
7
MA 86
8
CT

sented. The dealers, putting their best foot forward, display books in good to fine condition. Prepare to spend at least an hour (perhaps longer) browsing here. Book hunters will not want to overlook the glass case with some rarer and more expensive items or the display of business cards and literature from other book dealers in the entryway. There's also a handy "Book Wanted" bulletin board for listing your hard-to-find wants. The only drawback we note (a drawback common to many group shops) is that if the visitor has a very specific interest, that interest may be duplicated in several sections, requiring the visitor to spend more time then would ordinarily be the case in a single dealer shop. We certainly believe that this is an establishment that should not be missed.

Worcester

Another Story (MA107) 508-752-3566
1145 Main Street 01603

Collection:	General stock of hardcover and paperback and ephemera.
# of Volumes:	20,000+
Hours:	Monday & Tuesday 10-6. Wednesday-Friday 10-8. Saturday 10-6. Sunday 1-6.
Services:	Appraisals, search service, accepts want lists.
Travel:	On Main Street at Webster Square. Across from Merit gas station. Map 12.
Credit Cards:	No
Owner:	Manasha Bilsey
Year Estab:	1990

Ben Franklin's Annex (MA108) 508-754-3322
80 Franklin Street 01608

Collection:	General stock.
# of Volumes:	30,000
Specialties:	Literature; American history; local history; art.
Hours:	Monday-Friday 9:30-6. Saturday 9:30-5:30.
Services:	Search service, accepts want lists.
Travel:	Located in downtown Worcester on the Common. Map 12.
Credit Cards:	Yes
Owner:	Don Reid

Year Estab:	1989
Comments:	This large storefront shop on two levels carries a good general stock with some remainders and a few older volumes. The books are well displayed for easy browsing. Paperbacks, some hardcover titles and several bargain sections are located on the lower level. Most of the books are in good condition, many with their original dust jackets. In our judgment, the books are slightly overpriced.

Fabulous Fiction Book Store (MA109) 508-754-8826
984 Main Street 01603

Collection:	Specialty new and used, hardcover and paperback.
# of Volumes:	1,000 (used only)
Specialties:	Science fiction; fantasy, horror.
Hours:	Monday-Saturday 10-6:30. Sunday 12-6:30.
Services:	Mail order.
Travel:	Route 146 exit off I-290. Turn right onto Cambridge and proceed to Main Street. Make right onto Main. Shop is 1/4 ahead on left. Map 12.
Credit Cards:	No
Owner:	Bob Jennings
Year Estab:	1978

Yarmouth Port

Parnassus Book Service (MA110) 508-362-6420
Route 6A 02675

Collection:	General stock.
# of Volumes:	60,000+
Specialties:	Maritime; New England; fine arts; Russia; Latin America; Caribbean; Mexico; literature.
Hours:	Monday-Saturday 9-5. Sunday 12-5.
Services:	Appraisals, search service, catalog, accepts want lists.
Travel:	Heading east on Route 6, take exit 7. Turn right and proceed to Route 6A. Turn right on Route 6A and proceed for 1 1/2 miles. Map 14.
Credit Cards:	No
Owner:	Ben Muse
Year Estab:	1951

Comments: This very large and very good collection is housed on the first floor of a three story 19th century general store building. The floor to ceiling shelves make maximum use of the space, but unfortunately, unless you're very tall, it's difficult to read the titles on the upper shelves. Reaching the upper shelves could also be a problem, especially, as we only saw one ladder in sight during our visit. The collection appears to be well organized but neary a label is in sight to give the book hunter a clue as to what categories are shelved where. Despite the above, if you enjoy browsing, you could certainly spend considerable time in this shop. Although the owner estimates the size of the collection as "being in the eye of the beholder," we estimate the number of volumes in the 60,000-100,000 range. Don't overlook the special bargain book section located along the building's outside side wall.

Where's Waldo?

Acton

Henry Deeks 508-263-1861
468 Main Street
Mailing address: P.O. Box 2260 01720

Collection:	Specialty books and ephemera.
# of Volumes:	200
Specialties:	Civil War.
Services:	Image catalog, appraisals.
Credit Cards:	No
Owner:	Henry Deeks
Year Estab:	1969

Alford

George Robert Minkoff, Inc. 413-528-4575
26 Rowe Road 01230 Fax: 413-528-1866

Collection:	Specialty
Specialties:	19th century English and American literature; presentation copies; manuscripts; letters; illustrated; modern first editions.
Services:	Appraisals, catalog.
Credit Cards:	Yes
Owner:	George Robert Minkoff
Year Estab:	1969

Amherst

Amherst Antiquarian Maps 413-256-8900
McClellan Street
Mailing address: P.O. Box 12 01004

Collection:	Maps
Specialties:	Old and rare maps, charts and prints from 16th-19th centuries.
Services:	Catalog, accepts want lists.
Credit Cards:	No
Owner:	Jon Kimmel Rosenthal
Year Estab:	1977

Arlington

Scientia Books 617-643-5725
P.O. Box 433 02174

Collection:	Speciality
# of Volumes:	10,000
Specialties:	Medicine; science; evolution.
Services:	Catalog, accepts want lists.
Credit Cards:	No
Owner:	Malcolm Jay Kottler
Year Estab:	1980

Assonet

Osee H. Brady Books 508-644-5073
12 Elm Street 02702

Collection:	General stock.
# of Volumes:	8,000-10,000
Specialties:	Vintage turn of century fiction; biography; regional; natural history; children's; poetry.
Services:	Accepts want lists.
Credit Cards:	No
Owner:	Althea H. Brady
Year Estab:	1975
Comments:	Primarily mail order but open to dealers by appointment.

Bernardston

Astronomy Books, Paul W. Luther 413-648-9500
P.O. Box 217 01337

Collection:	Speciality
# of Volumes:	750
Specialties:	Astronomy; physical sciences; optics; meteorology; geology; unconventional science.
Services:	Appraisals, catalog.
Credit Cards:	No
Owner:	Paul W. Luther
Year Estab:	1976

Bernardston Books 413-648-9864
219 South Street (Route 5)
Mailing address: P.O. Box 484 01337

Collection: General stock.
# of Volumes: 20,000
Specialties: History; biography; military; natural history; literature; religion; art; linguistics; travel; exploration; poetry; sociology; cooking; gardening; women; black literature.
Hours: Daily 9-5.
Services: Appraisals, search service, catalog, accepts want lists.
Credit Cards: No
Owner: A.L. Fullerton
Year Estab: 1986
Comments: The collection is located in a large heated barn that features a reading room and separate children's room. Picnic tables are available during the summer.

Beverly

Jean S. McKenna, Book 508-922-3182
P.O. Box 190 01915

Collection: General stock.
# of Volumes: 3,000
Specialties: Children's
Services: Appraisals, search service (specialized), accepts want lists.
Credit Cards: No
Owner: Jean S. McKenna
Year Estab: 1973

Boston

The Maury A. Bromsen Co. 617-266-7060
770 Boylston Street, Ste.23F 02199

Collection: Specialty
# of Volumes: 80,000-100,000
Specialties: Scholarly books dealing with South America; Mexico; Central America; Caribbean; Spain; Portugal; bibliography; travel; exploration; Americana; Civil War; rare books of all periods; manuscripts; autographs.

Services: Appraisals, special subject listings may be provided upon request.
Credit Cards: No
Owner: Maury Bromsen
Year Estab: 1954

Priscilla Juvelis, Inc. 617-424-1895
150 Huntington Ave. SD-L 02115 Fax: 617-424-7687

Collection: Speciality
# of Volumes: 4,000
Specialties: Artist's books; fine bindings; fine printing, first editions; illustrated.
Services: Appraisals, accepts want lists, catalog.
Credit Cards: Yes
Owner: Priscilla Juvelis
Year Estab: 1980

Brockton

All Photography Books 508-587-6074
40 Reservoir Street, #510 02401-1175

Collection: Specialty books and ephemera.
# of Volumes: 2,000
Specialties: Photography
Services: Search service, catalog, accepts want lists.
Credit Cards: No
Owner: Arnold Sadow
Year Estab: 1975

John William Pye, Rare Books 508-588-6566
79 Hollis Street 02402 Fax: 508-584-5338

Collection: Specialty
# of Volumes: 2,000
Specialties: Ancient Egypt (books, photographs and prints); 19th and early 20th century literature; children's; miniature books; press books; illustrated.
Services: Appraisals, catalog, accepts want lists.
Credit Cards: No
Owner: John William Pye
Year Estab: 1992

Brookline

Amphion Antiquarian Books 617-566-3425
1069 Beacon Street 02146

Collection: Specialty
# of Volumes: 1,250
Specialties: Architecture; theater architecture; stage design; private press (British).
Services: Catalog, accepts want lists.
Credit Cards: No
Owner: Anthony Lee
Year Estab: 1987

Dan Miranda 617-739-1306
P.O. Box 145 02146

Collection: Specialty and ephemera.
Specialties: Black stereotypes; women's stereotypes and suffrage; Judaica; anti semitism; children's illustrated; ephemera and antique picture postcards 1890-1930.
Services: Appraisals, accepts want lists, mail order.
Credit Cards: No
Owner: Dan Miranda
Year Estab: 1970

Christopher Morgan Rare Books 617-739-3352
P.O. Box 1872 02146

Collection: Specialty
# of Volumes: 3,000
Specialties: History of computer science.
Services: Catalog, appraisals, accepts want lists.
Credit Cards: No
Owner: Christopher Morgan
Year Estab: 1988

Robert H. Rubin - Books 617-277-7677
P.O. Box 267 02146

Collection: Specialty
# of Volumes: 2,000

Specialties:	Law; economics.
Services:	Catalog, accepts want lists.
Credit Cards:	No
Owner:	Robert H. Rubin
Year Estab:	1978

Byfield

Hans E. Rohr
75 Main Street
Mailing address: P.O. Box 331 01922

Collection:	Specialty
Specialties:	Illustrated; rare books; prints.
Services:	Appraisals, accepts want lists.
Credit Cards:	No
Owner:	Hans E. Rohr
Year Estab:	1946
Comments:	Sells to trade only.

Cambridge

Maurizio Martino 617-661-4221
10 Magazine Street, #306 02139 Fax: 617-868-6090

Collection:	Speciality
# of Volumes:	500
Specialties:	Bibliography; illustrated (modern and antiquarian).
Services:	Accepts want lists.
Credit Cards:	No
Owner:	Maurizio Martino
Year Estab:	1987

Matinee House 617-665-2383
P.O. Box 381908 02238

Collection:	Specialty books and ephemera.
Specialties:	Film; theatre; radio; mystery; science fiction.
Services:	Mail order, accepts want lists.
Credit Cards:	No
Owner:	Janet Strazdes & Keith Gamble
Year Estab:	1990

Worldwide Antiquarian 617-876-6220
357 Cambridge Street 02141 Fax: 617-876-0839

Collection:	Specialty
# of Volumes:	25,000
Specialties:	Middle East; Far East; Africa; color plate books.
Services:	Catalog, appraisals, search service, accepts want lists.
Credit Cards:	No
Owner:	M. B. Alwan
Year Estab:	1978

Carver

Willoughby Books 508-866-9770
90 Rochester Road 02330

Collection:	General stock.
# of Volumes:	3,000
Specialties:	Children's; horticulture; first editions; vintage paperbacks; mystery; detective fiction.
Hours:	By chance or appointment.
Services:	Search service, accepts want lists, mail order, catalog (in planning stage).
Credit Cards:	No
Owner:	Tom O'Connell & Sandy Holbrook
Year Estab:	1988

Chelmsford

Cheryl Needle 508-256-0455
212 North Road 01824 Fax: 508-463-0482

Collection:	General stock (mostly 19th century).
# of Volumes:	5,000
Specialties:	Americana; travel; pamphlets.
Services:	Accepts want lists.
Credit Cards:	No
Owner:	Cheryl Needle
Year Estab:	1969

Chestnut Hill

Magda Tisza, Rare Books 617-527-5312
130 Woodchester Drive 02167

Collection:	Specialty
# of Volumes:	3,000
Specialties:	German literature; philosophy; Judaica; illustrated (German and French).
Services:	Appraisals, catalog.
Credit Cards:	No
Owner:	Magda Tisza
Year Estab:	1977

Concord

Joslin Hall Rare Books 508-371-3101
P.O. Box 516 01742

Collection:	Specialty
# of Volumes:	1,000
Specialties:	Decorative and fine arts reference; applied arts technologies.
Services:	Search service, catalog, accepts want lists.
Credit Cards:	Yes
Owner:	Forrest & Elizabeth Proper
Year Estab:	1985

The Thoreau Lyceum 508-369-5912
156 Belknap Street 01742

Collection:	Speciality new and used books.
# of Volumes:	260
Specialties:	Henry Thoreau and related subjects; transcendentalism; nature; New England history; local authors.
Hours:	Monday-Saturday 10-5. Sunday 2-5. Closed (mostly) in January.
Services:	Appraisals, accepts want lists, mail order.
Credit Cards:	Yes
Owner:	Thoreau Society, Inc.
Year Estab:	1966

Conway

Robert L. Merriam, Rare, Used and Old Books 413-369-4052
Newhall Road 01341

Collection:	Specialty
# of Volumes:	10,000
Specialties:	Books on books; decorative arts; military.
Services:	Catalog, appraisals, accepts want lists.
Credit Cards:	No
Owner:	Robert L. Merriam
Year Estab:	1955
Comments:	The owner also operates a bed and breakfast.

Southpaw Books 413-369-4406
Box 155 01341

Collection:	General stock and ephemera.
# of Volumes:	13,000
Specialties:	Labor; social reform; African-American; women; first editions; photography.
Services:	Appraisals, search service, catalog, accepts want lists.
Credit Cards:	No
Owner:	Eugene Povirk
Year Estab:	1982

East Orleans

Sea Watch Booklook 508-255-2742
P.O. Box 251 02643

Collection:	Specialty
# of Volumes:	10,000+
Specialties:	Civil War; World War I & II; maritime; financial; Cape Cod; New England; children's; cooking.
Services:	Catalog, search service, accepts want lists.
Credit Cards:	No
Owner:	Robert G. Edwards
Year Estab:	1982

East Otis

Lyman Books 413-269-6311
P.O. Box 853 01029

Collection:	Specialty
# of Volumes:	4,000
Specialties:	Theatre of many countries, including plays, histories and biographies.
Services:	Catalog.
Credit Cards:	Yes
Owner:	Samuel & Margola Freedman
Year Estab:	1982

Fairhaven

Edward J. Lefkowicz, Inc. 508-997-6839
43 Fort Street Fax: 508-996-6407
Mailing address: P.O. Box 63 02719

Collection:	Specialty
# of Volumes:	1,000
Specialties:	Nautical rare and antiquarian books and manuscripts.
Services:	Catalog, appraisals, accepts want lists.
Credit Cards:	Yes
Owner:	Edward J. Lefkowicz
Year Estab:	1974

Fall River

Dorcas Books 508-675-1904
133 Keeley Street 02723

Collection:	General stock.
# of Volumes:	15,000
Specialties:	American first editions; detective; travel; exploration; Americana.
Services:	Appraisals, search service, accepts want lists, catalog.
Credit Cards:	No
Owner:	Stanley R. Kay
Year Estab:	1972

Framingham

Miriam Redlo, Books 508-872-0297
11 Forest Avenue 01701

Collection: General stock.
# of Volumes: 5,000
Specialties: Psychology
Services: Appraisals, search service, accepts want lists.
Credit Cards: No
Owner: Miriam Redlo
Year Estab: 1983

Georgetown

Jane Field, Books 508-352-6641
14th North Street 01833

Collection: General stock.
# of Volumes: 6,000
Specialties: Non fiction.
Services: Accepts want lists.
Credit Cards: No
Owner: Kenneth & Marcia Jane Field
Year Estab: 1962
Comments: Although we didn't have an appointment, we were fortunate that the owner was in when we were passing through Georgetown. The collection, located in a tightly packed rear room of the owner's house plus a loft area in the adjacent garage, is modest in size but very reasonably priced. We found the owner extremely helpful.

Great Barrington

Greenmeadow Books 413-528-3897
117 Division Street 01230

Collection: Speciality
Specialties: Judaica
Services: Catalog, accepts want lists.
Credit Cards: No
Owner: Susie Kaufman
Year Estab: 1987

J. & J. Lubrano 413-528-5799
39 Hollenbeck Avenue 01230 Fax: 413-528-4164

Collection:	Specialty
# of Volumes:	5,000
Specialties:	Music, including early and rare printed music and musical literature; autographed letters of composers and musicians; autographed musical manuscripts; rare dance books.
Services:	Catalog, appraisals, accepts want lists.
Credit Cards:	Yes
Owner:	John & Jude Lubrano
Year Estab:	1977

Selzer & Selzer, Antiquarian Booksellers 413-528 -6079
388 State Road Fax: 413-528-4717
Mailing address: P.O. Box 595 01230

Collection:	Speciality
# of Volumes:	1,000
Specialties:	Rare, unique and imaginative antiquarian books.
Services:	Appraisals, search service, catalog, accepts want lists.
Credit Cards:	No
Owner:	Michael I. & Helen Selzer
Year Estab:	1990

Greenfield

Glass Mountain Books 413-772-6760
P.O. Box 1284 01302

Collection:	General stock.
# of Volumes:	2,000
Specialties:	Children's; illustrated.
Services:	Accepts want lists.
Credit Cards:	No
Owner:	Bobbie Glassenberg
Year Estab:	1985

The Selective Reader 413-774-5594
658 Bernardston Road 01301

Collection:	Specialty

# of Volumes: 5,000-6,000
Specialties: Automobilia; aeronautica.
Services: Appraisals, search service, catalog, accepts want lists.
Credit Cards: No
Owner: Earl & Gwendolyn Kelton
Year Estab: 1989

Hadley

Ken Lopez, Bookseller 413-584-4827
51 Huntington Road 01035

Collection: General stock.
# of Volumes: 15,000
Specialties: First editions; modern literature; Vietnam War literature; American Indian literature; Latin American literature; black literature.
Services: Appraisals, catalog, accepts want lists.
Credit Cards: Yes
Owner: Ken Lopez

Waiting for Godot Books 413-585-5126
P.O. Box 331 01035 Fax: 413-586-1731

Collection: Specialty
Volumes: 15,000
Specialties: First editions; 19th and 20th century English and American literature; art; photography; black literature; Vietnam War; Latin American literature.
Services: Catalog, appraisals, accepts want lists.
Credit Cards: Yes
Owner: Gary Oleson & Francine L. Ness
Year Estab: 1979

Haverhill

Constance Morelle, Books 508-374-7256
1282 Broadway 01832

Collection: General stock.
# of Volumes: 10,000

Hours:	By chance or appointment.
Services:	Search service, catalog, accepts want lists.
Credit Cards:	Yes
Owner:	Constance Morelle
Year Estab:	1972

Holliston

Brainerd F. Phillipson, Rare Books 508-429-5762
83 Locust Street 01746

Collection:	Speciality
# of Volumes:	20,000
Specialties:	Fiction, including first editions, signed and proofs, specializing in John Updike, Ernest Hemingway, Jack London, Mark Twain, detective and F. Scott Fitzgerald.
Services:	Search service, accepts want lists, mail order.
Credit Cards:	No
Owner:	Brainerd F. Phillipson
Year Estab:	1982

Holyoke

Janet Egelhofer, Rare Rooks 413-532-1295
36 Fairfield Avenue 01040

Collection:	Specialty
# of Volumes:	1,500
Specialties:	English and American literary first editions; poetry; signed and limited editions; literary criticism.
Services:	Catalog
Credit Cards:	No
Owner:	Janet Egelhofer
Year Estab:	1988

Hubbardston

Timothy B. Wilder, Rare Books 508-928-5864
Box 292 01452

Collection:	General stock
# of Volumes:	1,500
Specialties:	History of philosophy.

Hours: By chance or appointment.
Services: Appraisal, catalog, accepts want lists.
Credit Cards: No
Owner: Timothy B. Wilder
Year Estab: 1984

Hull

University Book Reserve 617-925-0570
75 Main Street & 815 Nantasket Avenue 02045

Collection: General stock.
# of Volumes: 250,000
Specialties: Psychology; sociology; religion; philosophy.
Services: Accepts want lists, mail order.
Credit Cards: No
Owner: Anne E. Maxted & Paul Bassinor
Year Estab: 1941

Jamaica Plain

F. R. Joslin - Bookseller 617-524-4863
9 Goodrich Road, Apt. 2
Mailing address: P.O. Box 358 02130-0358

Collection: General stock
# of Volumes: 4,000
Specialties: Bears; modern literature; first editions; women; anthropology; counter culture; history; politics.
Services: Appraisals, search service, catalog, accepts want lists.
Credit Cards: No
Owner: F.R. Joslin
Year Estab: 1992

Lame Duck Books 617-522-6657
90 Moraine Street 02130 Fax: 617-522-7827

Collection: Specialty
# of Volumes: 5,000
Specialties: Literary first editions; Latin American literature; European literature; philosophy; intellectual history.
Services: Catalog, accepts want lists.

Credit Cards: Yes
Owner: John W. Wronoski
Year Estab: 1984

Lanesborough

Savoy Books 413-499-9968
88 Bailey Road
Mailing address: P.O. Box 271 01237

Collection: General stock.
# of Volumes: 3,000-5,000
Specialties: Early agriculture; early horticulture.
Services: Appraisals, occasional catalog, accepts want lists.
Credit Cards: No
Owner: Robert & Lillian Fraker
Year Estab: 1971

Second Life Books, Inc. 413-447-8010
55 Quarry Road Fax: 413-499-1540
Mailing address: P.O. Box 242 01237

Collection: Specialty
# of Volumes: 5,000
Specialties: Gender studies; first editions; autographs; press books; agriculture; horticulture.
Hours: By chance or appointment, 8 AM-10 PM.
Services: Appraisals, search service, catalog, accepts want lists.
Credit Cards: Yes
Owner: Russell Freedman
Year Estab: 1972

Lexington

Eva Arond 617-862-6379
52 Turning Mill Road 02173

Collection: Specialty
# of Volumes: 7,000
Specialties: Children's; performing arts; domestic arts.
Services: Appraisals, search service, accepts want lists, catalog.
Credit Cards: No

Owner: Eva Arond
Year Estab: 1980

Leyden

Leif Laudamus, Rare Books 413-774-5722
752 Greenfield Road 01301-9418

Collection: General stock of rare and unusual books (15th-19th Century).
# of Volumes: 500
Specialties: Science; medicine; early printing; bibliography and reference; rare bibles, foreign language.
Services: Appraisals, catalog.
Credit Cards: No
Owner: Leif Laudamus
Year Estab: 1981

Lincoln

Garden Works 617-259-1110
31 Old Winter Street 01773

Collection: Speciality
# of Volumes: 1,500
Specialties: Gardening; landscape design; horticulture; decorated trade bindings.
Services: Appraisals, search service, catalog, accepts want lists.
Credit Cards: No
Owner: Robin Wilkerson
Year Estab: 1977
Comments: Owner maintains a display garden that is open for viewing.

Lowell

Anthony G. Ziagos, Bookseller 508-459-4694
P.O. Box 28 01853

Collection: General stock.
Specialties: Masonic; hypnosis; regional history; boy scouts.
Services: Appraisals, search service, accepts want lists, mail order.
Credit Cards: No

Owner:	Anthony G. Ziagos, Sr.
Year Estab:	1971

Lynn

Biblio Et Nummis 617-595-3499
171 Lewis Street 01902

Collection:	Specialty
# of Volumes:	4,000
Specialties:	Numismatics
Credit Cards:	No
Owner:	John P. Donoghue
Year Estab:	1985

Marblehead

Irving Galis 617-631-5351
357B Atlantic Avenue 01945

Collection:	General stock.
# of Volumes:	5,000+
Specialties:	Jazz; military; Bostonia; presidents; aviation; automobiles; royalty; Judaica; espionage; biography.
Services:	Mail order, search service, accepts want lists.
Credit Cards:	No
Owner:	Irving Galis
Year Estab:	1979

Marlborough

Gately Bros. Books 508-485-0047
37 Fairmount Street 01752

Collection:	General stock.
# of Volumes:	3,000-4,000
Specialties:	American history; theology; philosophy; reform.
Services:	Appraisals, search service, accepts want lists, mail order.
Credit Cards:	No
Owner:	Edward & John Gately
Year Estab:	1988

Page And Parchment 508-481-2282
20 Fay Court 01752

Collection: General stock.
# of Volumes: 10,000+
Specialties: Technology; manufacturing; design; handicrafts.
Services: Accepts want lists, mail order.
Credit Cards: No
Owner: Val Paul Auger
Year Estab: 1977

Melrose

Robinson Murray III 617-665-3094
150 Lynde Street 02176

Collection: Specialty
# of Volumes: 2,000
Specialties: American history and culture to 1860, including books, imprints, broadsides and pamphlets.
Services: Appraisals, accepts want lists, catalog.
Credit Cards: No
Owner: Robinson Murray, III
Year Estab: 1984

Montague

Peter L. Masi, Books 413-367-2628
17 Central Street
Mailing address: P.O. Box B 01351

Collection: Speciality
# of Volumes: 15,000
Specialties: Architecture; decorative arts; technology; early children's; agriculture; medicine; Americana.
Hours: By chance or appointment.
Services: Catalog, accepts want lists.
Credit Cards: No
Owner: Peter L. Masi
Year Estab: 1978

Needham

Esther Tuveson Out of Print Books & Ephemera
30 Brookside Road 02192 617-444-5533

Collection:	General stock.
# of Volumes:	2,000-2,500
Specialties:	Children's; literary first editions; illustrated; art.
Services:	Search service, accepts want lists.
Credit Cards:	No
Owner:	Esther Tuveson
Year Estab:	1977

Newton

Hard-To-Find Needlework Books 617-969-0942
96 Roundwood Road 02164

Collection:	Specialty new, used and remainders.
# of Volumes:	12,000
Specialties:	Embroidery; needlework; lace; knitting; textiles; fashion; crocheting; dolls.
Services:	Appraisals, search service, catalog, accepts want lists.
Credit Cards:	No
Owner:	Bette S. Feinstein
Year Estab:	1978

Sunderland Books 617-332-9880
457 Centre Street 02158

Collection:	Specialty
# of Volumes:	5,000
Specialties:	Children's; modern first editions; quality non fiction.
Services:	Appraisals, catalog, accepts want lists.
Credit Cards:	No
Owner:	Sheila Brownstein
Year Estab:	1986

North Abington

Antiques Americana 617-857-1655
P.O Box 19 02382

Collection:	Speciality
Specialties:	Americana
Hours:	Best to call several days in advance.
Services:	Catalog, accepts want lists.
Credit Cards:	Yes
Owner:	K.C. Owings
Year Estab:	1974

North Andover

Time and Again Books 508-689-0629
364 Main Street 01845

Collection:	Specialty
# of Volumes:	6,000
Specialties:	Mystery; detective; some science fiction.
Services:	Search service, catalog, accepts want lists.
Credit Cards:	No
Owner:	Kathy Phillips
Year Estab:	1984

North Weymouth

British Stamp Exchange 617-335-3675
12 Fairlawn Avenue 02191

Collection:	General stock and magazines.
# of Volumes:	20,000
Specialties:	Women; motion pictures; magazines, including Rockwells, illustrated; technical.
Services:	Mail order.
Credit Cards:	No
Owner:	Frank Mosher
Comments:	The owner describes his collection as "a wild array of boxes, rooms and shelves to explore."

Northampton

American Decorative Arts 413-584-6804
3 Olive Street
Mailing address: P.O. Box 751 01060

Collection:	Specialty
# of Volumes:	1,000
Specialties:	20th century applied and decorative art design.
Hours:	Saturday 11-5.
Services:	Accepts want lists.
Credit Cards:	No
Owner:	Chris Kennedy

L. & T. Respess Books 413-585-8764
68F Bradford Street
Mailing address: P.O. Box 1238 01061

Collection:	General stock.
# of Volumes:	4,000
Specialties:	Americana; southern Americana and literature; English and American literature; fishing; hunting.
Hours:	By chance or appointment.
Services:	Catalog, accepts want lists.
Credit Cards:	Yes
Owner:	Lin & Tucker Respess
Year Estab:	1980

Seth Nemeroff, Bookseller 413-586-2220
46 Green Street 01060

Collection:	General stock.
# of Volumes:	3,000
Specialties:	Antiquity; art; design; photography; Asia; travel, classical and medieval studies; 19th century books; symbolism; psychology; philosophy.
Hours:	By chance most afternoons and by appointment anytime.
Services:	Search service, accepts want lists, collection development.
Travel:	Located across from Smith College.
Credit Cards:	No
Owner:	Seth Nemeroff
Year Estab:	1984

Barbara E. Smith - Books 413-586-1453
P.O. Box 1185 01061

Collection:	General stock and ephemera.
# of Volumes:	5,000-8,000
Specialties:	Children's; illustrated; cooking; classics.
Services:	Search service (children's only), catalog, accepts want lists. Special "open house" sales in May and October.
Credit Cards:	Yes
Owner:	Barbara E. Smith
Year Estab:	1984

Taurus Books (Northampton Rare Books) 413-586-2023
3 King Avenue
Mailing address: P.O. Box 716 01061

Collection:	Specialty books and prints.
# of Volumes:	1,500
Specialties:	Press books; Americana; art; framed and unframed prints. Prices range from $35-$500.
Services:	Appraisals, catalog.
Credit Cards:	No
Owner:	Gordon A. Cronin
Year Estab:	1973

Northboro

Sugar Plum 508-393-8405
Box 779 01532

Collection:	General stock.
# of Volumes:	5,000
Services:	Appraisals, search service, accepts want lists.
Credit Cards:	No
Owner:	Addie & Joe Hebert

Onset

Joseph A. Dermont, Bookseller 508-295-4760
13 Arthur Street
Mailing address: P.O. Box 654 02558

Collection:	Speciality

# of Volumes:	5,000
Specialties:	Modern literary first editions; literary autographs; children's; science fiction; poetry; poetry broadsides.
Services:	Appraisals, search service, catalog, accepts want lists.
Credit Cards:	Yes
Owner:	Joseph A. Dermont
Year Estab:	1981

Reading

H & T Bond, Booksellers 617-944-9044
33 Hartshorn Street 01867

Collection:	General stock.
# of Volumes:	5,000
Specialties:	American social history 1870-1920 (labor, immigration, reforms, etc.); poetry; modern first editions; children's.
Services:	Search service, catalog, accepts want lists.
Credit Cards:	No
Owner:	Harold & Theresa Bond
Year Estab:	1983

Royalston

Dower House 508-249-2335
14 The Common
Mailing address: Box 76 Athol 01331

Collection:	Specialty
# of Volumes:	2,000
Specialties:	Children's; fairies; fairy tales; illustrated; Arthurian.
Services:	Appraisals, search service, catalog, accepts want lists.
Credit Cards:	No
Owner:	Ann G. Swindells
Year Estab:	1980

Sandwich

Retloks Book Store 508-888-8437
137 Merchants Square 02563

Collection:	General stock

# of Volumes: 12,000
Specialties: Concord authors; maritime.
Hours: By chance or appointment.
Services: Appraisals, search service, catalog, accepts want lists.
Credit Cards: No
Owner: Silas Retlok
Year Estab: 1986

Sharon

Michael Ginsberg Books, Inc. 617-784-8181
P.O. Box 402 02067 Fax: 617-784-1826

Collection: Speciality
Specialties: Rare Americana.
Services: Appraisals, catalog.
Credit Cards: Yes
Owner: Michael Ginsberg
Year Estab: 1975

Sheffield

Howard S. Mott, Inc. 413-229-2019
170 South Main Street Fax: 413-229-8553
Mailing address: P.O. Box 309 01257

Collection: General stock
# of Volumes: 15,000
Specialties: First editions; autographs.
Services: Catalog, appraisals, accepts want lists.
Credit Cards: Yes
Owner: Donald, Howard & Phyllis Mott
Year Estab 1936

Shrewsbury

Charles Lindberg - Books 508-842-1671
11 Liberty Drive
Mailing address: M.O. Box 623 01545

Collection: General stock.
# of Volumes: 2,500

Specialties:	New England authors.
Services:	Search service, mail order.
Credit Cards:	No
Owner:	Charles Lindberg
Year Estab:	1976

Somerville

Webb Dorick 617-776-1365
15 Ash Avenue 02145

Collection:	Specialty
# of Volumes:	1,500
Specialties:	Medicine; medical history; 17th century medical monographs.
Services:	Catalog, appraisals, accepts want lists.
Credit Cards:	No
Owner:	Webb Dorick
Year Estab:	1983

South Harwich

The Cape Collector 508-432-3701
1012 Main Street (Route 28) 02661

Collection:	General stock.
# of Volumes:	25,000
Specialties:	New England; Cape Cod; maritime; classics; children's; art; sports; Civil War; World War I & II.
Services:	Search service, accepts want lists.
Credit Cards:	No
Owner:	H. Jewel Geberth
Year Estab:	1968

South Natick

Kenneth W. Rendell, Inc. 617-431-1776
46 Eliot Street Fax: 617-0237-1492
Mailing address: P.O. Box 9001 Wellesley 02181

Collection:	Speciality
Specialties:	Autographs; letters; manuscripts; portraits.

Hours: Monday-Friday 9-5.
Credit Cards: Yes
Owner: Kenneth W. Rendell
Year Estab: 1959
Comments: Similar material also available at Kenneth W. Rendell Gallery, Place des Antiquaires, 125 East 57th Street, New York, NY 10002.

Southboro

Ten Eyck Books 508-481-3517
P.O. Box 84 01772

Collection: Specialty
# of Volumes: 3,000-4,000
Specialties: Children's; illustrated; hunting; fishing.
Services: Appraisals, catalog, accepts want lists.
Credit Cards: No
Owner: Catherine & Arthur Ten Eyck
Year Estab: 1985

Stockbridge

M.F. Adler, Books 413-298-3559
P.O. Box 627 01262

Collection: Specialty
# of Volumes: 1,500
Specialties: Children's (1890 to present).
Services: Search service, accepts want lists, mail order.
Credit Cards: No
Owner: Marion F. Adler
Year Estab: 1975

Overlee Farm Books 413-637-2277
Box 1155 01262

Collection: Specialty
Specialties: Voyages; travel; exploration; cartography; maritime; nautical; Herman Melville.
Services: Catalog, accepts want lists.
Credit Cards: Yes

Owner:	Martin & Sally Torodash
Year Estab:	1985

John R. Sanderson, Antiquarian Bookseller 413-298-5322
West Main Street Fax: 413-298-4466
Mailing address: P.O. Box 844 01262

Collection:	General stock (see Comments section) and specialty.
Specialties:	Rare and early books in most fields; Berkshire County; literary first editions; folklore; horticulture; psychology.
Services:	Appraisals, catalog, accepts want lists.
Credit Cards:	Yes
Owner:	John R. Sanderson
Year Estab:	1976
Comments:	The owner's general stock is located at Jenifer House in the Olde Antique Market on Route 7 in Great Barrington. Open Daily 10-5.

Stoughton

Western Hemisphere, Inc. 617-344-8200
144 West Street 02072 Fax: 617-344-8739

Collection:	Specialty
# of Volumes:	10,000
Specialties:	Business; economics; limited general stock.
Services:	Lists, appraisals, accepts want lists.
Credit Cards:	No
Owner:	Eugene L. Schwaab, Jr.
Year Estab:	1969

Templeton

Paul C. Richards, Autographs 508-630-1228
P.O. Box 298 01468 800-637-7711

Collection:	Speciality
# of Volumes:	1,500
Specialties:	Signed and inscribed books of authors and presidents; autograph letters; documents and signed photographs; financial Americana.

Services: Appraisals, catalog, accepts want lists.
Credit Cards: Yes
Owner: Paul C. Richards
Year Estab: 1961

Turners Falls

Woodbridge Brown, Bookseller 413-772-2509
312 Main Street 01376

Collection: Speciality and prints
# of Volumes: 4,500
Specialties: Americana; natural history; horticulture.
Services: Catalog, accepts want lists.
Credit Cards: No
Owner: Woodbridge Brown
Year Estab: 1989
Comments: The collection is housed in a restored old trolley office building.

Wales

From Hunger 413-245-3706
3 Main Street 01081

Collection: Specialty
Specialties: Cooking; domestic arts.
Hours: By appointment or chance.
Owner: Stephanie Hooker
Year Estab: 1992

Sheldon's Used Books 413-245-3365
Strafford Road (Route 19) 01081

Collection: General stock.
# of Volumes: 10,000
Specialties: Hunting; fishing; children's series; New England (small town histories).
Hours: 9-5 or whenever home.
Services: Accepts want lists.
Credit Cards: No
Owner: Lester & Doris Sheldon
Year Estab: 1984

The Wayward Bookman 413-245-3706
3 Main Street 01081

Collection:	General stock (limited) and speciality.
# of Volumes:	10,000
Specialties:	Literary American humor; modern literature.
Hours:	By appointment or chance.
Credit Cards:	No
Owner:	Kenneth Hooker
Year Estab:	1987
Comments:	The preponderance of the stock is scarce or first edition humor.

Waltham

Harold M. Burstein & Co. 617-893-7974
36 Riverside Drive 02154

Collection:	Specialty
# of Volumes:	10,000
Specialties:	Americana; 19th century American literature; children's.
Services:	Appraisals, search service, catalog, accepts want lists.
Credit Cards:	No
Owner:	Eunice K. & Michael D. Burstein
Year Estab:	1954

Wellesley

Terramedia Books 617-237-6485
19 Homestead Road 02181 Fax: 617-237-4833

Collection:	Specialty
# of Volumes:	1,000
Specialties:	Travel and exploration with emphasis on Africa, Asia and polar regions.
Services:	Appraisals, accepts want lists.
Credit Cards:	No
Owner:	Elias N. Saad
Year Estab:	1980

West Roxbury

Once Upon A Time Rare Books 617-469-2665
216 Perham Street 02132

Collection: Specialty and ephemera.
# of Volumes: 1,000
Specialties: Children's; illustrated.
Services: Appraisals, search service, accepts want lists.
Credit Cards: No
Owner: Suzanne Schlossberg
Year Estab: 1975

Westfield

Book-Tique 413-568-5627
81 Llewellyn Drive 01085

Collection: Specialty
# of Volumes: 5,000
Specialties: Hunting; fishing; guns; animals; birds; natural history.
Services: Mail order.
Credit Cards: No
Owner: Gustave H. Suhm
Year Estab: 1980

Weston

Jane Choras, Books 617-237-9828
225 Winter Street 02193

Collection: General stock.
# of Volumes: 10,000
Specialties: Illustrated books; children's; science fiction; horror; fantasy.
Services: Search service, accepts want lists.
Credit Cards: No
Owner: Jane Choras
Year Estab: 1982

Westport

Philip Lozinski Scholarly Books 508-636-2567
P.O. Box 3097 02790

Collection: Specialty
# of Volumes: 6,000
Specialties: Slavica (Russian, Polish, Czech, Serb, etc.), including history, linguistics and literature.
Services: Appraisals, search service, catalog, accepts want lists.
Credit Cards: No
Owner: Philip Lozinski
Year Estab: 1961

Wilbraham

Murray Books 413-596-9372
473 & 477 Main Street 01095

Collection: General stock and ephemera.
# of Volumes: 50,000
Specialties: Americana
Credit Cards: No
Owner: Paul Murray
Comments: Sells to dealers only.

Williamstown

William Wyer Rare Books 413-458-3369
P.O. Box 211 01267

Collection: Specialty
# of Volumes: 500
Specialties: First editions; illustrated (15th-20th centuries); museum quality rare books.
Services: Appraisals, catalog.
Owner: William James Wyer
Year Estab: 1980

Winchester

Lee Gallery 617-729-7445
1 Mount Vernon Street 01890

Collection:	Specialty
Specialties:	19th century books illustrated with original photographs; "Camera Work"; 19th and 20th century vintage photographs.
Services:	Appraisals, search service, accepts want lists.
Credit Cards:	Yes
Owner:	Mack Lee
Year Estab:	1980

Winthrop

James and Devon Gray Booksellers 617-846-0852
35 Charles Street 02152 Fax: 617-846-2472

Collection:	Specialty
# of Volumes:	100
Specialties:	16th century continental books; 17th century books; books before 1700.
Services:	Catalog, accepts want list.
Credit Cards:	No
Owner:	James & Devon Gray
Year Estab:	1992

Worcester

Jeffrey D. Mancevice, Inc. 508-755-7421
P.O. Box 413, West Side Station 01602 Fax: 508-753-2317

Collection:	Specialty
# of Volumes:	500
Specialties:	16th and 17th century.
Services:	Catalog
Credit Cards:	No
Owner:	Jeffrey D. Mancevice
Year Estab:	1977

Lorraine Allison, Bookseller 617-631-1121
235 Washington St. Marblehead 01945

Collection: Specialty
# of Volumes: 6,000
Specialties: New England; cookbooks; maritime; Marblehead.
Services: Search service, accepts want lists.
Credit Cards: No
Owner: Lorraine Allison
Year Estab: 1977

Kenneth Andersen 508-832-3524
P.O. Box 621 Auburn 01501

Collection: Specialty
Specialties: Hunting; fishing; mountaineering; golf; tennis.
Services: Appraisals, occasional catalog, specialized book lists (specify interest when inquiring).
Credit Cards: No
Owner: Kenneth Andersen
Year Estab: 1978

The Antiquarian Scientist 508-957-5267
P.O, Box 367 Dracut 01826

Collection: Speciality
# of Volumes: 1,250
Specialties: Science; medicine and technology; antique scientific instruments.
Services: Appraisals, catalog.
Credit Cards: No
Owner: Raymond V. Giordano
Year Estab: 1976

Back Numbers Wilkins 508-531-5058
Box 247 Danvers 01923

Collection: Magazines only.
Specialties: Issues back to 1850. Also magazine covers and ads.
Services: Accepts want lists.
Credit Cards: No

Owner:	James T. Fleming
Year Estab:	1908

Bayskater Books 508-583-4451
72 Granite Street Avon 02322

Collection:	Specialty
# of Volumes:	300
Specialties:	Ice skating (books and magazines).
Credit Cards:	No
Owner:	Fred & Eleanor Hunter
Year Estab:	1991

Richard Robert Caprio, Books, Prints & Collectibles 617-289-4198
43A Vivien Street Revere 02151

Collection:	Specialty
Specialties:	Sports memorabilia and autographs; E.A. Poe; historical leaves (King James Bible, Shakespeare folios); 18th and 19th century newspapers.
Services:	Appraisals, catalog, accepts want lists.
Credit Cards:	No
Owner:	Richard Robert Caprio
Year Estab:	1978

Roger F. Casavant 508-653-4104
88 Dudley Road Wayland 01778

Collection:	Specialty
# of Volumes:	7,000
Specialties:	19th century Americana, including government pamphlets; western Americana; American literature; children's; science fiction (paperback); illustrated. All either first editions or collectibles.
Services:	Appraisals, accepts want lists.
Credit Cards:	No
Owner:	Roger F. Casavant
Year Estab:	1962

Russell R. duPont, Bookseller 617-447-4091
41 Star Street Whitman 02382

Collection: General stock.
# of Volumes: 1,000-1,500
Specialties: New England; local histories; some genealogies.
Services: Catalog, accepts want lists; book repair, bookbinding.
Credit Cards: No
Owner: Russell R. duPont
Year Estab: 1991

Ex Libris 508-842-3291
257 Main Street Shrewsbury 01545

Collection: General stock.
# of Volumes: 4,000
Specialties: Art; biography.
Credit Cards: No
Owner: Cushing C. Bozenhard
Year Estab: 1978

Gidley Geographic 617-871-5380
P.O. Box 115 Accord 02018

Collection: Speciality
Specialties: *National Geographic* material, including magazines, books and ephemera.
Services: Search service, catalog, accepts want lists.
Credit Cards: No
Owner: Robert Gidley

Jeanne Kocsis 413-665-7057
Box 128 Whately 01093

Collection: Specialty
# of Volumes: 1,000
Specialties: Horticulture; botany; art; photography.
Services: Accepts want lists.
Credit Cards: No
Owner: Jeanne Kocsis
Year Estab: 1989

Mattakeesett Books 617-934-5564
65 Bay View Road Duxbury 02332

Collection:	Speciality
# of Volumes:	1,000
Specialties:	American fiction; Robert Frost; J.D. Salinger; angling.
Services:	Appraisals, search service, accepts want lists.
Credit Cards:	No
Owner:	David Pallai
Year Estab:	1986

Gail McDonald - Dog Books 617-871-5380
766 Willard St, A10 Quincy 02169

Collection:	Speciality books and ephemera.
# of Volumes:	4,000-6,000
Specialties:	Everything relating to dogs in fact, fiction or art. Changing display of books at HKC Antiques in Henniker, NH. (See New Hampshire chapter.)
Services:	Search service, catalog, accepts want lists, list updates.
Credit Cards:	No
Owner:	Gail M. McDonald
Year Estab:	1989

Mostly Murder Mystery and Mayhem 508-839-3241
292 Providence Road South Grafton 01560

Collection:	Specialty
# of Volumes:	5,000+
Specialties:	Detective; mystery. (Mostly American authors).
Services:	Appraisals, search service, catalog, accepts want lists.
Credit Cards:	No
Owner:	Marshall W. Snow
Year Estab:	1990

Robert A. Murphy, Bookseller (Higginson Book Co.) 508-745-7170
14 Derby Square Salem 01970

Collection:	Specialty
Specialties:	Local history; genealogy.

Services: Search service, catalog, accepts want lists; books reprinted on request.
Credit Cards: Yes
Owner: Robert A. Murphy
Year Estab: 1969

Peacock Books 508-456-8404
P.O. Box 2024 Littleton 01460

Collection: Specialty
# of Volumes: 1,000
Specialties: Ornithology
Services: Catalog, accepts want lists.
Credit Cards: No
Owner: Phyllis T. Parkinson
Year Estab: 198

Regimentals 617-337-6106
P.O. Box 86 South Weymouth 02190

Collection: Specialty books and ephemera.
# of Volumes: 3,000-5,000
Specialties: Military (American and British, all periods).
Services: Search service, accepts want lists.
Credit Cards: No
Owner: Donald P. Lewis
Year Estab: 1972

Retired Books 508-655-4008
P.O. Box 487 Sherborn 01770

Collection: Specialty
# of Volumes: 6,000
Specialties: Fables; science; history of science.
Services: Accepts want lists.
Credit Cards: No
Owner: Dorothea Widmayer & Eleanor Webster
Year Estab: 1985

Charlotte Shumway, Bookseller 508-420-1319
P.O. Box 1040 Marstons Mills 02648

Collection: Specialty
# of Volumes: 2,000
Specialties: Children's
Services: Catalog, accepts want lists.
Credit Cards: No
Owner: Charlotte Shumway
Year Estab: 1987

Tew-Lem Books 508-858-0297
P.O. Box 488 Tewskbury 01876

Collection: Specialty and ephemera.
# of Volumes: 1,000
Specialties: New England; town and city histories; fiction and non fiction by and about New England authors or with a New England background.
Services: Search service, catalog, accepts want lists.
Credit Cards: No
Owner: Bill Corbett, Jr.
Year Estab: 1990

Trevian Book Company 508-829-3205
P.O. Box 335 Holden 01520

Collection: Specialty
Specialties: Gardening; garden history; landscape architecture; horticulture; design and decoration; music.
Services: Search service, catalog, accepts want lists.
Credit Cards: No
Owner: Geoff Baer

Trotting Hill Park Books 413-567-6466
P.O. Box 1324 Springfield 01101

Collection: Specialty books and ephemera.
# of Volumes: 3,000-5,000
Specialties: Americana; medicine; natural history; travel; exploration; sports; fishing; hunting.
Services: Catalog, appraisals, search service, accepts want lists.

Credit Cards:	No
Owner:	Barbara & Rocco Verrilli
Year Estab:	1979

Whalemen's Shipping List 508-994-6870
47 Alice Street North Dartmouth 02747 Fax: 508-997-9668

Collection:	Specialty
# of Volumes:	4,000
Specialties:	Whaling
Services:	Appraisals, search service, catalog, accepts want lists.
Credit Cards:	No
Owner:	Frederick Mitchell
Year Estab:	1988

World War I Aero Books
P.O. Box 142 West Roxbury 02132

Collection:	Specialty new and used.
# of Volumes:	10,000
Specialties:	World War I & II.
Services:	Appraisals, search service, catalog, accepts want lists.
Credit Cards:	No
Owner:	Robert D. McGrath, Sr.
Year Estab:	1955

Antique Dealers

Main Street Arts & Antiques 508-281-1531
124 Main Street Gloucester 01930

Sunsmith House "Open shop" Antiques + collectibles 508-896-7024
2926 Main Street (Route 6A) Brewster 02631
April – October

Walnuts Antiques/Antiques 608 508-385-2755
608 Main Street (Route 6A) Dennis
Mailing address: P.O. Box 754 Brewster 02631

New Hamphsire

Alphabetical Listing By Dealer

Alphabetical Listing By Location

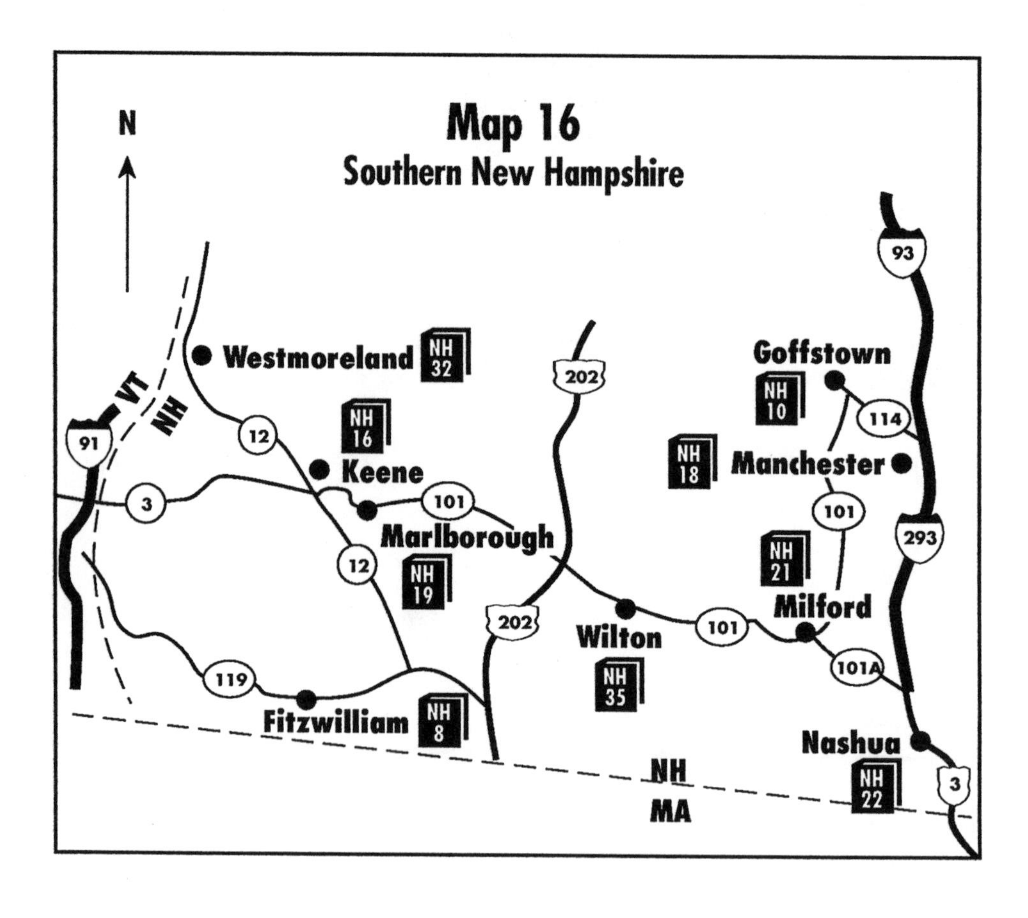
Map 16
Southern New Hampshire
N
VT
NH
91
93
Westmoreland
NH 32
202
Goffstown
NH 10
114
12
NH 16
NH 18
Manchester
Keene
3
101
Marlborough
101
12
NH 21
NH 19
293
202
Wilton
101
Milford
119
NH 35
101A
Fitzwilliam
NH 8
Nashua
NH 22
3
NH
MA

Bradford

Kalonbooks (NH1) 603-938-2380
P.O. Box 16, (Route 114) 03221

Collection:	General stock.
# of Volumes:	10,000
Specialties:	American history; science fiction; natural history.
Hours:	July & August: Wednesday-Sunday 1-5. Remainder of year: Saturday & Sunday 1-5.
Services:	Search service, accepts want lists.
Travel:	At junction of Route 103 & 114 proceed north on Route 114 for 1/2 mile. Turn right at blinking light. Turn right at end of red house. Map 18.
Credit Cards:	No
Owner:	Rod Jones
Year Estab:	1977

Brentwood

The New England Antiquarian Booksellers' Guild (NH2)
Route 101, The Castles 03833 1-800-457-5150 Fax: 603-679-8161

Collection:	General stock.
# of Volumes:	See comments
Hours:	Daily 10-5. Closed only Thanksgiving and Christmas.
Services:	Search service, accepts want lists.
Travel:	Hampton exit off I-95. Proceed west on Route 51 which becomes Route 101. Shop is on right. Look for a castle. Map 17.
Credit Cards:	Yes
Owner:	Piper Castles-O'Neill & Michael O'Neill
Year Estab:	1992
Comments:	A new group shop that opened for business in October, 1992. Owners anticipate having over 100 dealers in 3,000 square feet of space.

Center Sandwich

Hill Country Books (NH3) 603-284-7008
Village Historic District
Mailing address: Box 268 03227

Collection:	General stock.
# of Volumes:	20,000
Hours:	Memorial Day-Columbus Day: Wednesday-Saturday 10-5. Columbus Day-Christmas: Saturday 10-5. Other times by appointment.
Services:	Appraisals, accepts want lists.
Travel:	New Hampton exit off I-93. Proceed west on Route 104 toward Meredith. At traffic light, make left onto Route 25 toward Center Harbor. At Center Harbor, follow signs to Center Sandwich. Shop is in heart of village, about 1/5 mile from post office. Map 19.
Credit Cards:	Yes
Owner:	John E. Perkins
Year Estab:	1982
Comments:	A one-of-a-kind shop located in a barn attached to the owner's 18th century house in the heart of an historic New England village. The books, which the owner describes as "for the general reader," share space with a display of crafts and handmade quilts that are also for sale. Visitors will also enjoy the friendly menagerie of cats, dogs and sheep.

Concord

The Book Mill (NH4) 603-224-2770
485 North State Street 03301

Collection:	General stock of hardcover and paperback.
# of Volumes:	30,000
Hours:	Tuesday-Saturday 10-5:30.
Travel:	Exit 15 from Route I-93. Proceed to 2nd light. Take Route 3 to Penacock. Shop is about 3 miles ahead on left. Map 18.
Credit Cards:	Yes
Owner:	Christine M. Berg
Year Estab:	1986
Comments:	This spacious, well kept shop offers an interesting collection of newer used books, the majority of which are paper. There

is, however, a good selection of hardcover books, many with dust jackets. Although the book lover is not likely to find a rare used book here, the shop does offer a wide variety of books on all subjects.

Exeter

A Thousand Words (NH6) 603-778-1991
65 Water Street 03833

Collection: General stock, framed and unframed prints.
# of Volumes: 10,000
Specialties: New Hampshire; scholarly books in humanities and sciences; natural history; decorative prints.
Hours: Monday-Saturday 10-5:30.
Services: Appraisals, search service.
Travel: Exit 2 off I-95. Proceed west on Routes 51/101 4 miles to Exeter exit. Left off ramp and take Portsmouth Avenue to end. Right turn onto Water Street. Shop is 1/4 mile ahead on right after the Ioka Theatre in heart of business district. Map 17.
Credit Cards: Yes
Owner: John Segal
Year Estab: 1985
Comments: A small storefront shop that attractively combines used books and a picture framing business. The shop offers a small but quality collection of well organized books.

Exeter Rare Books (NH5) 603-772-0618
200 High Street 03833

Collection: General stock.
# of Volumes: 15,000
Specialties: Religion; European history.
Hours: Daily 10-5.
Travel: Exit 2 off I-95. Proceed west on Routes 51/101 for 4 miles to Exeter exit. Left off ramp and take Portsmouth Avenue to end. Left turn at light onto High Street. Barn is about 1 mile ahead on left. Look for a sign. Map 17.
Credit Cards: No
Owner: Anthony Moretti Tufts

Comments: The collection is divided between a large two story barn, some portions of which are poorly lit, and a smaller one story building. The books in the barn are inexpensively priced, not always in the best of condition and sometimes out of place. The books in the smaller building are in better condition. A shop where you may be able to find some bargains.

Framington

The Bookery (NH7) 603-755-4471
62 North Main Street 03835

Collection: General stock.
# of Volumes: 10,000
Specialties: Military.
Hours: Friday 10-6. By chance other times.
Services: Catalog, accepts want lists.
Travel: From Route 11, take Route 153 north. Shop is 2 blocks from town center on left. Map 19.
Credit Cards: No
Owner: Robert M. Colpitt
Year Estab: 1979

Fitzwilliam

Rainy Day Books (NH8) 603-585-3448
Route 119
Mailing address: P.O. Box 775 03447

Collection: General stock and ephemera.
# of Volumes: 25,000
Specialties: Arctic/Antarctic; aviation; children's; civil engineering; computer; cookbooks; electricity; electric power; machine tools; metallurgy; mountaineering; outdoor life; math; physics; New England; radio; railroads; European royalty; surveying; television; textile arts.
Hours: May 1st - November 1st: Thursday-Monday 11-5. Other times by appointment.
Services: Appraisals, catalog (technical), accepts want lists, mail order.

Travel:: From junction of Routes 12 and 119, 4th house on left going west on Route 119. Map 20.

Credit Cards: No

Owner: Lucia & Frank Bequaert

Year Estab: 1981

Comments: Easy to find, this two story shop offers a well organized stock arranged for easy browsing. The books are in good condition and are moderately priced. In our view, the radio collection is probably the finest available in any used book shop in this country. A children's corner can help occupy younger visitors while their parents are browsing.

Freedom

Freedom Bookshop & Gallery (NH9) 603-539-7265
P.O. Box 247, Maple Street 03836

Collection: General stock, literary periodicals and 19th and 20th century art.

# of Volumes: 15,000

Specialties: Literature; poetry; history; books on books; 19th and 20th century paintings, watercolors and prints. Literary periodicals viewed by appointment.

Hours: Late June-mid October: Sunday-Tuesday 11-5 and by appointment.

Services: Catalog, accepts want lists, mail order.

Travel: From junction of Routes 16 & 25 in Center Ossipee proceed 5 1/2 miles east on Route 25, then 3/4 mile north on Route 153. Turn right and follow signs to Freedom Village for about 1 1/2 miles. At center of village, take right fork and proceed across bridge. Shop is 1/4 mile ahead on left in barn behind large white house. Map 19.

Credit Cards: Yes

Owner: George L. Wrenn

Year Estab: 1987

Comments: A meticulously well organized and well cared for collection located in a barn that is divided into small cubicles off a wide center aisle. A book browser's dream. While the shop is somewhat out of the way and off by itself, it is well worth a visit for the serious book lover. Visitors may also enjoy viewing, and possibly purchasing, one of the paintings that are on display.

Goffstown

Sacred and Profane (NH10) 603-627-4477
Rt 13, New Boston Road
Mailing address: P.O. Box 321 03045

Collection:	General stock.
# of Volumes:	4,000
Specialties:	Theology; philosophy.
Hours:	Saturday & Sunday 12-5. Monday 3-7. Other times by appointment.
Services:	Catalog, accepts want lists, mail order.
Travel:	I-93 to Route 101 west. Go through traffic lights to Route 114. At small traffic circle in Goffstown, make left onto Route 13 towards New Boston. Shop is 1 1/2 miles ahead on left. Map 20.
Credit Cards:	No
Owner:	H. Donley Wray
Year Estab:	1981

Goshen

Nelson Books & Crafts (NE11) 603-863-4394
Brook Road
Mailing address: RR 2, Box 212 Newport 03773

Collection:	General stock of used books, antiques, handicrafts and juried art works.
# of Volumes:	60,000
Specialties:	Children's; antiques; technology; magazines; New Hampshire; Massachusetts; music; modern first editions; science fiction; horror (fiction & non fiction).
Hours:	March-June: Thursday-Monday 10-5. July-October: Monday-Saturday 10-8 and Sunday 10-5. November-February: Friday-Sunday 10-5. Other times by appointment.
Services:	Appraisals, search service, mail order, accepts want lists. Catalog is planned for near future.
Travel:	Exit 9 off I-89. West for 15 miles on Route 103. Go 1 mile past Sunapee traffic circle and turn right. Shop is 3 miles ahead on left. Map 18.
Credit Cards:	No
Owner:	Audrey Nelson & Paul Radion

Year Estab:	1984
Comments:	A 5,000 square foot "user friendly" shop attractively divided into a maze of rooms that are often separated from each other by a step or two. The collection is well organized, in excellent condition and reasonably priced. The shop is a browser's delight both for book lovers and lovers of handicrafts. The charming owners are helpful and enjoy chatting with their customers. A shop not to be missed.

Henniker

Book Farm (NH12) 603-428-3429
2 Old West Hopkinton Road 03242

Collection:	General stock.
# of Volumes:	30,000
Specialties:	Literature; literary biography and criticism; New England Americana; press books.
Hours:	May 1- September 30: Tuesday-Sunday 12-5. Remainder of year: Saturday & Sunday 1-5.
Services:	Appraisals, catalog, accepts want lists, mail order.
Travel:	1/4 mile off Route 202 on the right. Map 18.
Credit Cards:	No
Owner:	Walter Robinson
Year Estab:	1964
Comments:	A most congenial owner and a good selection of general books are to be found in this one story barn. The books are clean and reasonably priced. The owner delights in helping his visitors locate the books they've been searching for.

HKC Antiques (NH13) 603-428-7136
2 Old Ireland Road 03242

Collection:	Speciality
# of Volumes:	500+
Specialties:	All items are dog related: books, dishes, photography, jewelry, ceramics, etc.
Hours:	Wednesday-Saturday 10-5. Sunday 12-5. Other times by chance.
Services:	Appraisals, search service, accepts want lists, mail order.
Travel:	From Route 202 follow state signs to Route 114 south and HKC Antiques. Shop located off an unpaved road. Map 18.

Credit Cards: Yes
Owner: Nancy A. Bergendahl
Year Estab: 1989
Comments: If you love dogs, this place is a must. The shop, an extension of the owner's house, is filled with books and an amazing assortment of collectibles, all dealing with dogs. While you're chatting with the owner about your favorite breeds, take a few minutes to enjoy a cup of coffee at the shop's old fashioned soda fountain.

Old Number Six Book Depot (NH14) 603-428-3334
26 Depot Hill Road
Mailing address: P.O. Box 525 03242

Collection: General stock.
# of Volumes: 100,000+
Specialties: Scholarly works in all fields; history; psychology; sciences; mathematics; business; economics; religion.
Hours: Monday-Saturday 10-5. Sunday 12-5. Closed only Thanksgiving, Christmas and New Year's Day.
Travel: Route 114 south towards village. When Route 114 veers to the left (about 1/4 mile past bridge), take right fork onto Depot Street. Store is located about halfway up the hill on right in a private house. There's a sign just before the driveway but it's easy to miss. Map 18.
Credit Cards: Yes
Owner: Helen & Ian Morrison
Year Estab: 1975
Comments: A very modest entry through what was once a garage leads to 3,000 square feet of books and more books in this not to be missed shop. Books of more general interest and a children's corner are located on the first floor. More academic subject areas can be found upstairs. The aisles are a bit tight but the shop offers book hunters a vast collection covering virtually all areas of interest. Certainly one of the region's largest collections of solid academic titles as well as more popular subjects. The collection is exceptionally well organized with subcategories clearly labeled. The books are in good condition and are reasonably priced.

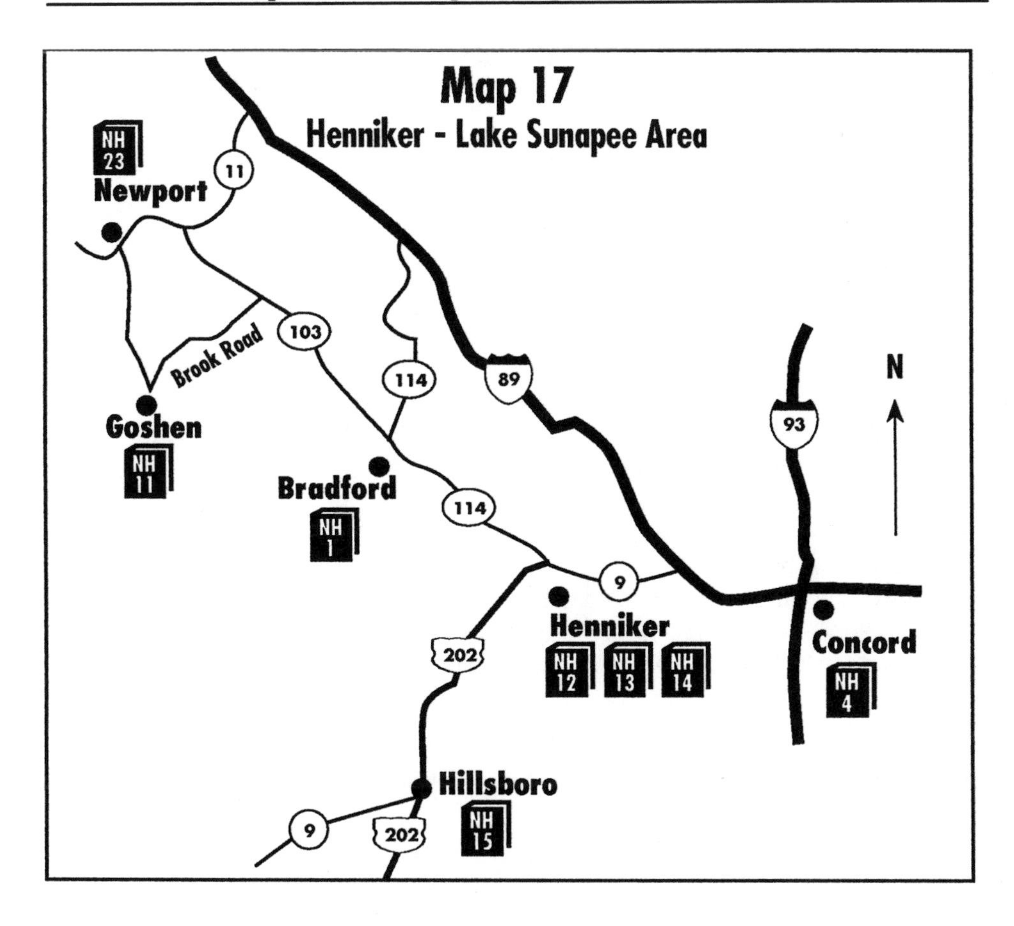

Hillsboro

Books, Antiques & Collectibles (NH15) 603-464-5771
27 Union Street 03244

Collection:	Specialty
# of Volumes:	3,000
Specialties:	Polar; mountain climbing; caves and caving; military (especially P.O.W.); South American exploration.
Hours:	Daily 10-4. Prior to March, 1993, by chance or appointment.
Services:	Appraisals, search service, catalog, accepts want lists.
Travel:	From U.S. Route 9 proceed south on Route 149 for 3 blocks. Turn right onto Union Street and watch for sign. Map 18.
Credit Cards:	Yes
Owner:	Jeff & Chris Abare

Keene

Eagle Books (NH16) 603-357-8721
19 West Street 03431

Collection:	General collection.
# of Volumes:	15,000
Specialties:	WPA; history; New England; natural history; art.
Hours:	Monday-Saturday 10-5.
Services:	Appraisals, search service, catalog, accepts want lists.
Travel:	From Route 101, proceed north on Main Street to Central Square. Go 3/4s around square to West Street. Shop is first store on north side of West Street. Map 20.
Credit Cards:	No
Owner:	Sylvia Felix
Year Estab:	1967
Comments:	This small but quality collection is located in a storefront shop in the heart of downtown Keene. The books are in good condition and are reasonably priced.

Littleton

Booklady (NH17) 603-444-1345
84 Main Street 03561

Collection:	General stock of hardcover and paperback.
# of Volumes:	10,000
Hours:	Monday-Saturday 11-5.
Travel:	Exit 41 off I-91. Proceed 1/2 mile on Route 302 into Littleton. Make left at light. Shop is about 2 blocks ahead on left. Map 24.
Credit Cards:	No
Owner:	Ervene Salan
Year Estab:	1989
Comments:	Located in the heart of downtown Littleton, this small but spaciously laid out storefront shop offers newer used books in good condition. Reasonably priced. Comfortable chairs encourage relaxed browsing.

Manchester

Amoskeag Books (NH18) 603-626-7954
809 Elm Street 03101

Collection:	General stock of used and new books.
# of Volumes:	5,000 (used)
Hours:	Monday-Saturday 9:30-5:30. Thursday till 8.
Services:	Search service, accepts want lists.
Travel:	Granite Street exit off I-93. Make left onto Elm Street. Shop is just ahead on right. Map 20.
Credit Cards:	Yes
Owner:	Laurie A. Saxon
Year Estab:	1990
Comments:	The used books are to be found in the rear portion of this otherwise new book shop located on the main thoroughfare of downtown Manchester. The shop offers book hunters a small but good selection of reasonably priced books in very good condition. A comfortable seating area and a complimentary cup of freshly brewed coffee add to the relaxed surroundings. The shop also displays books of other dealers.

Marlborough

Homestead Bookshop (NH19) 603-876-4213
221 East Main Street
Mailing address: P.O. Box 90 03455

Collection:	General stock.
# of Volumes:	45,000
Specialties:	Children's series; biography; fiction; regional.
Hours:	Monday-Friday 9-5. Saturday & Sunday 9-4:30. Closed only Christmas, New Year's Day, Thanksgiving and July 4th.
Services:	Appraisals, search service, accepts want lists, mail order, book repairs and rebinding.
Travel:	On Route 101, just east of Marlborough, next to Wilber Bros. Supermarket. Map 20.
Credit Cards:	Yes
Owner:	Robert J. Kenney
Year Estab:	1970

Comments: This one story shop, located along a major road, is crammed full of used book treasures. The collection is meticulously organized and the books are clean and moderately priced. This is a shop with something for everyone. In addition to the main room, don't miss the hidden nooks and crannies.

Meredith

Mary Robertson - Books (NH20) 603-279-8750
146 Daniel Webster Hwy (US Rt 3)
Mailing address: P.O. Box 296 03253

Collection: General collection and ephemera.
# of Volumes: 10,000+
Specialties: Needlework (new and used); crafts.
Hours: Mid May-July 1: Daily 12-4. July 1-Labor Day: Daily 10-5. Closed remainder of year.
Services: Search service.
Travel: From I-93 take Route 104 east to Route 3. Turn right on Route 3. Shop is in a big barn about 1/4 mile on right. Map 19.
Credit Cards: No
Owner: Mary Robertson
Year Estab: 1980
Comments: This large barn is spaciously laid out to facilitate leisurely browsing. The shop offers a well organized good general stock. Younger book lovers will enjoy the children's room thoughtfully furnished with appropriately sized chairs.

Milford

The Book Cellar (NH21) 603-672-4333
87 Union Square 03055

Collection: General stock of new and used hardcover and paperback.
# of Volumes: 8,000
Specialties: Christian education (home-schooling).
Hours: Monday-Friday 10-6. Sunday 9-5.
Travel: Exit 8 from Route 3. Take Route 101A to the end. Right turn onto Milford Oval. Shop is across from bandstand. Map 20.
Credit Cards: Yes

Owner: Allard & Kit Deu
Year Estab: 1992
Comments: Down one flight of steps, this relatively new shop offers a modest general stock of reasonably priced used books. There's also a good selection of children's books and classics. Comfortable chairs, placed in front of large picture windows overlooking a river, add to the shop's pleasing ambience.

Nashua

Burke's Books (NH22) 603-595-2557
255 Amherst Street (Turnpike Plaza) 03063

Collection: General stock of hardcover and paperback.
# of Volumes: 60,000
Specialties: Classics; history.
Hours: Monday-Friday 9:30. Saturday 9:30-6. Sunday 12-5.
Travel: Exit 7 off Route 3. Turn onto Route 101A west. Shop is located in a shopping center 1/4 mile ahead on right. Turn into center at light. Map 20.
Credit Cards: Yes
Owner: Edmund Burke
Year Estab: 1989
Comments: A most pleasant surprise to find a quality used book dealer in the middle of a shopping center. This good sized store stocks popular paperbacks in the middle aisles surrounded by a ring of moderately priced older books (including many classics) and newer used books. Don't miss the back room.

Newport

Paul & Rosemarie Majoros (NH23) 603-863-3165
Sunapee Road (Rts 11 & 103)
Mailing address: P.O. Box 36 03754

Collection: General stock.
# of Volumes: 5,000
Hours: Most days 10-5, but best to call.
Travel: 1/4 mile past junction of Routes 11 & 103. Map 18.
Credit Cards: No
Owner: Paul & Rosemarie Majoros

Comments:	A somewhat cluttered roadside shop that combines used books and collectibles. The collection consists primarily of reading copies not in the best of condition. We suggest a call before visiting as the owners may be relocating.

Northwood

Northwood Old Books (NH24) 603-942-8107
Routes 4, 9, 202 & 107
Mailing address: P.O. Box 525 Henniker 03242

Collection:	General stock.
# of Volumes:	20,000
Hours:	Monday-Saturday 10-6. Sunday 12-6. Open all holidays except Thanksgiving, Christmas, New Year's Day.
Services:	Appraisals.
Travel:	On south side of junction of Routes 4, 9, 202 & 107, west of Northwood Village and 4 1/2 miles east of Epsom Circle and Route 28. Map 18.
Credit Cards:	Yes
Owner:	Helen & Ian Morrison
Year Estab:	1992
Comments:	Don't be deceived by the shop's modest size as you walk in - there are lots more books downstairs. The collection is exceedingly well organized by category and subcategory. The books are in good condition and are moderately priced. The shop draws on the owners' stock in two other locations.

Ossipee

M. Daum Bookseller (NH25) 603-539-5640
Route 16 at Sunny Villa
Mailing address: P.O. Box 216 03864

Collection:	General stock, prints and ephemera.
# of Volumes:	7,500
Specialties:	New England; sports; children's; photography.
Hours:	July 15-October 15: Thursday-Monday 10-5. October 15-June 30: Friday-Sunday 10-5.
Services:	Appraisals, accepts want lists.
Travel:	Located on Route 16, 1/2 mile north of intersection with

Travel:	Located on Route 16, 1/2 mile north of intersection with Route 28. Look for the roadside sign: "The Bookmobile Used Books". Map 19.
Credit Cards:	Yes
Owner:	Michael Daum
Year Estab:	1988
Comments:	Although a two story shop, the hardcover volumes are located exclusively on the first floor. The shop offers a good sized collection with some sleepers. We noted a nice stock of mysteries, science fiction and books about foreign lands. The somewhat musty and unorganized basement is used to store paperbacks.

Portsmouth

The Antiquarian Bookstore (NH26) 603-436-7250
1070 Lafayette Road 03801

Collection:	General stock and popular and specialized magazines.
# of Volumes:	100,000+
Specialties:	Erotica (old and new) in most forms.
Hours:	Monday-Saturday 9:30-6 and other times by appointment.
Services:	Appraisals, search service, mail order.
Travel:	On U.S. Route 1, 2 miles south of Portsmouth traffic circle. Just before Comfort Inn. Map 17.
Credit Cards:	Yes
Owner:	John W. Foster, Manager
Year Estab:	1973
Comments:	100,000 books may be no exaggeration for this tightly packed shop with floor to ceiling shelves and books shelved behind books. This is an extensive general collection with all fields represented. Unfortunately, the narrow aisles can give the book hunter a sense of claustrophobia and the absence of stools or ladders limits access to the upper shelves. There's a $10 minimum on retail magazine sales.

Bob's Books (NH27) 603-427-1323
150 Congress Street 03801-4019

Collection:	General stock.
# of Volumes:	22,000
Specialties:	Religion; history; literature.

Hours:	Monday-Saturday 10-6.
Services:	Appraisals, search service, catalog, accepts want lists.
Travel:	Business Route (Woodbury Avenue) exit off I-95. Proceed on Bartlett Street to Islington and take Islington to intersection of Islington/Congress/Middle/Maplewood streets. Shop is across from library. Map 17.
Credit Cards:	Yes
Owner:	W. Robert Fowler
Year Estab:	1992 (see Comments)
Comments:	A brand new shop within walking distance of two other established shops. Although new to the area, the owner has been in the used book business since 1982.

Book Guild of Portsmouth (NH28) 603-436-1758
58 State Street 03801

Collection:	General stock and records.
# of Volumes:	40,000
Specialties:	New Hampshire; maritime.
Hours:	Monday-Saturday 9:30-5:30. Sunday 12-5.
Services:	Appraisals, search service, catalog.
Travel:	Exit 7 off I-95. Take Market Street toward downtown. Make left turn onto Bow Street and proceed to end. Make left turn onto State Street and proceed one block. Map 17.
Credit Cards:	Yes
Owner:	Doug Robertson & David Meikle
Year Estab:	1982
Comments:	A conveniently located two story storefront shop in downtown Portsmouth. The books are in good condition. Special bargain sections offer fiction, biography and presidential biography titles for under $5.00. The shop also displays books of other dealers.

The Portsmouth Bookshop (NH29) 603-433-4406
110 State Street 03801

Collection:	General stock and 18th and 19th century prints and maps.
# of Volumes:	8,000
Specialties:	Literature; first editions; art; illustrated; 19th century poetry; travel.
Hours:	Daily 10-5:30.
Services:	Appraisals, search service, accepts want lists, mail order.

Travel: Exit 7 off I-95. Take Market Street toward downtown. Make left onto Bow Street and proceed to end. Make left onto State Street and proceed one block. Map 17.
Credit Cards: Yes
Owner: Brian DiMambro
Year Estab: 1988
Comments: This storefront shop offers a well organized general collection with some interesting esoteric selections. The attractively decorated interior and soft music encourage leisurely browsing. A rear room is devoted exclusively to maps and prints.

West Lebanon

Colonial Plaza Books (NH30) 603-448-5880
Rt. 12A at Colonial Plaza Antiques
Mailing address: 23 Riverside Drive Lebanon 03766

Collection: General stock.
# of Volumes: 4,000
Hours: Daily 9-5.
Services: Accepts want lists.
Travel: Exit 20 off I-89.
Credit Cards: No
Owner: Karl & Kathleen Neary
Year Estab: 1967

West Ossipee

One More Time (NH31) 603-539-6187
Route 16 03890

Collection: General stock and ephemera.
# of Volumes: 5,000+
Hours: April 1-October 1: Daily except Thursday 9-5.
Travel: On Route 16 between Ossipee and West Ossipee. Proceeding west, shop is on left. Map 19.
Credit Cards: No
Owner: Eleanor Brown
Comments: While the shop, located in a barn behind the owner's house, offers a small selection, it does have an interesting mix of reading copies. Very reasonably priced.

Westmoreland

Hurley Books (NH32) 603-399-4342
Route 12, RR 1, Box 160 03467

Collection: Small general stock/large specialty stock.
# of Volumes: 35,000
Specialties: Farming; gardening; religion (large collection); miniature books.
Hours: Most weekdays 8-4. Weekends by chance or appointment.
Services: Catalog, accepts want lists.
Travel: On Route 12, 200 yards north of Route 63. Map 20.
Credit Cards: No
Owner: Henry Hurley
Year Estab: 1966
Comments: According to the owner, his mail order stock may be searched on computer and quotes can be given in subject areas.

Wilton

Crook's Books (NH35) 603-654-5688
Main Street 03086

Collection: General stock.
# of Volumes: 5,500
Hours: June 1-September 1: Monday-Saturday 10-7. Sunday 11-4. Remainder of year: Monday-Saturday 12-6.
Services: Accepts want lists.
Travel: About 15 miles west of Nashua on Route 101. As you enter Wilton, take right fork into business district. Shop is on left next to supermarket. Map 20.
Credit Cards: No
Owner: Gary Crooker
Year Estab: 1991
Comments: A small, unassuming shop with inexpensively priced books. Some winners among an otherwise ordinary collection.

Wolfeboro

The Wolfeboro Bookshop (NH34) 603-569-5438
Glendon & Depot Streets
Mailing address: P.O. Box 970 03894

Collection:	General stock of new and used hard cover and paperback.
# of Volumes:	7,000
Specialties:	Signed first editions.
Hours:	Monday-Saturday 9-5. Summer only: also Sunday 9-12.
Travel:	Route 28 to downtown Wolfeboro. Parking can be hard to find during the height of the tourist season. Shop is one block from main thoroughfare. Map 19.
Credit Cards:	Yes
Owner:	Cyndy Burt & Bob Brokaw
Year Estab:	1982

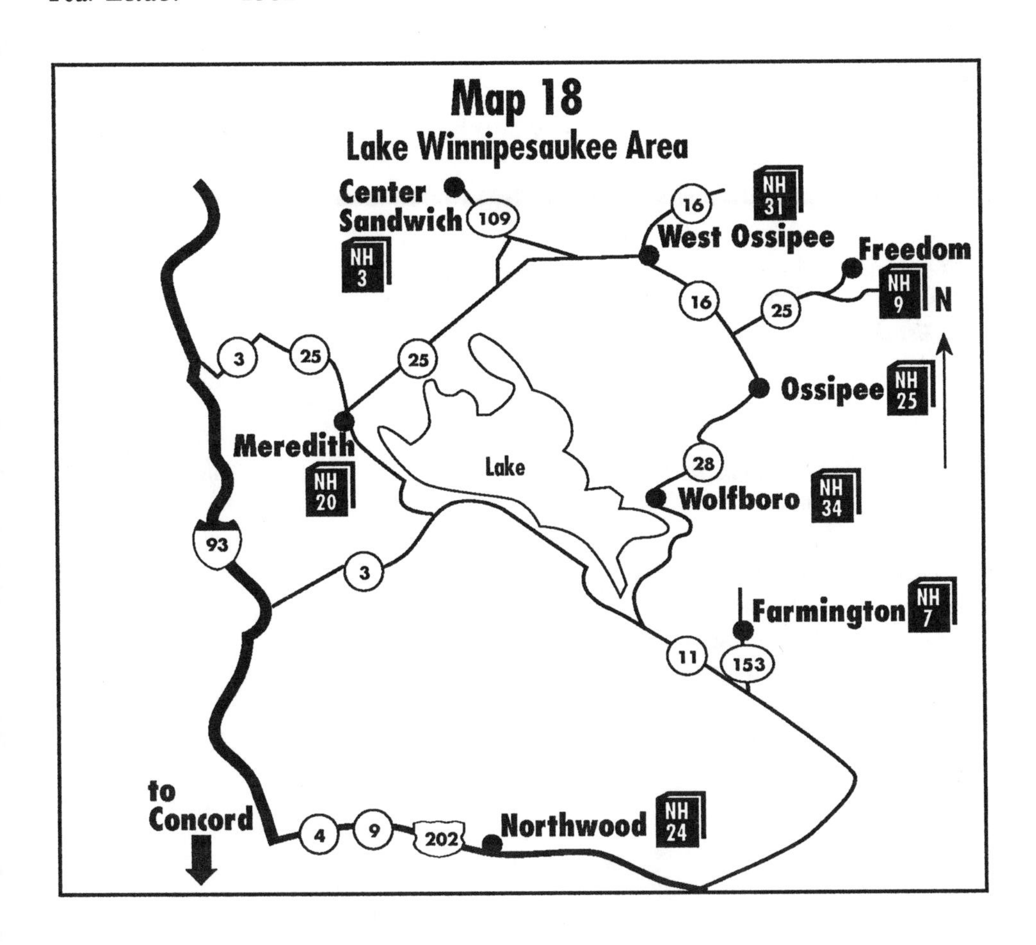

Alstead

Barb's Derrey Farm 603-835-6916
Main Street 03602

Collection: General stock.
# of Volumes: 2,000
Specialties: First editions; art; architecture; children's; country living.
Hours: By chance or appointment.
Services: Accepts want lists, search service.
Credit Cards: No
Owner: Barb Derrey
Year Estab: 1992

Alton

Fred Costello - Books 603-875-7684
Main Street 03809

Collection: General stock (mostly non fiction).
# of Volumes: 3,500
Hours: By chance daily 9-5 or by appointment.
Services: Accepts want lists.
Credit Cards: No
Owner: Fred Costello
Year Estab: 1970

Andover

The Cilleyville Bookstore 603-735-5667
P.O. Box 127 03216

Collection: General stock.
# of Volumes: 25,000-30,000
Hours: By chance or appointment.
Services: Appraisals, search service, accepts want lists.
Credit Cards: No
Owner: Sands B. Robart
Year Estab: 1977

Antrim

Ron Kurz 603-588-2916
P.O. Box 164 03440

Collection:	General stock.
# of Volumes:	2,000-4,000
Specialties:	Fine and rare books in all fields.
Services:	Accepts want lists, mail order.
Credit Cards:	No
Owner:	Ron Kurz
Year Estab:	1982

Bedford

Cloak and Dagger Books 603-668-1629
9 Eastman Avenue 03110-6701 Fax: 603-626-0626

Collection:	Speciality
# of Volumes:	10,000
Specialties:	Intelligence; true spy; counterintelligence; codes and ciphers; guerilla warfare; terrorism; political assassinations; secret police agencies. All non fiction.
Hours:	By chance or appointment.
Services:	Appraisals, search service, catalog, accepts want lists.
Credit Cards:	Yes
Owner:	Dan D. Halpin, Jr.
Year Estab:	1986
Comments:	Owner claims his stock is the largest inventory of its type anywhere in the world.

Concord

Carr Books 603-225-3109
51 North Spring Street 03301

Collection:	General stock and ephemera.
# of Volumes:	1,000+
Specialties:	18th century books.
Services:	Appraisals, accepts want lists.
Credit Cards:	No

Owner:	Roberta Carr
Year Estab:	1968

Robert M. O'Neill Fine Bindings 603-225-5530
27 Pinewood Trail 03301

Collection:	Speciality
Specialties:	Fine bindings; press books; limited editions.
Services:	Appraisals
Credit Cards:	No
Owner:	Robert O'Neill
Year Estab:	1971

Contoocook

The Arnolds 603-746-3624
Deer Path 03229

Collection:	Specialty
# of Volumes:	500
Specialties:	Civil War; western Americana; Indians.
Services:	Appraisals
Credit Cards:	No
Owner:	Don & Claire Arnold
Year Estab:	1977

Conway

La Tienda el Quetzal 603-447-5584
P.O. Box 298 03818

Collection:	Specialty
# of Volumes:	1,500
Specialties:	Central America with emphasis on Guatemala; Mayan Indians; William Walker period of Nicaragua. Also publishes some reprints.
Services:	Appraisals, search service, accepts want lists, mail order.
Credit Cards:	No
Owner:	James C. Andrews

Derry

Bert Babcock - Bookseller 603-432-9142
9 East Derry Road 03038
Mailing address: P.O. Box 1140 03038

Collection:	Speciality
# of Volumes:	7,000+
Specialties:	Modern and contemporary first editions; signed, limited and association literary; some press books; poetry; poetry broadsides.
Hours:	By chance or appointment.
Services:	Appraisals, catalog, accepts want lists, search service within areas of specialization.
Credit Cards:	Yes
Owner:	Bert Babcock
Year Estab:	1976

Dover

Kelley's Books 603-742-6497
2 Cheyenne Street 03820

Collection:	General stock.
# of Volumes:	9,000
Specialties:	Mystery; New England authors; 19th century; poetry.
Hours:	By chance or appointment.
Services:	Accepts want lists, mail order.
Travel:	1.5 miles from Exit 9 off Route 16 (Spaulding Turnpike). Take Rochester Road to Shawnee Street to Cheyenne Street.
Credit Cards:	No
Owner:	Eugene & Diane Kelley
Year Estab:	1990

Exeter

The Colophon Bookshop 603-772-8443
117 Water Street 03833

Collection:	Specialty

# of Volumes:	7,000
Specialties:	Books about books; history of printing; literary first editions; related bibliography; Civil War.
Services:	Catalog, accepts want lists.
Credit Cards:	Yes
Owner:	Robert Liska
Year Estab:	1971

Francestown

Typographeum Bookshop
Bennington Road 03043

Collection:	Specialty
# of Volumes:	1,500
Specialties:	20th century British and European literature; first editions; private press books; fine bindings.
Hours:	By chance or appointment.
Services:	Catalog
Credit Cards:	No
Owner:	R.T. Risk
Year Estab:	1976

Guilford

Louise Frazier - Books 603-524-2427
380 Morrill Street 03246

Collection:	General stock.
# of Volumes:	15,000+
Specialties:	Cooking
Hours:	By chance or appointment.
Services:	Appraisals, search service, accepts want lists.
Credit Cards:	No
Owner:	Louise Frazier
Year Estab:	1960's

Gorham

Tara 603-466-2624
Glen Road
Mailing address: P.O. Box 278 03581

Collection:	Speciality
Specialties:	White Mountain, New Hampshire maps and prints.
Hours:	By chance or appointment.
Services:	Accepts want lists.
Credit Cards:	No
Owner:	Doug & Andrea Philbrook
Year Estab:	1982

Hancock

Old Bennington Books 603-525-4035
P.O. Box 142 03449

Collection:	Specialty
# of Volumes:	3,000
Specialties:	Civil War; Americana; polar.
Services:	Appraisals
Credit Cards:	No
Owner:	Alan Lambert

Harrisville

Ben's Old Books 603-827-3639
P.O. Box 162 03450

Collection:	General stock.
# of Volumes:	1,000
Specialties:	Early American history and fiction to 1860.
Services:	Accepts want lists.
Credit Cards:	No
Owner:	Pat & Craig Brown
Year Estab:	1987

Hopkinton

Churchillbooks 603-746-5606
Rt. 1, Box 682 03229 Fax: 603-746-4260

Collection: Speciality
# of Volumes: 1,000
Specialties: By and about Winston S. Churchill.
Hours: By chance or appointment.
Services: Appraisals, accepts want lists, catalog.
Credit Cards: Yes (over $100)
Owner: Richard Langworth

Laconia

Barn Loft Bookshop 603-524-4839
96 Woodland Avenue 03246

Collection: General stock.
# of Volumes: 8,000
Specialties: Children's; New Hampshire; Maine.
Hours: By chance or appointment
Credit Cards: No
Owner: Lee Burt

Cotton Hill Books 603-524-4967
RFD 12, Box 298 03246

Collection: General stock.
# of Volumes: 2,500
Specialties: White Mountains; New England; gardening; cooking.
Services: Appraisals, search service, accepts want lists.
Credit Cards: No
Owner: Elizabeth Emery
Year Estab: 1973

Barbara B. Harris - Books 603-524-5405
RFD 1, Box 199A 03246

Collection: General stock.
# of Volumes: 3,000
Specialties: Children's; New England; biography; nature; gardening.

Services:	Mail order.
Credit Cards:	No
Owner:	Barbara B. Harris
Year Estab:	1981

Lancaster

Bretton Hall Antiquities 603-788-2202
12 Cottage Street 03584

Collection:	General stock.
# of Volumes:	5,000
Specialties:	New Hampshire; White Mountains; maritime; Americana; literature.
Hours:	By chance or appointment.
Services:	Catalog, accepts want lists.
Credit Cards:	Yes
Owner:	Richard C. & Louise Force
Year Estab:	1984

Lebanon

Thunder Road Books 603-448-4647
2 Chestnut Street 03766

Collection:	Specialty
# of Volumes:	3,000
Specialties:	Automotive, including racing and auto related biographies; Henry Ford.
Services:	Catalog, accepts want lists.
Credit Cards:	No
Owner:	Philip Clark
Year Estab:	1989

Manchester

Anita's Antiquarian Books 603-669-7695
97 Eddy Road, Unit C 03102

Collection:	General stock, ephemera, records, stamps and coins.
# of Volumes:	15,000+
Specialties:	New Hampshire.

Hours:	By chance or appointment.
Owner:	Anita & Michael Danello
Comments:	Owners have an additional 70,000 volumes in storage.

Nashua

Paul Henderson - Books 603-883-8918
50 Berkeley Street 03060

Collection:	Specialty
Specialties:	Local histories and genealogies.
Services:	Search service.
Credit Cards:	No
Owner:	Paul Henderson

New London

Burpee Hill Books 603-526-6654
Burpee Hill Road 03257

Collection:	General stock.
# of Volumes:	5,000
Hours:	By chance or appointment May 1-November 1 only.
Services:	Accepts want lists.
Credit Cards:	No
Owner:	Alf E. Jacobson
Year Estab:	1983

Northfield

Evelyn Clement - Dealer in Old Books 603-286-2381
98 Park Street 03276

Collection:	General stock.
Specialties:	Early technical; New Hampshire; White Mountains; rivers; railroad; logging.
Hours:	By chance or appointment.
Services:	Accepts want lists.
Credit Cards:	No
Owner:	Evelyn Clement
Year Estab:	1958

Comments:	The shop is located near a restored freight house with a vintage pullman car, seven cabooses and an alco engine.

Peterborough

Callahan & Company, Booksellers 603-924-3726
P.O. Box 505 03458

Collection:	Speciality :
Specialties:	Hunting; fishing; natural history. (Stock is primarily out-of-print titles.)
Services:	Catalog, accepts want lists.
Credit Cards:	No
Owner:	Ken & Diane Callahan

Pike

The Brass Hat and Menckeniana 603-989-5697
RR 2, Box 197A 03780

Collection:	Specialty
# of Volumes:	7,000
Specialties:	Military history; U.S. Marine Corps; general history; books by and about H.L. Mencken.
Services:	Catalog, accepts want lists.
Credit Cards:	No
Owner:	George B. & Jeanne J. Clark
Year Estab:	1972

Rumney

John F. Hendsey - Bookseller 603-786-2213
Box 437 03266

Collection:	General stock.
# of Volumes:	10,000
Specialties:	Fine and rare books.
Services:	Appraisals
Credit Cards:	No
Owner:	John F. Hendsey
Year Estab:	1960's

Village Books 603-786-9812
Main Street
Mailing address: P.O. Box 20 03266

Collection:	Specialty
# of Volumes:	2,000
Specialties:	New Hampshire; White Mountains; hunting; fishing.
Services:	Catalog, accepts want lists.
Credit Cards:	No
Owner:	Ann S. Kent
Year Estab:	1964

Somersworth

Book Shop at Great Falls 603-692-4196
P.O. Box 70 03878

Collection:	Speciality
# of Volumes:	5,000
Specialties:	New England, including histories, genealogy and 19th century fiction and non fiction dealing with New England; Sarah Orne Jewett.
Services:	Limited search service, catalog, accepts want lists.
Credit Cards:	No
Owner:	John Ballentine
Year Estab:	1982
Comments:	Owner also reprints 19th century books dealing with New England and sells new books in area of specialization.

Temple

Tainter Lane Dustycover Bookshop 603-878-1758
West Street 03084

Collection:	General stock.
# of Volumes:	40,000+
Services:	Search service, accepts want lists, mail order.
Credit Cards:	No
Owner:	Gary & Robin Doucette
Year Estab:	1950's

Warner

Old Paper World 603-456-3338
Box 246, Route 103 03278

Collection:	Specialty books and ephemera.
# of Volumes:	7,000
Specialties:	Western Americana; rare books.
Hours:	By chance or appointment.
Travel:	1 1/2 miles off I-89 on Route 103.
Credit Cards:	No
Owner:	Tom & Christopher Stotler
Comments:	The collection is housed in a somewhat messy barn that combines books and collectibles. Some ephemera is located in a back room, but the bulk of the collection is not readily accessible. The modest collection of books is not well organized and there are few if any labels on the shelves. The number of volumes we saw displayed during our visit appeared to be less than the owner's estimate. The owner claims to have the largest stock of ephemera in New England "if he can get to it." If you're in the area, the barn is worth a quick stop.

Weare

Sykes & Flanders, ABAA 603-529-7432
99 Concord Stage Road
Mailing address: P.O. Box 460 03281

Collection:	Books, maps and ephemera.
Services:	Appraisals, catalog (sporadic), accepts want lists.
Credit Cards:	No
Owner:	Richard & Mary Sykes
Year Estab:	1972

West Antrim

William Reilly - Rare Books 603-588-3082
West Street 03440

Collection:	General stock.
# of Volumes:	4,000

Specialties: Children's
Services: Appraisals, search service, accepts want lists, mail order.
Credit Cards: No
Owner: William Reilly
Year Estab: 1980

Mail Order Dealers

Abbott & Abbott Books 603-772-4464
58 River Road Stratham 03885

Collection: Specialty
# of Volumes: 3,000
Specialties: Birds; aviation.
Services: Accepts want lists.
Credit Cards: No
Owner: Terry & Denny Abbott
Year Estab: 1987

G. P. Ackerman, Books 603-756-4223
P.O. Box 26 Walpole 03608

Collection: Specialty
# of Volumes: 3,500
Specialties: Theater; English history; language; literature.
Services: Accepts want lists.
Credit Cards: No
Owner: G.P. Ackerman
Year Estab: 1982

The Book Bin 603-224-5609
4 Roger Avenue Concord 03301

Collection: Specialty
Specialties: New England; New Hampshire; old first editions.
Services: Accepts want lists.
Credit Cards: No
Owner: Dot O'Neil
Year Estab: 1965

The Bookman of Arcady 603-446-7475
HCR 32, Box 501 Stoddard 03464

Collection:	Specialty
# of Volumes:	500
Specialties:	Biography; fine print presses; poetry.
Services:	Search service, accepts want lists.
Credit Cards:	No
Owner:	Mary Zeller
Year Estab:	1981

Books & More 603-588-2415
P.O. Box 8 Milford 03055

Collection:	Speciality
# of Volumes:	6,000
Specialties:	Science fiction; fantasy. (Vintage and rare paperbacks and media related materials. Some hardcovers.)
Services:	Search service, catalog, accepts want lists.
Credit Cards:	No
Owner:	Judith Klein-Dial
Year Estab:	1989

Bump's Barn Bookshop 603-968-3354
23 Depot Street Ashland 03217

Collection:	General stock.
# of Volumes:	10,000
Specialties:	Art; photography.
Services:	Catalog, accepts want lists.
Credit Cards:	No
Owner:	Don Bump
Year Estab:	1958

Robert C. Campbell 603-888-1577
96 Langholm Drive Nashua 03062

Collection:	General stock.
Specialties:	Natural history.
# of Volumes:	1,500

Services: Catalog (in planning stage), search service, accepts want lists.
Credit Cards: No
Owner: Robert C. Campbell
Year Estab: 1990

Cellar Door Books 603-225-2012
62 Washington Street Concord 03301

Collection: Specialty
Specialties: Tasha Tudor; hot air ballooning.
Services: Accepts want lists.
Credit Cards: No
Owner: William John Hare
Year Estab: 1972

Landscape Books 603-964-9333
P.O. Box 483 Exeter 03833

Collection: Speciality
# of Volumes: 2,000
Specialties: Landscape design; garden history and design.
Services: Appraisals, search service, catalog, accepts want lists.
Credit Cards: No
Owner: Jane W. Robie
Year Estab: 1972

John LeBow - Bookseller 603-627-7544
P.O. Box 1390 Manchester 03105

Collection: Speciality
# of Volumes: 2,000
Specialties: Modern first editions; signed limited editions; "beat" literature; 1960's ephemera.
Services: Catalog, appraisals, search service, accepts want lists.
Credit Cards: Yes
Owner: John LeBow
Year Estab: 1986

Ronald Purmort 603-863-1810
39 Laurel Street Newport 03773

Collection: General stock.

# of Volumes:	10,000
Specialties:	Children's; hunting; fishing.
Services:	Accepts want lists.
Credit Cards:	No
Owner:	Ronald Purmort
Year Estab:	1982

Richardson Books, Ltd. 603-772-7993
P.O. Box 1198 Manchester 03105

Collection:	Speciality
# of Volumes:	1,500
Specialties:	English and American literature; Jane Austen; Virginia Woolf & Bloomsbury Group; modern literature (1900-1940).
Services:	Catalog, accepts want lists.
Credit Cards:	No
Owner:	Peggy & Jon Richardson
Year Estab:	1982

1791 House Books 603-469-3636
Main Street Meriden 03770

Collection:	Books and ephemera, including baseball and trade cards.
# of Volumes:	35,000
Specialties:	Sports (especially baseball); British royalty; first editions; Americana; magic; early comic books.
Credit Cards:	No
Owner:	Erich & Jane Witzel
Year Estab:	1978
Comments:	Occasionally open by appointment.

Edward F. Smiley 603-472-5800
43 Liberty Hill Road Bedford 03110

Collection:	Speciality
# of Volumes:	2,000
Specialties:	Gardening
Services:	Search service, catalog.
Credit Cards:	No
Owner:	Edward F. Smiley

Steinbrueck Books 603-774-7588
47 Putney Road Bow 03304

Collection:	Speciality
# of Volumes:	1,500
Specialties:	Architecture; engineering; business; industrial history; gardening.
Services:	Catalog, accepts want lists.
Credit Cards:	No
Owner:	Achim Steinbrueck
Year Estab:	1991

TransAction (After 7PM) 603-788-2441
34 Bridge Street Lancaster 03584

Collection:	Speciality
Specialties:	Magazines; paper.
Services:	Accepts want lists.
Credit Cards:	No
Owner:	Stan Pearson
Year Estab:	1987

Women's Words Books 603-228-8000
Route 4, Box 322, Straw Road Hopkinton 03229

Collection:	Specialty
# of Volumes:	3,000
Specialties:	Women's studies.
Services:	Appraisals, search service, accepts want lists.
Credit Cards:	Yes
Owner:	Nancy L. Needham
Year Estab:	1976

Antique Dealers

Burlwood Antique Center
Route 3 Meredith

Sunny Villa Shops 603-539-2253
Route 16 at Sunny Villa Ossipee

Rhode Island

Alphabetical Listing By Dealer

Alphabetical Listing By Location

Newport

The Armchair Sailor Bookshop (RI1) 401-847-4252 800-292-4278
543 Thames Street 02840 Fax: 401-847-1219

Collection: Speciality new and used books, charts and other nautical items.
# of Volumes: Under 500
Specialties: Nautical
Hours: Monday-Saturday 9-6. Sunday 12-5.
Services: Appraisals, catalog.
Travel: Map 21.
Credit Cards: Yes
Owner: Ronald Barr
Year Estab: 1978
Comments: Primarily a new book store with a limited used book section.

The Book Store On Van Zandt (RI2) 401-849-7370
95 Van Zandt Avenue 02840

Collection: General stock.
# of Volumes: 7,000
Specialties: Literature; history; biography; religion.
Hours: Thursday-Saturday 12-6.
Travel: Map 21.
Credit Cards: No
Owner: James I. Huston
Year Estab: 1990

Corner Book Shop (RI3) 401-846-1086
418 Spring Street 02840

Collection: General stock of hardcover and paperback.
# of Volumes: 16,000
Hours: Monday-Saturday 1-5 & 6:30-9.
Services: Appraisals
Travel: I-195 to Route 138 to Route 114. Spring Street is second major street from the waterfront. Map 21.
Credit Cards: No
Owner: Lawrence R. Whitford
Year Estab: 1962

Comments: A compact shop with a limited collection but some potential finds. The books are not all in the best of condition.

The Newport Book Store (RI4) 401-847-3400
116 Bellevue Avenue 02840

Collection: General stock.
# of Volumes: 12,000-15,000
Specialties: Americana; Rhode Island; New England; military; naval history and strategy; American Revolution; Middle East; fine bindings.
Hours: Daily 12-6 and other times by appointment.
Services: Appraisals, search service, catalog, accepts want lists.
Travel: In heart of Newport historic district, next to Newport Art Museum and two blocks from waterfront. Map 21.
Credit Cards: Yes
Owner: Donald G. Magee
Year Estab: 1982
Comments: This is a new location for a long established book seller. The spacious, well lit storefront shop has a home library atmosphere that invites leisurely browsing. Timely exhibits, e.g., political cartoons and buttons during a presidential election year, give the shop added flavor and distinctiveness. The stock has been carefully selected for both its content and condition. The owner is planning to set up a group shop on the lower level.

The Scribe's Perch (RI5) 401-849-8426
316 Broadway Fax: 401-848-2529
Mailing address: P.O. Box 3295 02840

Collection: General stock.
# of Volumes: 10,000
Hours: Summer: Daily 11-6. Winter: Daily 11-5.
Services: Appraisals, search service, catalog, accepts want lists, book auctions.
Travel: I-195 north to Route 138 east. Follow highway to end. Continue on Route 114 which becomes Broadway in Newport. Shop is on right, next to Broadway Florist and The Annex. Map 21.
Credit Cards: No
Owner: *Jim Weyant*

Comments: Most of the books in this storefront shop are of a common variety and are priced accordingly. We saw few rare books when we visited. The entire collection is not readily available for browsing.

Simmons & Simmons (RI6) 401-848-0339
223 Spring Street 02840

Collection:	General stock.
# of Volumes:	1,000
Specialties:	Exploration; polar.
Hours:	Daily 11-4.
Services:	Appraisals
Travel:	Map 21.
Credit Cards:	No
Owner:	Eric Simmons
Year Estab:	1975

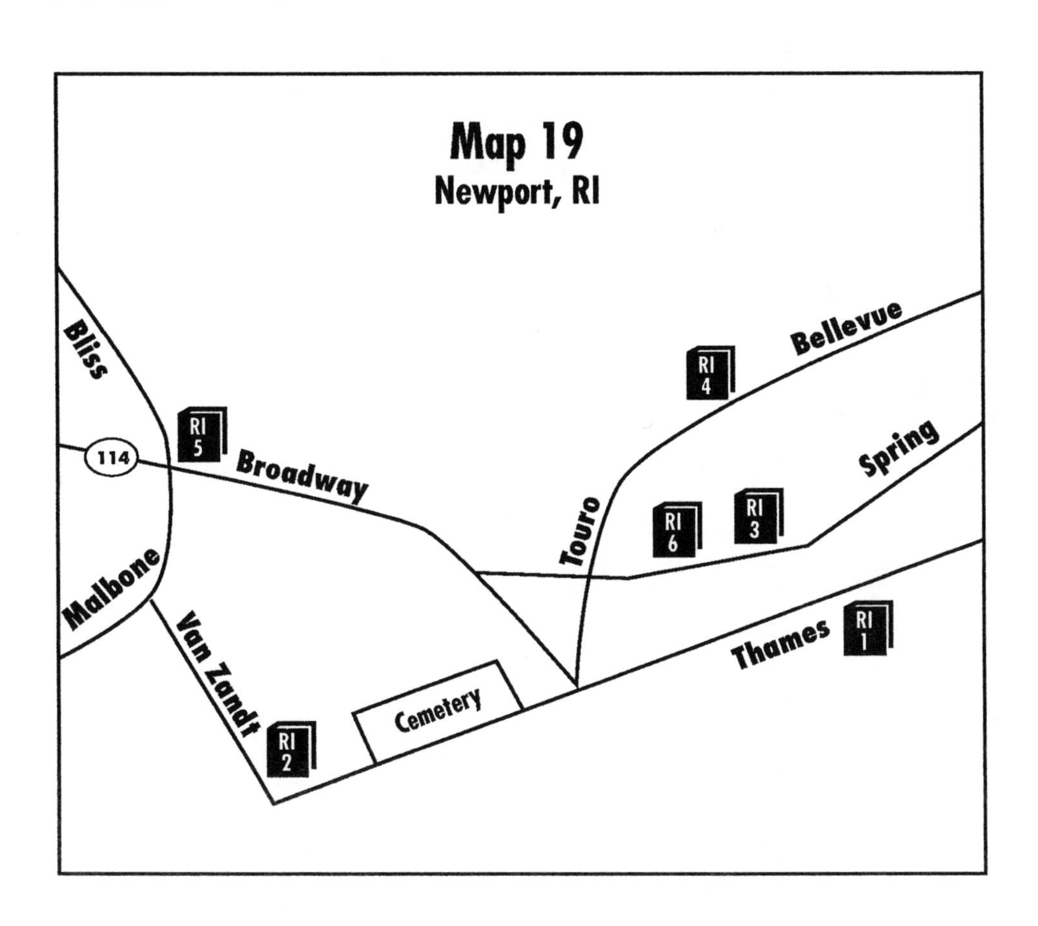

Providence

Cellar Stories Book Store (RI7) 401-521-2665
190 Mathewson Street 02903

Collection:	General stock of hardcover and paperback, magazines and ephemera.
# of Volumes:	50,000
Specialties:	Rhode Island history; literature; modern first editions; nautical; art; fantasy; science fiction.
Hours:	Monday-Saturday 10-6.
Services:	Appraisals, search service, catalog, accepts want lists.
Travel:	Exit 21 off I-95. Right turn at end of ramp. Bear right onto Empire Street. Left onto Weybosset and second right onto Mathewson. Map 22.
Credit Cards:	Yes
Owner:	Michael K. Chandley
Year Estab:	1981
Comments:	Despite its name, this shop is located one flight up. The collection is well organized with large brightly colored signs in the aisles to guide the book hunter. Better science fiction books are in a glass cabinet and behind the front desk. Fantasy books are mostly paperbacks. In addition to the specialties listed above, we noted a strong cooking section. According to the owner, the shop is "Rhode Island's largest used book store." Based on our travels through the state, we are inclined to agree with him.

Cornerstone Books (RI8) 401-331-1340
127 Thayer Street (ans. mach.) 401-861-7244
Mailing address: P.O. Box 2591 02906

Collection:	General stock.
# of Volumes:	10,000
Specialties:	Black American literature.
Hours:	Monday-Saturday 12-5.
Services:	Appraisals, search service, catalog, accepts want lists.
Travel:	Gano Street exit off I-95. At end of ramp, make right onto Gano. Make left onto Angell, then left onto Thayer. Shop is on the left, after Brown University buildings. Map 22.
Credit Cards:	No
Owner:	Ray Rickman

Year Estab: 1984
Comments: A modest general collection in a very modest sized store. In addition to Afro American literature, the specialty collection includes titles dealing with contemporary Afro American culture.

Murder By The Book (RI9) 401-331-9140
1281 North Main Street 02904 Fax: 401-751-4980

Collection: Speciality used and new hardcover and paperback.
# of Volumes: 10,000-12,000
Specialties: Mysteries; detective; spy.
Hours: Monday-Friday 12-7. Saturday 11-7.
Services: Search service, catalog, accepts want lists.
Travel: Exit 25 (North Main Street) off I-95. At North Main Street take left at light. Shop is on right after third set of lights. Map 22.
Credit Cards: Yes
Owner: Kevin J. Barbero
Year Estab: 1978
Comments: One of the largest and best organized shops specializing in mystery and detective books we have seen in the New England area. The collection ranges from reading copies to collectibles and includes an excellent selection of hardcover books in addition to the usual paperback selections. The shop shares space with an equally outstanding specialty shop. (See below)

Other Worlds Bookstore (RI10) 401-331-9140
1281 North Main Street 02904

Collection: General stock.
# of Volumes: 30,000+
Specialties: Science fiction; fantasy; horror.
Hours: Monday-Friday 12-7. Saturday 11-7. Other times by chance or appointment.
Services: Appraisals, search service, catalog (science fiction/horror.)
Travel: North Main Street exit off I-95. Left onto North Main. Shop is on right after the third set of lights. Map 22.
Credit Cards: Yes
Owner: Paul Dobish, Jr.
Year Estab: 1983

Comments: Much like the shop it shares space with (see above), this is one of the largest and best organized shops specializing in science fiction and horror that we have seen in the New England area. For a change, the shelves are filled with an excellent selection of hardcover books representing all periods, in addition to the usual paperback selections. Books are priced fairly.

Providence Bookstore Cafe (RI11) 401-521-5533
500 Angell Street 02906

Collection: General stock of used and new books.
# of Volumes: 20,000 (combined)
Specialties: Modern first editions; art.
Hours: Daily 11-10.
Services: Search service, accepts want lists.
Travel: Gano Street exit off I-95. Right onto Gano and proceed to first light. Right onto Pitman then first left onto Wayland. Proceed to second light. Cafe is on far right corner in the Wayland Manor, a large red brick residential building. Look for a long gray awning. Map 22.
Credit Cards: Yes
Owner: Michael K. Chandley
Year Estab: 1991
Comments: An attractively decorated shop with a limited collection of used books, most of which fall into the newer used category. Some sets. New books can be purchased for half price. If you decide to stop for lunch or dinner in the adjoining restaurant while you're book hunting, you'll appreciate the menu -- it's divided into Chapters with an appropriate Introduction and Conclusion. According to the owner, "customers are encouraged to consume books with their meals and browse while they wait for the food." We spotted a billiards table and two chess tables in a rear room. The entrance is down a few steps.

Sewards' Folly, Books (RI12) 401-272-4454
139 Brook Street 02906

Collection: General stock.
# of Volumes: 12,000
Specialties: Rhode Islandiana; scholarly.

Hours:	Daily 12-6.
Services:	Search service.
Travel:	2nd Providence exit (Wickenden Street) off I-95. Left at bottom of ramp. Left at Brook Street (second stop light). Map 22.
Credit Cards:	No
Owner:	Schuyler & Peterkin Seward
Year Estab:	1976
Comments:	Unfortunately, neither the aisles or shelves in this crowded shop are labeled and a glance at the shelves will give the book hunter a hint, but only a hint, as to what can be found on the shelves. The books are moderately priced. In addition to the specialties listed above, we noted a strong biography section. The fiction section was somewhat limited. The owner seems quite erudite and chatty.

Tyson's Old & Rare Books (RI13) 401-421-3939
334 Westminster Street 02903

Collection:	General stock.
# of Volumes:	10,000+
Specialties:	Americana; local history (with emphasis on colonial history).
Hours:	Most Wednesdays 11-5. Most Saturdays 11-4.
Services:	Appraisals, catalog, search service.
Travel:	Exit 21 off I-95. Turn right at end of ramp and bear right onto Empire Street. Turn onto Westminster according to direction of one way streets. The shop is on the third floor of an office building. Map 22.
Credit Cards:	No
Owner:	Mariette P. Bedard
Year Estab:	1931

Warwick

Fortunate Finds Bookstore (RI14) 401-737-8160
16 West Natick Road 02886

Collection:	General stock and ephemera.
# of Volumes:	15,000
Specialties:	Trade catalogs; children's; New England.

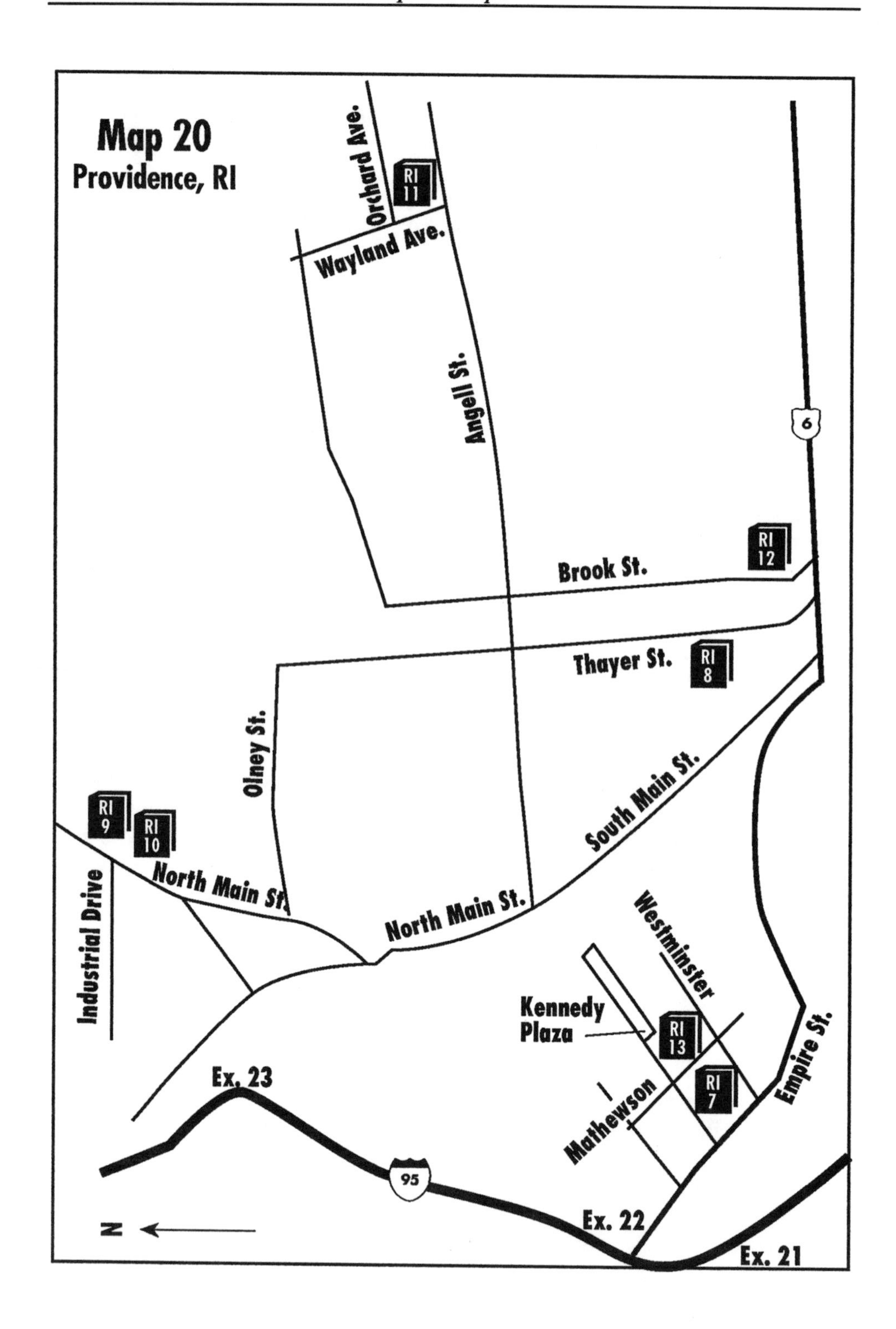
Map 20
Providence, RI
Orchard Ave.
RI 11
Wayland Ave.
Angell St.
6
Brook St.
RI 12
Thayer St.
RI 8
Olney St.
South Main St.
RI 9
RI 10
North Main St.
North Main St.
Industrial Drive
Westminster
Kennedy Plaza
RI 13
RI 7
Mathewson
Empire St.
Ex. 23
95
Ex. 22
Ex. 21
N

Hours: Friday & Saturday 10-4.
Services: Mail order, appraisals, accepts want lists.
Travel: Off Route 5 near Warwick Mall.
Credit Cards: No
Owner: Mildred Santille
Year Estab: 1952

Watch Hill

Book & Tackle Shop (RI15) 401-596-0700
7 Bay Street
Mailing address: P.O. Box 1462 02891

Collection: General stock and ephemera.
# of Volumes: 50,000
Specialties: Children's; medical; nautical; fishing; art; music; history; gardening; science.
Hours: June-September: Daily 9-9.
Services: Appraisals, search service, an occasional catalog, accepts want lists.
Travel: From Westerly, proceed on Route 1A to village. Map 2.
Credit Cards: Yes
Owner: Bernie Gordon
Year Estab: 1953
Comments: Located in an old storefront shop in the heart of a quaint seaside village, this shop offers a mix of some older items related to regional history as well as a general stock representing most subject areas. We found the books to be over priced and some were in less than satisfactory condition. A few library discards were noted and even these were priced above what a seasoned book hunter would find elsewhere. Despite the above caveats, the shop does have many one-of-a-kind items which may not be found elsewhere and which could complete a book hunter's want list.

Cranston

The Owl at the Bridge 401-467-7362
25 Berwick Lane 02905 Fax: same

Collection:	General stock.
Specialties:	Italian culture.
Services:	Appraisals, mail order.
Credit Cards:	No
Owner:	Samuel J. & Penelope R. O. Hough

Newport

Anchor & Dolphin Books 401-846-6890
30 Franklin Street
Mailing address: P.O. Box 823 02840

Collection:	Speciality with some general stock.
# of Volumes:	2,500
Specialties:	Garden history; landscape architecture; horticulture; architecture; design; domestic arts; city planning.
Hours:	Most afternoons, March-December.
Services:	Appraisals, catalog.
Travel:	Memorial Boulevard (Route 138) to Spring Street. Turn north onto Spring Street and make first left onto Franklin Street.
Credit Cards:	No
Owner:	Ann Marie Wall & James A. Hink
Year Estab:	1977
Comments:	A modest but quality collection in immaculately cared for surroundings.

Providence

M & S Rare Books, Inc. 401-421-1050
245 Waterman Street, Suite 303 Fax: 401-272-0831
Mailing address: P.O. Box 2594, East Side Sta. 02906

Collection:	General stock.
# of Volumes:	7,500

Specialties:	Rare American 18th-19th century books; black history; medicine; philosophy; history; literature; pamphlets, broadsides and manuscripts.
Services:	Appraisals, catalog.
Credit Cards:	No
Owner:	Daniel G. Siegel
Year Estab:	1969
Comments:	The owner notes that his stock offers a collection of "rare, important and valuable books for the collector, researcher and institution."

Metacomet Books 401-421-5750
143 Elton Street
Mailing address: P.O. Box 2479 02906

Collection:	General stock.
# of Volumes:	4,000
Specialties:	Americana; literature (mostly pre-1950); first editions; science; technology.
Hours:	All times."
Credit Cards:	No
Owner:	James Sanford
Year Estab:	1980
Comments:	The owner states that most of his stock is in the $10-$50 range, with a few shelves of over $100 books.

Smithfield

Smithfield Rare Books 401-231-8225
20 Deer Run Trail 02917

Collection:	Speciality
# of Volumes:	1,000
Specialties:	Medical; science.
Services:	Catalog, accepts want lists.
Credit Cards:	No
Owner:	Michael Elmer
Year Estab:	1985

AAAA Books 401-467-3644
P.O. Box 2817 Providence 02097

Collection:	Speciality
# of Volumes:	15,000 items
Specialties:	Jehovah Witness and Watchtower Bible and Tract Society materials.
Services:	Search service, accepts want lists.
Credit Cards:	No
Year Estab:	1986

Michael Borden, Book Dealer 401-683-4872
2774 East Main Road Portsmouth 02871

Collection:	General stock.
# of Volumes:	35,000
Specialties:	Science fiction (rare, first editions and paper); mystery; illustrated books; children's; books about books; pulps; fine bindings; autographs; advance and review copies.
Services:	Appraisals, catalog, accepts want lists.
Credit Cards:	No
Owner:	Michael Gordon
Year Estab:	1969

Lincoln Out-Of-Print Book Search 401-647-2825
33 Mt. Hygeia Road Foster 02825

Collection:	General stock.
# of Volumes:	60,000
Services:	Search service, accepts want lists.
Credit Cards:	Yes
Owner:	Harold & Linda Ephraim
Year Estab:	1931

The Two Front Rooms 401-732-9668
1349 West Shore Road Warwick 02889

Collection:	Speciality
Specialties:	Children's; fantasy; horror.
Services:	Catalog, accepts want lists.
Credit Cards:	No

Owner: Holly Van Wye
Year Estab: 1992

Donald W. Winland, Books 401-245-2551
P.O. Box 324 Portsmouth 02871

Collection: Speciality
# of Volumes: 3,000-5,000
Specialties: Rhode Island history; maritime; military; Japan, China; Americana; antiques reference; travel; archeology; biography.
Services: Search service, catalog, accepts want lists.
Credit Cards: No
Owner: Donald W. Winland
Year Estab: 1976

A stairway to heaven

Vermont

Alphabetical Listing By Dealer

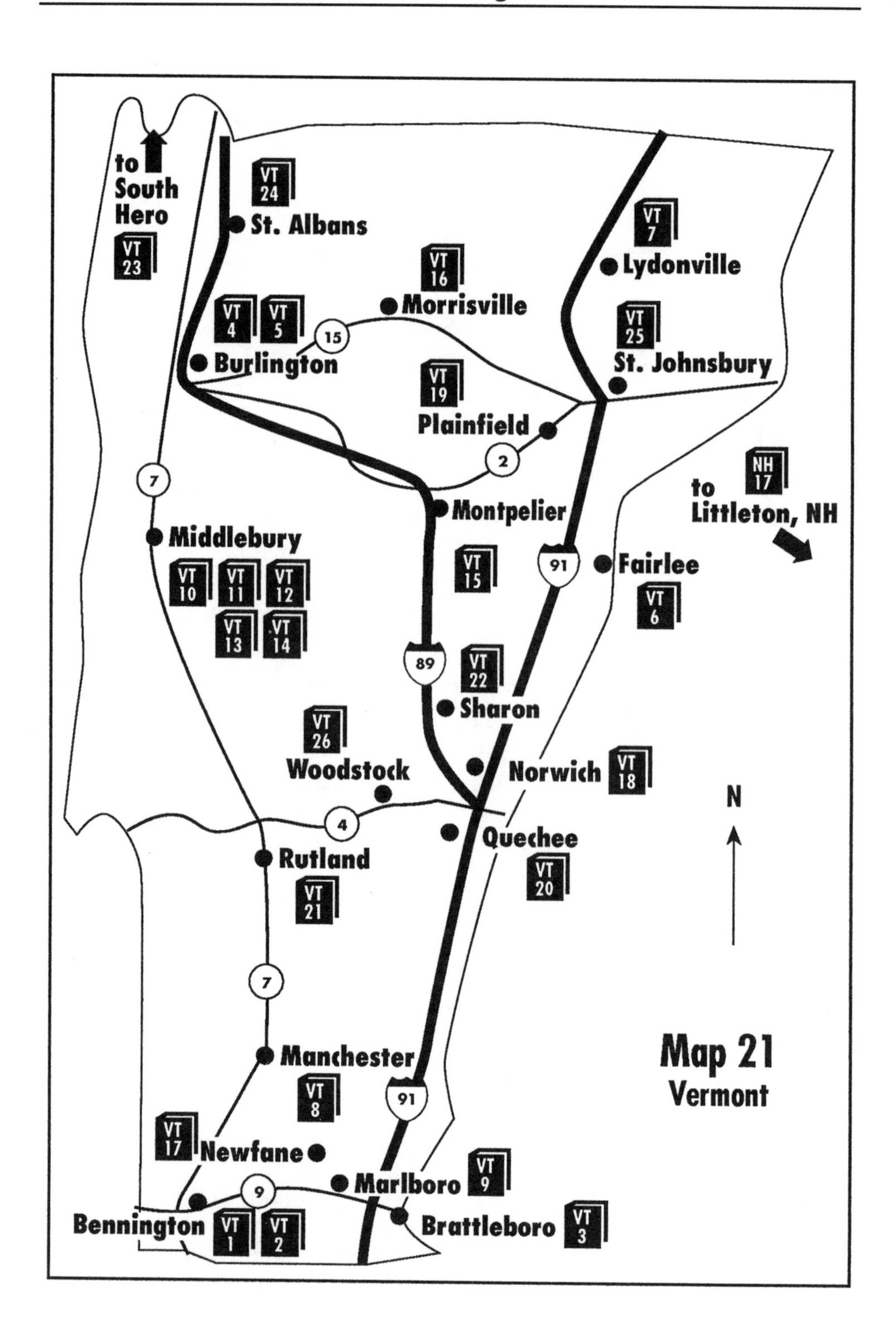
to South Hero
VT 23
VT 24
St. Albans
VT 7
Lydonville
VT 16
Morrisville
VT 4
VT 5
15
Burlington
VT 25
St. Johnsbury
VT 19
Plainfield
2
NH 17
to Littleton, NH
7
Montpelier
Middlebury
91
Fairlee
VT 15
VT 10
VT 11
VT 12
VT 6
VT 13
VT 14
89
VT 22
Sharon
VT 26
Woodstock
Norwich
VT 18
N
4
Quechee
Rutland
VT 20
VT 21
7
Manchester
Map 21
Vermont
VT 8
91
VT 17
Newfane
VT 9
Marlboro
9
Bennington
VT 1
VT 2
Brattleboro
VT 3

Alphabetical Listing By Location

Bennington

New Englandiana (VT1) 802-447-1695
121 Benmont Avenue Fax: 802-442-8526
Mailing address: P.O. Box 589 05201

Collection:	General stock.
# of Volumes:	7,500
Specialties:	Biography; history.
Hours:	Monday 8-4:30. Other weekdays by chance.
Services:	Catalog
Travel:	From Vermont Route 9 west, proceed 1 block on Benmont to corner of River Street. From US Route 7 north, take River Street 2 blocks to intersection with Benmont. Look for a 2 story red brick building. Map 24.
Credit Cards:	No
Owner:	Roger D. Harris
Year Estab:	1961
Comments:	If you don't mind a lot of bending and finding some books slightly out of place, you can get some real bargains in this one story warehouse like shop. All subjects are represented and the books are in relatively good condition. Don't overlook the large new arrivals section.

Now and Then Books (VT2) 802-447-1470
439 Main Street 05201

Collection:	General stock of hardcover, paperback and pulps.
# of Volumes:	30,000+
Specialties:	Cooking; children's.
Hours:	Monday-Saturday 10-5:30. Sunday by chance.
Services:	Accepts want lists, informal search service.
Travel:	On Route 9 (Main Street), one block east of Route 7, in downtown Bennington. Map 24.
Credit Cards:	No
Owner:	Wolfgang Roxon
Year Estab:	1983
Comments:	Located one flight up in a multi tenant office building, the shop is divided into a series of small well lit rooms. The stock is as large as the owner claims and the books are in good condition. All categories are represented and the books are priced most reasonably.

Brattleboro

Brattleboro Books (VT3) 802-257-0177
34-36 Eliot Street 05301

Collection:	General stock.
# of Volumes:	35,000
Specialties:	Vermont; Civil War; military.
Hours:	Monday-Saturday 9:30-6. Sunday 11-4.
Services:	Appraisals, search service, accepts want lists.
Travel:	Exit 1 off Route I-91. Take Canal Street to downtown. Eliot Street is in heart of downtown. Parking can be a problem. Map 24.
Credit Cards:	Yes
Owner:	Barbara Milani, Ken Nims & Duane Whitehead
Year Estab:	1979
Comments:	A large bi-level store with a good selection of hard to find books. The collection on the street level features more recent used books, books in better condition and a separate and spacious children's/young adult room. The books downstairs are older and less well organized due to lack of space. If you're looking for bargains, don't skip the downstairs.

Burlington

Bygone Books (VT4 802-862-4397
31 Main Street 05401

Collection:	General stock of hardcover and paperback and records.
# of Volumes:	12,000
Specialties:	Vermont
Hours:	Monday-Saturday 9:30-5:30.
Services:	Appraisals, search service, accepts want lists.
Travel:	Exit 14 W off I-89. Proceed west toward Lake Champlain. Shop is on south side (left) of Main Street, 1 block from lake. Map 24.
Credit Cards:	Yes
Owner:	5 partners
Year Estab:	1978

Comments: A roomy shop with a warm, pleasing interior that encourages leisurely browsing. The entrance is up a few steps. The collection consists of mostly popular titles in all subjects with few if any rare items.

Codex Books (VT5) 802-862-6413
148 Cherry Street 05401

Collection: General stock.
# of Volumes: 12,000
Specialties: Science fiction; fantasy; new age; occult; oriental.
Hours: Monday-Saturday 10:30-5:30.
Travel: Located in downtown Burlington one block from Burlington Mall. Map 24.
Credit Cards: Yes
Owner: Don Norford
Year Estab: 1988
Comments: Located in the basement of a retail building (look for the name of the shop on the street level door), this shop contains a nice assortment of newer and some older used books, almost all in very fine condition. If you have the time, you might also want to visit one of the two "new" book stores just footsteps away in an outdoor mall. One of the stores features a cafe.

Fairlee

Old Book Store (VT6) 802-333-9709
Main Street 05045

Collection: General stock.
# of Volumes: 5,000+
Hours: Daily 8-6.
Services: Accepts want lists.
Travel: Exit 15 off I-91. Make right at exit and then a left onto Route 5 north. Shop is 1/2 mile ahead on the left in a large white building. Map 24.
Credit Cards: No
Owner: John Larson & Adele Chapman
Year Estab: 1924

Comments:	A one-of-a-kind book store. The books are in a large general store that also sells fishing supplies, wine, toys and sundries. While the collection is limited in size, it does include a broad selection of categories. The books are in mixed condition ranging from near new to well worn. Because of its limited size, the shop may not be worth going out of your way for. But, if you're in the area, it would certainly make for a pleasant stop.

Lydonville

Green Mountain Books & Prints (VT7) 802-626-5051
100 Broad Street 05851

Collection:	General stock of new and used books.
# of Volumes:	30,000
Hours:	Monday-Thursday 10-4. Friday 10-5. Saturday 10-1.
Travel:	Exit 23 off I-91. Follow Route 5 north into center of village. Shop is on left next to post office, directly across from a small war memorial park. Map 24.
Credit Cards:	Yes
Owner:	Ellen Doyle & Ralph Secord
Year Estab:	1976
Comments:	A roomy street level shop with the used book collection located in the rear of the store. A convenient children's corner can help occupy the younger set while the adults are browsing. The collection includes some interesting titles with few if any rarities. Reasonably priced.

Manchester

Johnny Appleseed Bookshop (VT8) 802-362-2458
Main Street 05254

Collection:	General stock.
# of Volumes:	15,000
Specialties:	Regional; hunting; fishing; sports; first editions.
Hours:	Monday-Saturday 9:30-5. Sunday & holidays 10-5.
Travel:	On Route 7A, next to Equinox Hotel and across from monument. Map 24.
Credit Cards:	Yes

Owner:	Frederic F. Taylor
Year Estab:	1930
Comments:	This two story shop is located in an 1832 bank building. The owner makes creative use of every square inch of space to store his books, including the original bank vault. The first floor contains many sets and historical items, some newer books and greeting cards. Older books and several rare items are located on the second floor. Most subject areas are covered and prices are quite reasonable.

Marlboro

The Bear Bookshop (VT9) 802-464-2260
Butterfield Road
Mailing address: RD#4, Box 446 Brattleboro 05301

Collection:	General stock.
# of Volumes:	25,000
Specialties:	Music; scholarly books; bibliography.
Hours:	Late spring-Labor Day: Generally daily 10-5 but best to call ahead. Labor Day-Columbus Day: By appointment.
Travel:	Proceeding west on Route 9 from Brattleboro, watch for state sign (about 2 miles after turnoff to Marlboro). Make first left after sign onto unmarked unpaved road. Shop is about 1 mile ahead on left. Map 24.
Credit Cards:	Yes
Owner:	John Greenberg
Year Estab:	1975
Comments:	A large clean multi level barn where book lovers could easily spend several hours browsing. A quality collection that is well organized and reasonably priced.

Middlebury

Alley Beat (VT10) 802-388-2743
8 Mill Street 05753

Collection:	General stock of new and used books and records.
# of Volumes:	7,000
Hours:	Daily 10-5.
Travel:	Off Route 7 in downtown Middlebury. Map 23.
Credit Cards:	Yes

Owner:	Keith Conklin & Garland Martin
Year Estab:	1987
Comments:	A small collection in a small street level store that's worth a stop when visiting the other used book shops in Middlebury.

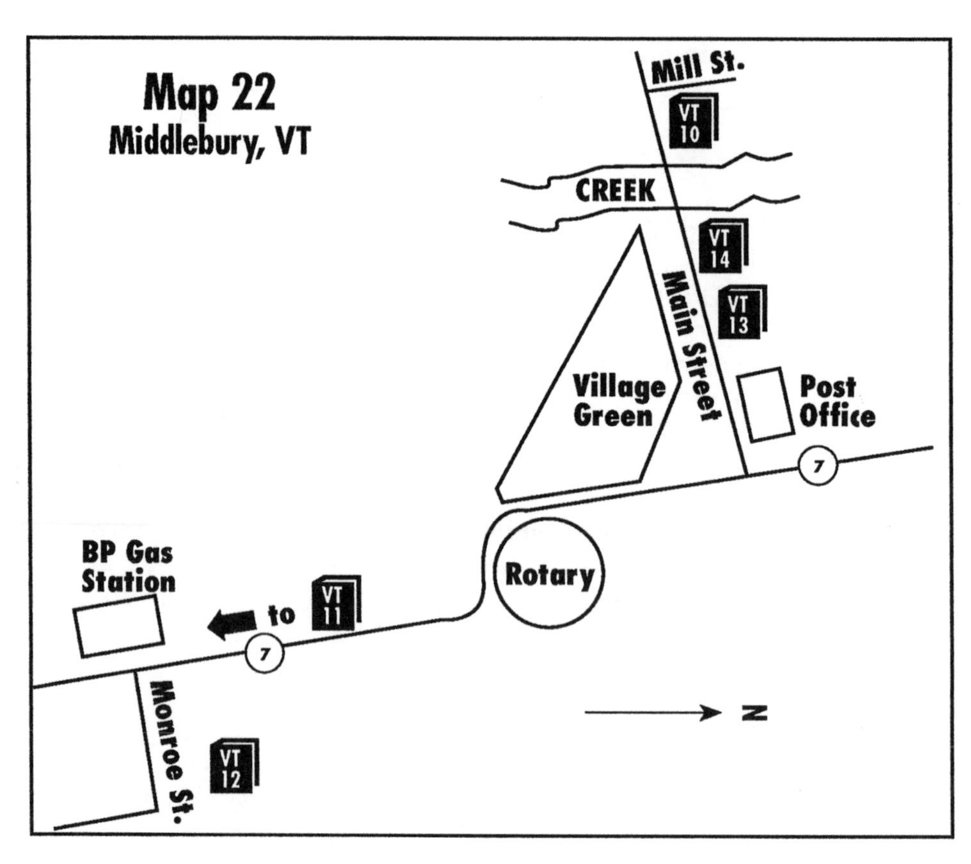

Terry Harper, Bookseller (VT11) 802-453-5088
Middlebury Antiques Center (Route 7)
Mailing address: P.O. Box 37 Bristol 05443-0037

Collection:	General stock.
# of Volumes:	6,000-7,000
Specialties:	Americana; uncommon.
Hours:	Daily 9-6. Additional stock at owner's home in nearby Bristol can be viewed by appointment.
Services:	Accepts want lists, mail order.

Travel:	Middlebury Antiques Center located at junction of Routes 7 & 116. For owner's home, take Route 116 to Bristol. Turn left at red light in village. House is ahead 1 mile (117 North Street.) Map 23.
Credit Cards:	Yes (at Center only)
Owner:	Terry Harper
Year Estab:	1968
Comments:	The booth at the Antiques Center carries a limited selection of books.

Monroe Street Books (VT12) 802-388-1622
7 Monroe Street 05753 Fax: 802-388-1608

Collection:	General stock, ephemera and prints.
# of Volumes:	20,000
Specialties:	Children's; illustrated photography; cartoon and comic art; modern fiction; graphic arts.
Hours:	Memorial Day-October 30: Daily 10-6 but best to call ahead. Remainder of year by appointment.
Services:	Accepts want lists.
Travel:	3/4 mile from downtown Middlebury. Proceed south on Route 7. Turn left at BP gas station and look for sign four houses down on right. Parking is in rear. Map 23
Credit Cards:	Yes
Owner:	Dick & Flanzy Chodkowski
Year Estab:	1991
Comments:	The shop is located in a small two story building behind the owner's house. An absolute "must see" for any book lover. In addition to the specialties listed above, the collection is also strong in humor. Most of the books are of relatively recent vintage (post World War II) but many items pre date the war. All are in excellent condition. Not inexpensive; you pay for what you get.

Otter Creek Old and Rare Books (VT13) 802-388-3241
20 Main Street, Box 871 05753

Collection:	General stock and some ephemera.
# of Volumes:	25,000
Hours:	Monday-Saturday 10-5. Sunday by chance. Closed Wednesdays November 1-April 30.
Services:	Accepts want lists.

Travel:	Off Route 7 in downtown Middlebury. Map 23.
Credit Cards:	No
Owner:	Sharon Harter Washington
Year Estab:	1989 (see comments)
Comments:	What a surprise to find this spacious and well stocked book store in a basement setting. The shop is divided into two large rooms with a well equipped children's corner. The fiction section is particularly large and the offerings in every other category are quite adequate. The books are primarily reading copies and are moderately priced. The shop was formerly known as the Breadloaf Bookshop, East Middlebury, VT.

The Vermont Book Shop (VT14) 802-388-2061
38 Main Street 05753

Collection:	Specialty
# of Volumes:	150 (used)
Specialties:	Vermont; Robert Frost, including signed and limited editions; William Upson Alexander.
Hours:	Monday-Saturday 8:30-5:30. Sunday 11-4.
Services:	Search service.
Travel:	Off Route 7 in downtown Middlebury. Map 23.
Credit Cards:	Yes
Owner:	Dick Blair
Year Estab:	1949
Comments:	Although primarily a new book shop, this street level shop is worth a visit if you're looking for used books dealing with Vermontiana, or if you also enjoy browsing new book stores whenever you're in a new area.

Montpelier

Rivendell Books (VT15) 802-223-3928
100 Main Street 05602

Collection:	General stock of used books and remainders.
# of Volumes:	10,000+
Hours:	Monday-Saturday 9:30-6. Sunday 10:30-4.
Services:	Appraisals, search service, accepts want lists.

Travel:	Montpelier exit off I-89. Proceed on Route 2 into Montpelier. Left turn at third bridge which becomes Main Street. Shop is on left, at corner of Main and Langdon, 1/2 block from State Street in heart of downtown Montpelier. Map 24.
Credit Cards:	Yes
Owner:	Mikael A. Batten Michael Grimaldi
Year Estab:	1991
Comments:	Most of the used books in this street level shop are of more recent vintage with a few older items sprinkled in. No rarities for the true afficionado.

Morrisville

Brick House Bookshop (VT16) 802-888-4300
RFD 3, Box 3020 05661

Collection:	General stock.
# of Volumes:	50,000
Hours:	Monday-Saturday 10-5. Sunday 12-5. For Monday only, best to call ahead.
Services:	Appraisals, search service, accepts want lists, mail order.
Travel:	Route 100 north to Morrisville. As you approach Morrisville, watch for state signs on the right. Make left at sign and left at fork. Shop is about 1/4 mile ahead on right in a red brick house. Map 24.
Credit Cards:	Yes
Owner:	Alexandra Heller
Year Estab:	1975
Comments:	Located on the first floor of a private residence, this shop offers a good selection in every category. For the most part, the books are in good condition and reasonably priced. A cup of tea is always available upon request.

Newfane

NU-tique Shop (VT17) 802-365-7677
P.O. Box 35 05345

Collection:	General stock, records and collectibles.
# of Volumes:	10,000
Hours:	Late May-November: Saturday-Wednesday 10:30-4:30.

Travel:	On Route 30. Proceeding north, shop is on left. Map 24.
Credit Cards:	No
Owner:	Don & Phyllis Kent
Comments:	A combination collectibles/used book shop, with the books tightly packed in the rear portion of the building. The shop offers a nice selection in all categories with some sleepers. Very moderately priced.

Norwich

Lilac Hedge Bookshop (VT18) 802-649-2921
Main Street
Mailing address: P.O. Box 712 05055

Collection:	General stock.
# of Volumes:	10,000
Specialties:	Literature; art.
Hours:	Thursday-Sunday 10-5. Other times by chance or appointment.
Services:	Appraisals, search service.
Travel:	1/2 mile from I-91 and 1 mile from Dartmouth College. Look for house with a white picket fence on right. Map 24.
Credit Cards:	No
Owner:	Robert P. Ericson
Year Estab:	1980
Comments:	A truly lovely shop filled with scholarly books. The collection is housed in a portion of a private house surrounded by well kept gardens. In addition to the specialties listed above, the collection is also strong in biography. A pleasure to visit.

Plainfield

The Country Bookshop (VT19) 802-454-8439
RFD 2, Box 1260 05667

Collection:	General stock and ephemera.
# of Volumes:	10,000
Specialties:	Folk music; folklore; bells.
Hours:	June 1-Labor Day: Daily 10-5. Remainder of year: Friday & Saturday 10-5.
Services:	Appraisals, catalog, accepts want lists.

Travel:	Route 2 to Plainfield. Turn at blinking light and proceed down hill 1 block. Shop is to the right, located next to a church. Map 24.
Credit Cards:	Yes
Owner:	Benjamin Koenig
Year Estab:	1974
Comments:	A well stocked, well kept and well organized shop located on the first floor of a 100 year old house. The books are in excellent condition and are moderately priced. The shop is easy to find and well worth a visit.

Quechee

Quechee Books (VT20) 802-295-1681
Route 4 at I-89
Mailing address: P.O. Box 525 Henniker 03242

Collection:	General stock of hardcover and paperback.
# of Volumes:	25,000
Specialties:	Scholarly books in all fields.
Hours:	Daily 10-5 except Memorial Day-Columbus Day: 9-6. Closed only Thanksgiving, Christmas and New Year.
Services:	Appraisals.
Travel:	Next to Quechee Mobil at Quechee exit off I-89. Map 24.
Credit Cards:	Yes
Owner:	Helen & Ian Morrison
Year Estab:	1986
Comments:	A compact two story shop with narrow aisles and a small children's corner to interest the younger set. The collection is very well stocked and organized. In addition to scholarly books, the collection is also strong in horror, science fiction and mystery. The shop has a high turnover of titles, facilitated by access to owners' stock in two other shops.

Rutland

Tuttle Antiquarian Books, Inc. (VT21) 802-773-8229
26 South Main Street Fax: 802-773-1493
Mailing address: P.O. Box 541 05702

Collection:	General stock and ephemera.
# of Volumes:	40,000+

Specialties: Genealogies; town and county histories.
Hours: Monday-Saturday 8-5.
Services: Catalog (for genealogical material and town histories), accepts want lists.
Travel: Located on east side of Routes 4 & 7, opposite park and 1 block south of Chaffee Art Gallery. Map 24.
Credit Cards: Yes
Owner: Charles E. Tuttle
Year Estab: 1832
Comments: The collection is housed in two old Rutland houses, each with two floors. A large directory sign in the entry foyer of the first building points book hunters in the right direction. The rooms are spaciously laid out and well lit. The collection is strong in most areas and the books are moderately priced. One section features older books, some over 150 years old. According to the owner, the shop is "Vermont's largest old, rare and second-hand book shop."

Sharon

Old Schoolhouse Books (VT22) 802-763-2434
Old Schoolhouse Center (Route 132)
Mailing address: P.O. Box 190 05065

Collection: General stock of used and some new books, framed fine art prints and driftwood art.
# of Volumes: 18,000+
Specialties: Nature; history; children's; classics; New England.
Hours: Wednesday-Saturday 10-5.
Services: Search service, accepts wants lists.
Travel: Exit 2 off I-89. As you turn left onto Route 14, schoolhouse is on right. Map 24.
Credit Cards: No
Owner: William Jackson
Year Estab: 1990
Comments: A modest collection of books, all in good condition, has replaced the desks and chairs in one classroom of this recycled schoolhouse. Additional books are displayed in the hallway. The stock is general with no areas of deep strength. The owners also have a booth at nearby Timber Village on Route 4 in Quechee.

South Hero

Frances L. Robinson Books (VT23) 802-372-4343
at Robinson Hardware 05486 802-372-6622
Mailing address: RR #1, Box 238 05486

Collection:	General stock.
# of Volumes:	2,500-3,000
Hours:	Monday-Saturday 8-5.
Travel:	On Route 2 through Champlain Islands. Exit 17 off I-89. Map 24.
Credit Cards:	No
Owner:	Frances L. Robinson
Year Estab:	1985
Comments:	This book collection is located in a corner of the owner's hardware store.

St. Albans

The Eloquent Page (VT24) 802-527-7243
21 Catherine Street 05478

Collection:	General stock.
# of Volumes:	8,000-10,000
Specialties:	Children's; science fiction; fantasy.
Hours:	Daily 10-6.
Services:	Search service, accepts want lists, mail order.
Travel:	Exit 19 off I-89. Go through first stop sign. At second stop sign, turn right. Left turn onto Lake Street. Catherine Street is first left. Shop is on right in small brick mall. Map 24.
Credit Cards:	No
Owner:	Donna Howard & Kheya Ganguly-Kiefner
Year Estab:	1992
Comments:	The owners invite their customers to "sit, read and have a cup of coffee or tea."

St. Johnsbury

Dave's Diner Books (VT25) 802-748-8888
69 Portland Street 05819

Collection:	General stock.
# of Volumes:	3,000-4,000
Specialties:	C.S. Lewis; biography; religion.
Hours:	May 1-December 25: Daily 12-5 and by appointment. Best to call ahead.
Services:	Accepts want lists.
Travel:	On Route 2, about 1/4 mile east of center of St. Johnsbury. Next to Yankee Traveler Motel. Map 24.
Credit Cards:	No
Owner:	David Montague
Year Estab:	1992
Comments:	A truly unique setting for a used book shop: an old diner, circa 1950. This is a fledgling shop with a modest general stock.

Woodstock

Pleasant Street Books, Cards, Ephemera (VT26) 802-457-4050
48 Pleasant Street 05091

Collection:	General stock, ephemera and old baseball cards.
# of Volumes:	7,000
Specialties:	First editions; fine bindings; Vermont.
Hours:	Summer-Fall: Daily 11-5. Winter-Spring: Thursday-Sunday 11-5.
Travel:	Exit 9 (Woodstock) of Route 91. Proceed on Route 12N into Woodstock. Shop is in rear of white house on right. Map 24.
Credit Cards:	Yes
Owner:	Harry Saul, Jr.
Year Estab:	1986
Comments:	Don't be fooled by the sign outside this shop that reads "Baseball Cards." Located in the historic village of Woodstock, this two story barn like building contains a plethora of interesting and unusual used books representing every genre. Prices are moderate. Much of the ephemera is tucked away in ornately carved antique chests.

Bellows Falls

Arch Bridge Bookshop 802-463-9395
142 Westminster Street 05101

Collection:	General stock.
# of Volumes:	6,000
Specialties:	World War II; Civil War; western Americana; Arctic and Antarctic; aviation; sports.
Hours:	By chance or appointment
Credit Cards:	No
Owner:	Duane & Barbara Whitehead
Year Estab:	1980

Brattleboro

Ken Leach Rare Books 802-257-7918
14 Elm Street
Mailing address: P.O. Box 1561 05301

Collection:	Specialty
# of Volumes:	5,000-50,000
Specialties:	18th and 19th century American printings dealing with every subject of the period.
Credit Cards:	No
Owner:	Ken Leach
Year Estab:	1968

Burlington

Ashley Book Company 802-863-3854
P.O. Box 534 05402

Collection:	Specialty
# of Volumes:	2,000-2,500
Specialties:	Rare books; private press; skiing; books about books; bibliography; illustrated.
Credit Cards:	No
Owner:	Gloria B. & George C. Singer
Year Estab:	1982

Fraser Publishing Co. 802-658-0322
309 South Willard Street 05401 Fax: 802-658-0260

Collection: Specialty
# of Volumes: 4,000
Specialties: Stock market; investing; business histories; commodities; money and banking; economics. (Majority of books are out-of-print titles.)
Hours: 9-4.
Services: Search service, catalog, accepts want lists.
Credit Cards: Yes
Owner: James L. Fraser
Year Estab: 1968

Chittenden

Hugh's Irish Books 802-483-2884
Box 75 05737

Collection: Specialty
# of Volumes: 3,000
Specialties: Ireland; athletics.
Services: Accepts want lists.
Credit Cards: No
Owner: Hugh Short
Year Estab: 1989

Derby Line

Tranquil Things 802-873-3454
43 Main Street 05830

Collection: General stock of hardcover and paperback.
# of Volumes: 3,000-5,000
Hours: By chance most afternoons or by appointment.
Services: Accepts want lists.
Travel: Derby Line exit off I-91 (the last exit before Canada). Proceed south on Main Street for 3 blocks. Shop is on left.
Credit Cards: Yes
Owner: Richard & Pat Wright
Year Estab: 1988
Comments: The shop also sells fine crafts and gift items.

Fairlee

John Larson 802-333-4784
Box 3, Main Street 05045

Collection: General stock and ephemera.
Credit Cards: No
Owner: John Larson

Ferrisburgh

Good Earth Used and Rare Books 802-425-2101
4 Winds Road 05456

Collection: Specialty
# of Volumes: 2,000+
Specialties: Classical literature; geography; country life; art; children's; health; nutrition.
Services: Appraisals, accepts want lists.
Credit Cards: Yes
Owner: Barry Gorden
Year Estab: 1984
Comments: The book shop shares quarters with a fine art gallery and gourmet tea shop.

Greensboro

Recovery Books-The Robert Frost Book Shop 802-586-2846
Box 232 05841

Collection: General stock.
# of Volumes: 4,000-5,000
Specialties: Robert Frost.
Services: Appraisals (Frost only), search service, accepts want lists.
Credit Cards: No
Owner: Jeff & Mary Anne Jeffrey
Year Estab: 1982

Hartford

Rays Antiquarian Books 802-295-2267
3 Depot Square, Box 323 05047

Collection: General stock of hardcover and used books.
# of Volumes: 15,000
Hours: By chance most anytime or by appointment.
Services: Accepts want lists, mail order.
Travel: From White River Junction, proceed on VA cutoff road to Hartford.
Credit Cards: No
Owner: Leslie R. Ray
Year Estab: 1985

Newbury

Oxbow Books 802-866-5940
U.S. Route 5, RD Box 196 05051

Collection: General stock and ephemera.
# of Volumes: 2,000
Specialties: Vermont; Frances Parkinson Keyes; postcards.
Services: Search service, accepts want lists.
Credit Cards: No
Owner: Peter Keyes
Year Estab: 1983
Comments: The owner also displays books at the Antiques Collaborative in Quechee.

North Pomfret

Richard H. Adelson, Antiquarian Booksellers 802-457-2608
HC 69, Box 23 05053

Collection: General stock.
Specialties: Voyages; travel; illustrated; children's; Pacific; Africa.
Services: Appraisals, catalog, accepts want lists.
Credit Cards: No
Owner: Jane & Richard Adelson
Year Estab: 1971

Comments:	Owners note that their collection is "not set up for browsing."

Norwich

G.B. Manasek 802-649-3962 603-643-2227
P.O. Box 1204 05055 Fax: 603-643-5634

Collection:	Specialty
# of Volumes:	500
Specialties:	Rare maps (pre 1800), atlases and antiquarian books only. No general stock.
Services:	Catalog

Putney

The Unique Antique 802-387-4488
Main Street
Mailing address: P.O. Box 485 05346

Collection:	General stock, ephemera and some antiques.
# of Volumes:	3,000+
Specialties:	Art; photography; children's; Americana.
Hours:	By chance 9-6 or by appointment.
Services:	Appraisals, accepts want lists.
Travel:	1 minute from Exit 4 off I-91. On left, four houses after garden nursery.
Credit Cards:	No
Owner:	Jonathan Flaccus
Year Estab:	1977
Comments:	Located on the first floor of a Victorian house, this combination used book/antique shop offers a quality selection of not inexpensive books. The entrance is up a few steps.

Waitsfield

Rare and Well Done Books 802-496-2791
Route 100
Mailing address: P.O. Box 274 Warren 05674

Collection:	Specialty
# of Volumes:	5,000

Specialties:	19th and 20th century literature; first editions; 19th century evolution and natural history.
Hours:	Fall & winter only.
Services:	Appraisals.
Credit Cards:	No
Owner:	Cathleen G. Miller
Year Estab:	1983

Wilder

Stanley Books 802-295-9058
29 Gillette Street, Box 434 05088

Collection:	General stock.
# of Volumes:	2,000-3,000
Services:	Accepts want lists.
Credit Cards:	No
Owner:	Thomas & Kathleen Stanley
Year Estab:	1977

Williston

Beliveau Books 802-482-2540
Rt. 2A, Box 458 05495

Collection:	General stock.
# of Volumes:	120,000
Specialties:	Vermont; military; history; nature.
Services:	Appraisals, accepts want lists.
Travel:	Shop located at Goose Creek Farms, 3 1/2 miles south of exit 12 off I-89. At exit, proceed toward Hinesberg. Turn left at farm sign. Book barn is 1/4 mile up the unpaved road.
Credit Cards:	No
Owner:	A.J. Beliveau
Year Estab:	1970
Comments:	This shop is located just outside Burlington on a working farm that also features a bed & breakfast. Most of the collection is stored in a large barn with narrow crowded aisles. The balance of the stock is divided between a second building and the owner's residence. The collection is stronger in non fiction than fiction. The condition

of the books is mixed and the owner's unique way of organizing his collection can be somewhat confusing at first. If you have lots of time to browse, you might find some sleepers here.

Top of the World Books 802-878-8737
20 Westview Circle 05495

Collection: Specialty
# of Volumes: 200
Specialties: Mountaineering; polar exploration.
Hours: Evenings only.
Services: Search service, catalog, accepts want lists.
Credit Cards: No
Owner: Gregory M. Glade
Year Estab: 1989

Mail Order Dealers

Adamant Books 802-223-2951
Box 46 Adamant 05640

Collection: Speciality books and ephemera.
# of Volumes: 3,000+
Specialties: Vermont; New England; agriculture; gardening.
Services: Search service.
Credit Cards: No
Owner: Weston A. Cate, Jr..

Aislinn Books & Research
P.O. Box 589 Bennington 05201

Collection: General stock.
# of Volumes: 20,000
Specialties: Ireland and other Celtic countries; Japan; poetry; women.
Services: Search service, catalog, accepts want lists; non genealogical research.
Credit Cards: No
Owner: J.M. Hays
Year Estab: 1983

Birch Bark Books 802-438-5079
RR 1, Box 1590 West Rutland 05777 201-228-3211

Collection:	General stock.
# of Volumes:	2,000
Specialties:	P.G. Wodehouse; modern first editions; medical.
Credit Cards:	No
Owner:	Joan & Jay Weiss
Year Estab:	1989

Michael Dunn Books 802-334-2768
P.O. Box 436 Newport 05855 Fax: 802-334-7815

Collection:	Specialty
# of Volumes:	5,000
Specialties:	Americana; Vermont; Canada.
Services:	Catalog, search service, accepts want lists.
Credit Cards:	No
Owner:	Michael Dunn
Year Estab:	1978

John Johnson Natural History Books 802-44 2-6738
RR 1, Box 513 North Bennington 05257

Collection:	Speciality
# of Volumes:	5,000+
Specialties:	Natural history.
Services:	Catalog
Credit Cards:	No
Owner:	John Johnson
Year Estab:	1949

Longhouse: Booksellers and Publishers 802-254-4242
277 Jacksonville Stage Guilford 05301

Collection:	Specialty
# of Volumes:	5,000
Specialties:	Modern literary first editions; counterculture; women; the uncommon; poetry; small press books and magazines; country life and trades.
Services:	Accepts want lists.
Credit Cards:	No

Owner: Bob & Susan Arnold
Year Estab: 1973

Whitney McDermott - Books 802-988-4349
RR #2, Cross Road, #176 Jay 05859

Collection: Specialty
# of Volumes: 5,000
Specialties: Books about bookplates; illustrated; original art of children's books; graphic arts.
Services: Search service, accepts want lists.
Credit Cards: No
Owner: Whitney McDermott
Year Estab: 1932

Middlebury Book Center 802-388-8063
51 Washington Street, #4 Middlebury 05753

Collection: Specialty
# of Volumes: 2,000
Specialties: Humanities; social sciences.
Services: Search service, accepts want lists.
Credit Cards: No
Owner: Rachel Barrett & Patrick Hayes
Year Estab: 1992

Mountain Reverie 802-899-4447
P.O. Box 26 Underhill Center 05490

Collection: General stock.
# of Volumes: 3,000
Services: Appraisals, accepts want lists.
Credit Cards: No
Owner: Marie Tedford
Year Estab: 1975

William L. Parkinson Books 802-482-3113
RR 1, Box 1330 Shelburne 05482

Collection: Specialty
# of Volumes: 25,000
Specialties: Vermont, including books, maps, ephemera and prints.

Credit Cards: No
Owner: William L. Parkinson
Year Estab: 1980

Bradford DeWolfe Sheff 802-485-8239
P.O. Box 246 Northfield 05663

Collection: Speciality
# of Volumes: 1,000
Specialties: Philatelic literature; Thornton Burgess; U.S. postal history.
Credit Cards: No
Owner: Bradford DeWolfe Sheff

The Yankee Trader 802-644-2908
Box 219 Jeffersonville 05464

Collection: General stock.
Services: Search service, accepts want lists, appraisals.
Credit Cards: No
Owner: Roger Mann
Year Estab: 1950

A room with a view - if you can find the window

Specialty Index

The Used Book Lover's Guide To New York, New Jersey, Pennsylvannia and Delaware will be available in the near future.

If you have found this volume useful in your book hunting endeavors and would like to be notified about the publication date of the next volume, send your name and address to: